Yale Studies in Political Science, 8

David Horne, Editor

Published under the direction of the Department of Political Science

James Mill

and the Art of Revolution

JOSEPH HAMBURGER

New Haven and London, Yale University Press, 1963

FOR LOTTE

Preface

This book grew out of (and interrupted) a study of Philosophic Radicalism. Examining James Mill's views of political change raised questions about the way the Reform Bill was passed, and from there I was drawn to the problem of evaluating the threat of revolution that was said to exist at that time. The book deals with James Mill solely as a theoretician of Radical strategy, and it examines the efforts made by him and other Radicals to shape the governing classes' image of public feeling and especially their image of the popular disposition to violence.

There are many political situations in which efforts are made to influence perceptions of the potential for violence in a society and to manipulate anxieties about revolution among one's political antagonists. These are not confined to international politics, where the use of violence is within the range of expected responses, but also are to be found in domestic politics, especially where the legitimacy of a political order is sufficiently discredited that restraints on the use of violence become seriously weakened. In such situations efforts will be made, more or less consciously, to gain political ends by attempting to influence the government's assessment of social cleavages and the possibility of open conflict. James Mill is notable for having formulated a theory of political change that provides for the use of such tactics. Indeed, since he thought of the press as the main instrument of intimidation, he may be seen as an early advocate of the tactics that look upon the press and the distribution of "news" as part of the "overall weaponry" of politics. Although the press was widely used in this way during the struggle over the Reform Bill, Mill and a small group of associates were unique for having done so self-consciously, systematically, with skill, and with a degree of success.

Statements of fact often become intertwined with rhetorical purpose, opening the door to exaggeration and even dissimulation. Even if participants are misled, political analysis should not accept rhetorical statements as necessarily accurate descriptions. With regard to the situation in 1831–32, this raises a question about the reality of the threat of revolution that was said to exist, and an attempt is made to determine the validity of such claims. In doing so it is impossible to avoid consideration of many details connected with the passing of the Reform Bill, for they provide the immediate context for this inquiry; but it is not my purpose to re-tell that familiar story. So far as the historical treatment of the Reform Bill is concerned, my only purpose is to suggest and even nourish doubts about certain interpretations of that event.

Many persons and institutions have kindly allowed me to publish extracts of manuscripts in their possession, and I would like to record my gratitude to them: Viscount Lambton (the Lambton Papers located at the Estate Office at Chester-le-Street, County Durham); Sir Fergus Graham (the Graham Papers); Mr. Russell Ellice (the Ellice Papers on deposit at the National Library of Scotland); the Newcastle Trustees (Newcastle Papers at the University of Nottingham); University College, London (the Parkes Papers and Brougham Papers); the University of Durham (Grey of Howick Collection); the Trustees of the British Museum (Bentham, Cobden, Napier, Place Papers). The British Library of Political and Economic Science and the National Provincial Bank have given permission to publish extracts of a James Mill letter. The governors of Dunford have given permission to quote from three letters among the Cobden Papers at the County Record Office at Chichester, Sussex. The portrait sketch of Joseph Parkes by Benjamin Robert Haydon is reproduced on the jacket by kind permission of the Birmingham Reference Library, which also has allowed me to quote from various documents in its collections. Unpublished Crown-copyright material in the Public Record Office, London, has been reproduced by permission of the Controller of H. M. Stationery Office. All of these institutions have kindly sent microfilm copies of some of the manuscripts used. Microfilm copies of Graham Papers and Ellice Papers were borrowed, respectively, from the Newberry Library, Chicago, and the Public Archives of Canada. I am greatly obliged to Miss Skerl of University College Library for having sent microfilm copies of letters in the Brougham Papers when that collection was still only partially catalogued. Mrs. Anne Granger typed the manuscript with her usual efficiency and was helpful in many ways. The Billings Memorial Award, granted by Yale University, allowed me to conduct some of the research in England during the summer of 1960. I also owe thanks to the Rockefeller Foundation and the Morse Fund at Yale University, as their support this past year of a study of John Stuart Mill and Philosophic Radicalism also provided time for the final revision of this book. Finally, I wish to record my indebtedness to Professor F. Hayek for having encouraged and nourished my interest in nineteenth-century political thought.

J. H.

New Haven, Connecticut
March 1963

Contents

Abbreviations

Birm. J.	*Birmingham Journal*
Exam.	*Examiner* (London)
Hansard	*Hansard's Parliamentary Debates,* 3d series
Manch. Guard.	*Manchester Guardian*
Morn. Chr.	*Morning Chronicle* (London)
PP	*Parliamentary Papers*
PCN	Place Collections of Newscuttings, in the British Museum

Had I taken notes of such matters as have come to my knowledge during the last eighteen months, had I noticed the many persons whom the agitation brought me acquainted with, the multitude of things within and without doors in which I have been engaged with other men, the relation would have been at least somewhat curious and extraordinary. . . .

FRANCIS PLACE

For to exaggerate with judgment one must begin by measuring with nicety.

JOSEPH CONRAD

To use, and not to be used by, the Aristocracy has been my theory; and for accomplishment of that purpose a little chicanery in a Lawyer is permissible.

JOSEPH PARKES

CHAPTER 1

Radicalism and the Constitution

"Steam alone could do the business." So said Joseph Parkes, explaining how Tory opposition to the Municipal Corporation Bill was overcome.[1] By steam, of course, he meant the pressure of public opinion as expressed through petitions, public meetings, and especially the press. The generation of such steam for political purposes had greatly increased during the first half of the nineteenth century. Popular agitation had begun to reflect a widening political consciousness among ordinary men, and there were sophisticated efforts to organize the expression of public feelings in order to influence the course of Parliamentary deliberations. Such organization was evident in the successful agitations that led to Catholic Emancipation and the passing of the Reform Bill, as it was in agitation still to come, like that of the Anti Corn Law League. Changes in the law and in the constitution itself were being brought about by mobilizing the opinions and feelings of the unenfranchised masses through the use of petitions, meetings, associations, and the press. Parkes, who was one of the most experienced and proficient of the Radical politicians, confidently said, "the public mind in this country will ultimately right everything." And after playing a major role in managing

1. Parkes to Durham and Ellice, Sept. 6, 1835: Lambton Papers. Parkes frequently used this and related metaphors. Sending certain "cheap" political publications to Place, he said they would illustrate "the working of *the* Engine—the Press": Parkes to Place, Dec. 5, 1830, Place Papers (British Museum), Add. MSS 35,148, f. 77. Daniel Whittle Harvey in 1835 referred to "the excitement of the people, or, as the phrase was, . . . keep[ing] the steam up": *Hansard's Parliamentary Debates,* 3d ser., *30,* 1208.

two successful agitations he even felt that "the British constitution is as elastic as a ball of India rubber!"[2]

This great expansion of extra-Parliamentary politics was one of the significant developments of the early nineteenth century. It grew out of the claims of the excluded who were seeking access to the established political institutions, and it was the means by which the governing classes were confronted with these claims. The rationale for the eighteenth-century constitution had provided that all the varied "interests" in the nation were represented in Parliament. Thus, according to Sir Robert Inglis, Parliament "comprehends within itself, those who can urge the wants and defend the claims of the landed, the commercial, the professional classes of the country; those who are bound to uphold the prerogatives of the Crown, the privileges of the nobility, the interests of the lower classes, . . . the rights of the distant dependencies, of the East Indies, of the West Indies, of the Colonies, of the great corporations."[3] But this rationale, which had been shared by Whigs and Tories alike, became inadequate with the rise to political consciousness of sections of the populace who did not feel themselves genuinely represented in the House of Commons. Thus there arose the voice "out of doors." This voice came from the manufacturing towns where, as Lord John Russell described them, "There sprang up a people whom it was easy to inflame and excite by popular harangues, and by the press, by large meetings, and by inflammatory newspapers." The situation was such that Lord Eldon said, if he had to begin life again, he "would begin as an agitator."[4]

The voice sometimes demanded particular changes, such as law reform, free trade, or changes in the Poor Law. But more typically, because of the growth of democratic ideas and also be-

2. Parkes to Durham, May 11, 1834, and Parkes to Durham and Ellice, Sept. 6, 1835: Lambton Papers.

3. Quoted in Samuel H. Beer, "The Representation of Interests in British Government: Historical Background," *American Political Science Review, 51* (1957), 618. Inglis' remarks were made in a speech of March 1, 1831.

4. *Hansard, 51* (Jan. 31, 1840), 1051; Eldon, quoted in Walter Bagehot, *The English Constitution* (London, Oxford, 1955), pp. 143–44.

cause some reformers realized that wider representation would carry with it redress for particular grievances, it called for changes in the constitution of Parliament itself. Thus the typical Radical made reform in the direction of democratic representation his first cause—Major Cartwright, Cobbett, Bentham, Burdett, James Mill, Joseph Sturge, and Henry Hetherington all come to mind. When these demands for changes in the constitution were finally satisfied, Radicalism as a political movement dominating extra-Parliamentary politics would practically disappear.

The governing class recognized the democratic implications of Radicalism, and the Radicals looked upon the governing class as its antagonist and as the main obstacle to revising a constitution that in Radical eyes needed fundamental change. But the lines of battle were not clearly drawn, nor was the issue dividing the two sides clearly defined, for the Radicals derived some of their rhetoric and many of their methods of agitation from the very constitution they were seeking to transform. Their claim on behalf of "the People" was in part derived from the traditional rhetoric of the constitution, though they, of course, invested it with new meaning. The widespread use of this ambiguous term, meaning to some a small, propertied electorate, but to others signifying the entire populace, obscured real differences in outlook; yet it also blunted the edge of political conflict, causing no little confusion as well.[5] Also, the very methods of extra-Parliamentary agitation on which Radicals depended were part of the constitution, although again they refashioned these traditional practices. Among the ideas borrowed by the Radicals from the constitution was the ambiguous right to resist oppression, and acknowledgment of this right, at least among the Whigs, further reduced the governing classes' confidence that Radicalism might be suppressed.[6] Because they borrowed so heavily from the

5. C. S. Emden, *The People and the Constitution. Being a History of the Development of the People's Influence in British Government* (2d ed., London, Oxford, 1956), appendix 1, pp. 317–20.

6. For an example of Radical interpretation of this right, see *The Objects and Laws of the National Union of the Working Classes and Others,* Article XI: "When a government violates the right of the people, resistance becomes the most sacred, and the most indispensable of duties"

eighteenth-century constitution, the Radicals were able to justify their extra-Parliamentary agitation by reference to "rights" provided by it. Consequently, even though they saw Radical claims as a threat to the traditional constitution, the governing classes, especially the Whig politicians, instead of simply assuming the role of aristocratic defenders of the traditional order, felt obliged to acknowledge the legitimacy of much Radical activity, and thus there was a reluctance to pursue a policy of outright repression.[7]

While the governing classes had to acknowledge certain constitutional "rights," they also could recall an aspect of constitutional tradition that allowed them to be skeptical of such Radical claims. The eighteenth-century constitution, it is true, recognized petitioning, public meeting, and liberty of the press as rights and liberties of all Englishmen, and these rights had been widely eulogized long before the appearance of modern Radicalism in the late eighteenth century. In the eighteenth century, however, these practices were not viewed as being intimately connected

---

(n.d. but ca. 1831), p. 3. For acknowledgment of this right as an "extreme remedy against the abuse of power," see Lord John Russell, *An Essay on the History of the English Government and Constitution* (London, 1865), pp. 190–94 (original ed., 1823); J. L. De Lolme, *The Constitution of England; or, An Account of the English Government,* ed. W. H. Hughes (London, 1834), pp. 269–80; Elie Halevy, *England in 1815,* English tr. by E. L. Watkins and D. A. Barker (London, Benn, 1949), p. 148; on its acknowledgment in Blackstone, see J. W. Gough, *Fundamental Law in English Constitutional History* (Oxford, Clarendon, 1955), pp. 186, 190–91.

7. The way in which the Radicals borrowed from traditional writings, many of which expressed British constitutional beliefs, is illustrated in a Radical anthology put together by Thomas Dolby. It gave extracts from the writings of Algernon Sidney, Milton, Charles James Fox, and Erskine (especially from his speeches on behalf of defendants in libel suits), as well as from Bentham, Paine, and Major Cartwright. In all cases, of course, the passage quoted gives support to the Radical position. Under the category "Agitation," Burke is quoted: "I like a clamour where there is an abuse. The fire-bell at midnight disturbs your sleep, but it keeps you from being burned in your bed" (from speech of March 7, 1771). Thomas Dolby, *The Cyclopaedia of Laconics; or, School of Reform in Church and State, being the best things from the best authors, alphabetically arranged, with their applicability to the present times* (London, n.d. but between 1832 and 1840), p. 9 and passim.

with claims by the unenfranchised masses for a share of sovereignty. Extra-Parliamentary politics was merely a sort of political barometer that the government would prudently consult but which it could also ignore. De Lolme, an enthusiast for English liberties who was widely read in England, observed that since "the end of legislation is not . . . to have the particular intentions of individuals, upon every case, known and complied with, but solely to have what is most conducive to the public good found out and established, it is not an essential requisite in legislative operations that every individual should be called upon to deliver his opinion"; on the contrary, he reports that this leads "to the greatest inconveniences."[8] Reflecting this view, Peel in 1831 held that, "We [in Parliament] are here to consult the interests, and not to obey the will of the people, if we honestly believe that that will conflict with those interests."[9] The emphasis was on the checking and constitutionalist but not democratic function of public opinion. The main outlines of the constitution were thought to have been established; public opinion could help it to function, but not in a way that might lead to fundamental change. The law, reflecting these constitutional ideas, therefore placed limits on the use of extra-Parliamentary practices, limits that existed in spite of the widely held belief in the rights and liberties of all Englishmen. As a result, in the contest between Radicalism and the governing classes, it was unclear whether the Radicals were enemies of the constitution because they were seeking to make it more democratic or whether, despite this goal, they had a legitimate role because they were exercising rights it in some sense provided.

Radicalism thus had a dual status in the constitution. The constitution encouraged Radical activity and the extension of Radical claims; but it also possessed the means of restraining Radicalism. As a result, there was much uncertainty about the political effectiveness and the personal consequences of the Radicals' use of the techniques of extra-Parliamentary agitation. This is exemplified by the Radicals' use of the press, for until well into the nineteenth century they could not have used it with confidence that

8. De Lolme, *Constitution of England,* pp. 250–51.
9. Speech of Sept. 21, 1831, quoted in R. J. White, ed., *The Conservative Tradition* (London, Kaye, 1950), p. 132.

they would go unpenalized. The liberty of the press, it is true, was generally acknowledged as a principle of the constitution— had not Blackstone said that it was "essential to the nature of a free state"? And yet while it was praised by lawyers as well as politicians of all parties, Dicey, at the end of the nineteenth century, could still say that the phrase was "not to be found in any part of the statute-book nor among the maxims of the common law."[10] The basis of the claim for its existence was in the final abolition of the Licensing Act in 1694; but since this did not remove responsibility for publication, the extent to which a free press was effectively achieved depended upon the way libel law defined that responsibility and the manner in which the law was enforced. The situation was summed up by the authoritative Blackstone; liberty of the press, he said, "consists in laying no *previous* restraints upon publications, and not in freedom from censure for criminal matter when published. Every freeman has an undoubted right to lay what sentiments he pleases before the public: to forbid this, is to destroy the freedom of the press: but if he publishes what is improper, mischievous, or illegal, he must take the consequences of his own Temerity."[11] Libel law is therefore the key to the reality behind the phrase "liberty of the press."

While the law defined several kinds of libel, the offence most relevant to the legal foundation of liberty of the press was seditious libel. In the eighteenth century this was defined "(omitting technicalities) as written censure upon public men for their conduct as such, or upon the laws, or upon the institutions of the country." This definition reflected theories of government that were current when the law took shape; the doctrine of divine right clearly implies the impropriety of censure by subjects. If literally applied it was, as Stephen has observed, "wholly incon-

10. A. V. Dicey, *Law of the Constitution* (4th ed., London, Macmillan, 1893), p. 227. Stephen suggests that "the rhetoric commonly used about liberty of the press derived some part of its energy and vivacity from the consciousness which the lawyers who employed it must have had of the insecurity of its legal foundations": James Fitzjames Stephen, *A History of the Criminal Law of England, 2* (London, Macmillan, 1883), 349.

11. William Blackstone, *Commentaries on the Laws of England, 4* (Oxford, 1773), 151–53.

sistent with any serious public discussion of political affairs," and "so long as it was recognized as the law of the land all such discussion existed only on sufferance."[12] In fact the law was not enforced, or at least not consistently. Political controversy often flourished, protected somewhat by the prevailing belief in liberty of the press, but also by the belief, fostered by the legends of 1688, that government by consent necessarily involved free discussion. However, while there was a discrepancy between popular belief and the law, governments retained the legal authority to punish and therefore discourage publications that censured public officials, the laws, or the institutions of government. Much moderate and some immoderate criticism went untouched, but in the background there always lurked the legal authority to prosecute those responsible (i.e. author, editor, printer, publisher) for a publication that posed a threat to civil peace or the stability of institutions. Even Blackstone, a firm believer in liberty of the press, justified this consequence of the libel law. He wrote: "to punish (as the law does at present) any dangerous or offensive writings which, when published, shall on a fair and impartial trial be adjudged of a pernicious tendency, is necessary for the preservation of peace and good order, of government and religion—the only solid foundations of civil liberty."[13] Thus libel law was justified as a means of protecting the established order, not excluding the constitution itself, the value of which was not questioned. As long as libel law continued to have this function and as long as something approximating the established definition was maintained, it was hazardous for Radicals to use the press fully. That the law was sometimes enforced is indicated by the 27 convictions between 1819 and 1821. This figure does not include the 25 prosecutions that were unsuccessful but which nonetheless exacted severe penalties from the impecunious editors who typically were the victims.[14] Jonathan Wooler, editor of the

12. Stephen, *History, 2,* 299, 348; W. S. Holdsworth, *A History of English Law, 10* (London, Methuen, 1927, 1938), 673; *6,* 375.
13. *Commentaries, 4,* 152.
14. "Prosecutions for Libel, Blasphemy, and Sedition, 1813–1822," *Parliamentary Papers* (hereafter *PP*), 1823 (562), XV, 239–71. The 27 convictions do not include 2 convictions for both blasphemous and sedi-

Black Dwarf and on one occasion Bentham's printer, was in this situation, as was William Hone who, in 1817, was three times acquitted. Furthermore, those who won acquittals from juries unwilling to find editors guilty on political grounds often found their chances greatly reduced when the government prosecuted for blasphemous libel. Thus, between 1821 and 1834, while there were only 18 convictions for seditious libel, for blasphemous libel there were 75.[15] Looking back to this period, John Stuart Mill noted that "freedom of discussion even in politics, much more in religion, was at that time [1820's] far from being, even in theory, the conceded point which it at least *seems* to be now [1851]."[16]

The situation was such that Bentham was urged by his friends to avoid publication of certain pamphlets in order to avoid the near certainty of prosecution. During the Reform Bill agitation Peel and other Tories frequently urged the government to prosecute. And although the Whig government, long the friend to the principle of a free press, generally resisted these suggestions, it did prosecute Cobbett (unsuccessfully) and Carlile (successfully) in 1831; and it also sent literally hundreds of vendors of unstamped, extreme, radical newspapers to prison during the early thirties.[17] It was only in the mid and late 1830's that Radicals

---

tious libel, nor 16 cases not tried but in which the "defendent suffered judgment by default." The 25 unsuccessful cases include only 1 acquittal, 1 case of a hung jury, and 23 cases not tried. Not included were 8 prosecutions for both blasphemous and seditious libel which were initiated but not tried.

15. *PP*, 1834 (410), XLVIII, 269–72.

16. *The Early Draft of John Stuart Mill's Autobiography*, ed. Jack Stillinger (Urbana, Univ. of Illinois, 1961), p. 88.

17. The *Poor Man's Guardian* claimed that "upwards of five hundred persons" were convicted for selling it as an unstamped paper: W. J. Linton, *James Watson* (Manchester, 1880), p. 33. The *Union* (n.d., but ca. Jan. 1832), p. 133, listed 67 persons convicted by magistrates in metropolitan London during 1831 for selling unstamped papers or almanacs: British Museum, Place Collection of Newscuttings (hereafter PCN), Set 17, *3*, f. 80b.

An attempt has been made to identify the location of documents in the Place Collection of Newscuttings even though some of the pages are not

could feel somewhat secure against conviction. During much of the Radical agitation before this time there was genuine uncertainty as to how free the press really was.

Of all the extra-Parliamentary practices available to the Radicals, petitioning had greater protection than any of the others. The Bill of Rights provided that subjects had the right to petition the King, but even this right was qualified by the continuance of a Restoration statute that disqualified most persons from petitioning for political changes. Before 1779, whereas there were many petitions from private persons and organizations, there was very little genuine political petitioning. With the petition of the Yorkshire freeholders in 1779 there was an example of organized effort to gather very large numbers of signatures, and this is thought to have been the "origin of the modern system of petitioning, by which public measures and matters of general policy, have been forced upon the attention of Parliament."[18] While the right of petitioning had an especially important place in the Whig tradition, by the end of the eighteenth century it was willingly affirmed as a right by men of all views. Pitt, in 1795, affirmed "the right of the people to express their opinions on political men and measures, and to discuss and assert their right of petitioning all branches of the legislature." The number and size of petitions greatly increased (interrupted only by the war and the repressive measures attending it), and they reached their height with reform petitions in 1831–32.[19] However, while this right was well estab-

---

numbered. Wherever unfoliated leaves appear between numbered pages a number is attributed if appropriate; otherwise a letter. For example, if reference is made to the first of several unfoliated leaves between ff. 100 and 101, it is cited as f. 100a; the second, f. 100b; etc.

18. The Restoration statute provided that petitions with 20 or more signatures urging political change could come only from a county meeting convened by the gentry; or in London, a meeting convened by the Common Council: Peter Fraser, "Public Petitioning and Parliament Before 1832," *History, 46* (1961), 200–01; Thomas Erskine May, *The Constitutional History of England, 2* (London, 1873), 61–63; 63, n. 2.

19. Emden, *People and Constitution*, pp. 75–77; Fraser, "Public Petitioning," *History, 46* (1961), 204. Croker reported that petitions calling for Parliamentary reform numbered 19 in 1821, 12 in 1822, 29 in 1823,

lished, as late as 1831–32 there was no general consensus as to what function petitions had in the political system. The presentation of petitions frequently led to debates about their significance. A pro-Reform petition signed by many thousands would be presented as evidence of "public opinion" in a certain county or town; but this would provoke an anti-Reformer to contend that the real opinion of the county or town, by which he would mean the opinion of the educated and propertied persons, was opposed to the Reform Bill.[20] Thus, while the right to petition undoubtedly existed, the exercise of this right was made somewhat less effective by the absence of consensus as to the composition of the public that should exercise it.

To select another and more important example, that of public meetings, again, as with the press, there was much uncertainty about the consequences of engaging in this activity. Fox argued— and this language was widely used—that "the people out of doors . . . possessed a right to declare their opinion of men and things, in order to do which they might meet and consult together, provided they did it in a peaceable, orderly manner."[21] Although his reference to public order appears to be a reasonable criterion of the conditions under which the right might be exercised, in practice the statement was dangerously imprecise, for the crimi-

---

none for 1824 through 1829, 14 in 1830, and 650 up to March 1831: *Hansard*, 3 (March 4, 1831), 88. Colin Leys, "Petitioning in the Nineteenth and Twentieth Centuries," *Political Studies, 3* (1955), 47–49.

20. "Petitions in thousand,—using the same language,—inscribed in the same handwriting, and on the same description of paper,—and signed by fabulous numbers,—have marked the activity of agents rather than the unanimity of petitioners; and, instead of being received as the expression of public opinion, have been reprobated as an abuse of a popular privilege": May, *Constitutional History, 2,* 68. Fraser observes that the "game had been overplayed, and it had become common to despise the signatories and insinuate that they included paupers, prisoners, dependents, servants, women, or minors. The exploitation of petitions for party purposes encouraged many questionable devices for multiplying signatures." Discussion of petitions also became a nuisance, and in 1831 there was agreement to restrict the times for presenting them: Fraser, "Public Petitioning," p. 209.

21. Emden, *People and Constitution*, pp. 82–83.

nal law defined offences in connection with public meetings in such a way that, when the law was vigorously enforced, it discouraged attempts to organize meetings. In addition, when established legal procedures seemed inadequate, special legislation and executive action could effect the same purpose. First, with regard to the law, any speaker at a public meeting risked being charged with the use of seditious words, which were defined the same as seditious libel. In addition, seditious conspiracy was an offence with which those organizing certain public meetings were liable to be charged. Henry Hunt, the leading speaker at the famed Peterloo meeting, and others were tried for a seditious conspiracy in connection with that meeting; and several Chartist leaders and Daniel O'Connell (in connection with Irish agitation) were charged for the same offence. Stephen noted "how wide the legal notion of a seditious conspiracy is. It includes every sort of attempt, by violent language either spoken or written, or by a show of force calculated to produce fear, to effect any public object of an evil character, and no precise or complete definition has ever been given of objects which are to be regarded as evil." Still another provision of law that allowed the government to prosecute and thus discourage the organizers of public meetings was the common law offence of unlawful assembly. This consisted of any meeting convened under circumstances or conducted in a way "such as to produce reasonable fear of a breach of the peace."[22] Although these provisions of the law did not make all public meetings illegal, they did make those who organized and led the meetings vulnerable, for the offences were defined with sufficient breadth to allow considerable discretion as to whether prosecution would be initiated. This discretion was in fact exercised, notably during the five years following Waterloo and again during some of the Chartist agitations when several persons were

22. Stephen, *History*, 2, 378, 380, 386. For a description of the law by a spokesman for moderate radicalism see John Wade, *The Cabinet Lawyer: A Popular Digest of the Laws of England* (London, 1840), pp. 345–46, 355–56. Wade observes that "the general rule of law in regard to public meetings is that—numbers constitute force—force, terror—terror, illegality."

convicted for using seditious words.[23] On other occasions when from nervousness the usual machinery of the law was thought to be inadequate, the government resorted to other devices. For example, in 1795 and 1819, special legislation was passed to restrict public meetings.[24] And in 1831 the Home Secretary effectively discouraged leaders of the National Union of the Working Classes from carrying out their widely advertised plan to hold a public meeting by threatening them with full enforcement of the law. So here again, while the "right" to hold public meetings was widely acknowledged, its exercise in practice was limited.[25]

Finally, turning to political associations, we come to a device like the public meeting, with which they were closely connected, that became particularly important from about 1780 onward and which by the early nineteenth century also became the source of a constitutional dilemma. This is evident in the King's Speech at the opening of Parliament on December 6, 1831, when he alluded to the political unions that had a prominent part in the Reform Bill agitation. "Sincerely attached to our free Constitution," he said, "I never can sanction any interference with the legitimate exercise of those rights which secure to my people the privileges of discussing and making known their grievances; but, in respecting these rights, it is also my duty to prevent combinations, under whatever pretext, which in their form and character are incompatible with all regular government, and are equally opposed to the spirit and to the provisions of the law."[26] A Proclamation had been issued (November 22, 1831), pointing to the illegality of associations that were composed of various divisions, under leaders with gradation of rank and authority, suggestive of military organization. This had been provoked by proposals that

23. Stephen, *History, 2,* 378.

24. Emden, *People and Constitution,* p. 83.

25. Dicey says, "it can hardly be said that our constitution knows of such a thing as any specific right of public meeting": *Law of the Constitution,* pp. 257–59. "The law did not guarantee the right of public assembly, but did not deny it either, unless laws were infringed, in which case the meeting could become an unlawful assembly, or a riot, or a rebellion": E. N. Williams, *The Eighteenth Century Constitution, 1688–1815* (Cambridge Univ. Press, 1960), p. 408.

26. *Hansard, 9* (Dec. 6, 1831), 4–5.

certain unions organize along quasi-military lines and while it silenced the allusions to such organization, it did not put an end to the unions' other activities. The law provided fewer means, however, for discouraging political associations than it did for meetings and the press; yet even without the quasi-military organization they were sufficiently uncertain of legitimacy that Burdett felt uneasy about his membership in the National Political Union on the ground that it was a permanent body speaking for the people and therefore was a rival to Parliament. Thus the unions posed a constitutional dilemma that troubled thoughtful Radicals and caused anxiety among public officials.[27]

The techniques of the extra-Parliamentary politicians had, then, an uncertain status in the law and the constitution. Although acknowledged as rights, there was liability of violating the law if the rights were exercised. The risk was greater in the case of public meetings and the press, less with petitioning and in organizing political associations. The legal uncertainty reflected constitutional ambiguity that was an uneasy blend of two opposing views. At one extreme was the view that the main lines of the constitution are permanently established, and that they provided government by rulers who are "the superior of the subject, as being . . . wise and good, the rightful ruler and guide of the whole population." Hence it is "wrong to censure him openly, that even if he is mistaken his mistakes should be pointed out with the utmost respect, and that whether mistaken or not no censure should be cast upon him likely or designed to diminish his authority." On the other hand there was the opposing view that regarded the ruler "as the agent and servant, and the subject as the wise and good master who is obliged to delegate his power to the so-called ruler because being a multitude he cannot use it himself." From this it follows that any censure is legitimate; indeed, in this view "there can be no such offence as sedition."

27. Parkes also felt that unions ought not to be permanent; he gave this as one of the reasons for not joining the union: *Birm. J.,* Nov. 26, 1831, p. 4; Dec. 3, 1831, p. 2; M. W. Patterson, *Sir Francis Burdett and His Times, 2* (London, Macmillan, 1931), 599–600. Sir James Scarlett held the same view, only more firmly; see *Despatches, Correspondence, and Memoranda of Arthur Duke of Wellington, 8* (London, 1880), 57–58.

These were, of course, extreme views; and Stephen, noting that each had a share in shaping English law, sees the result as a compromise (which of course does not mean that each view contributed equally).[28] During the early nineteenth century, however, when the two views were to be found at the source of many political struggles, their relationship was one of tension, or even conflict, and not an established compromise. But the conflict was not reflected in any of the established political alignments. There were, indeed, persons who advocated one of the two extreme views—Paine or Dr. Price, on one side, and Croker, perhaps, at the other. Most politicians, however, were not so easily typed, and the two views, mixed, but rarely in discernible proportions, are to be found over the entire range of the political spectrum. Both Whigs and Tories, but the Whigs more so, acknowledged the propriety of allowing the "voice of the People" to be heard by the government. But even the Whigs did not face as a theoretical problem the question of the effect, if any, that public opinion was to have on the decisions of government. Their tradition—and this was a national not a party tradition—gave emphasis to a belief in consent and rights, including even a right to resistance, but it also saw Parliament as sovereign and the nondemocratic element in its constitution as being permanently established. The disinclination to settle the question in theory was accompanied by a tendency to settle it in practice, not by reference to conflicting first principles, but empirically, which meant that sometimes the democratic view prevailed and sometimes not.[29] This made it unlikely that the theoretical question would ever be articulated, thus perpetuating in the constitution the ambiguity as to the status of the unenfranchised masses of the "People" and the Radicals who were their spokesmen.

This was the situation facing the Radicals in the early nine-

28. Stephen, *History*, 2, 299–300.

29. Thus the Whigs appeared inconsistent by asserting the obligation to yield to public opinion while also preventing, in certain cases, its free expression. For example, they advocated a free press and resisted most suggestions that the extreme Reform press be prosecuted, yet they maintained the newspaper stamp tax and prosecuted Cobbett and Carlile as well as many vendors of unstamped papers.

teenth century. The constitution allowed them to stimulate popular desires, but it did not assure that government would respond to them. The constitution encouraged the government to permit the Radicals to agitate discontents and mobilize public opinion; but it also gave it discretion to place limitations on such agitation. Furthermore, the government's decision was to be based on its estimate of the intensity of emotion and disposition to violence that Radicalism embodied; the fate of the social order depended on an estimate of these imponderables. Timidity on either side —among the Radicals or the Parliamentary politicians—might assure civil peace, but at the sacrifice of other goals. On the other hand, boldness on either side would bring the risk of violence and perhaps revolution. In these circumstances, as the example of Catholic Emancipation seemed to suggest, attitudes toward risks of violence became an important facet of the political situation.[30] Skillful observers of the political scene instinctively recognized this. Francis Place quickly saw the significance of the cancelation of the King's visit to the City in November 1830. "This is the first time, observe, that apprehension of violence by the people against an administration [operated] as to induce them openly to change their plan of proceeding . . . [it is] the first step in the BRITISH REVOLUTION."[31] It is notable that James Mill, in the course of advocating tactics for Radicalism, emphasized the importance of attitudes toward violence as one of the most important variables in the political situation.

30. Thus Lord Wellesley said of his brother, the Duke of Wellington, "His confession [in 1829] that it was fear of civil war which induced him to grant that boon was a premium upon future agitation. Whatever he thought, he ought not to have put forward such a cause": Broughton, *Recollections of a Long Life, 5* (London, 1911), 31. Of course, as Gash has shown, it was not only fear of being unable to govern Ireland, but domestic political considerations as well, that led to the Emancipation decision: Norman Gash, *Mr. Secretary Peel: The Life of Sir Robert Peel to 1830* (London, Longmans, 1961), pp. 570–74, 587.

31. Place to Hobhouse, Nov. 8, 1830. Add. MSS 35,148, f. 69. Copies and drafts of letters in the Place Papers at the British Museum are not identified as such, even though most of the letters in the collection (other than those addressed to Place) are copies or drafts in Place's handwriting.

CHAPTER 2

Revolution Without Violence

The threat of violence or even revolution appeared quite possible during the early nineteenth century. Many persons felt that society was resting on crumbling foundations, and this made every expression of discontent, whether organized agitation or impassioned outbreak of rioting, appear ominous. Sensing a threat of revolution, men were quick to put into words their nervousness and their expectations. Greville, for example, having been reminded in 1829 of the poverty and drudgery that characterized the lives of many of his countrymen, thought "such an unnatural, artificial, and unjust state of things neither can nor ought to be permanent. I am convinced," he wrote, "that before many years elapse these things will produce some great convulsion." Hobhouse noted in his diary in 1832 that many of the aristocracy "believe themselves, and perhaps are, on the brink of destruction."[1] These expectations were more acute during crises, among the aristocracy especially, but they were also evident among other classes and at other times. There were many reasons for such feelings. Above all there was the rioting that occurred so fre-

1. Greville, quoted in O. F. Christie, *The Transition from Aristocracy 1832–1867* (London, 1927), p. 38; Broughton, *Recollections, 4,* 185. It is not certain that Hobhouse shared those fears. In June 1832 he noted, "We . . . opened our handsome drawing-rooms. How long for! . . . so we go on, even to the brink, so they say, of ruin and revolution": ibid., p. 240. For other examples see *The Greville Memoirs,* eds., Lytton Strachey and Roger Fulford, *2* (London, Macmillan, 1938), 138; J. R. M. Butler, *The Passing of the Great Reform Bill* (London, 1914), pp. 100, 136; Elie Halevy, *The Triumph of Reform 1830–1841,* Eng. tr., E. I. Watkin (London, Benn, 1950), p. 43; Christie, *Transition from Aristocracy,* pp. 48–51.

quently as to be called a "national pastime."[2] The Gordon riots, Birmingham riots in 1791, O.P. riots, Corn Law riots, Luddism, Peterloo, election rioting, and the disturbances in agricultural districts in 1830–31 were all well-remembered events that shaped the image of discontentedness among the populace. There was enough awareness of poverty to make discontent seem natural.[3] The existence of the urban mob—which has been called an "unknown or little known *residuum* of the population"[4]—made the possibility of violent revolution more plausible and increased the feeling of insecurity among the respectable classes. The absence of an adequate police force also meant a greater sense of dependence on moral restraints and on deferential attitudes among the populace, a circumstance that made violence appear to be the natural concomitant of discontent. Finally, all symptoms appeared especially ominous from the tendency to see them in the context of the French Revolution. All these circumstances shaped the feeling that violence existed just beneath the surface and might burst out at any moment.

Politicians were aware of such apprehensions and many shared them. Some experienced acute fear of revolution; others recognized a danger that, even if it were not imminent, made the political system vulnerable; still others, aware of such a sense of insecurity among their rivals, attempted to manipulate fears of revolution in order to achieve partisan goals. Although the mood of insecurity and fear affected politicians differently, for all alike it entered into their calculations and affected their judgments.

W. E. Houghton says, "The growing bitterness of class feeling, after issuing in physical violence and repressive force, made the threat of revolution tangible and immediate to an extent unknown in England or the United States today": *The Victorian Frame of Mind 1830–1870* (New Haven, Yale, 1957), p. 56.

2. Sir Carleton Kemp Allen, *The Queen's Peace* (London, Stevens, 1953), p. 114.

3. Canning thought that the Poor Laws, by protecting society from the consequences of complete pauperization, "saved England from revolution." The Liberal economist McCulloch shared this view: Beatrice and Sidney Webb, *English Local Government, 7* (London, 1906), 404–05.

4. Christie, *Transition from Aristocracy*, p. 49.

The Art of Revolution: James Mill

Almost all early nineteenth-century reformers, even the most radical of them, were aware of the possibility of violent revolution and, as a result, they faced a dilemma. They wished to bring about extensive changes yet, with the rest of the nation, they abhorred violence and felt skeptical about the value of reform achieved through its use. In these circumstances the apparently peaceful course lay in creating public pressure for reform. But the effectiveness and even the legitimacy of this line of conduct was uncertain during this predemocratic period. The precariousness of exercising such rights as liberty of the press or assemblage of public meetings was brought home by the many prosecutions for sedition. At the same time, the violent alternative was made more abhorrent to them by the French Revolution. That event is often cited, and rightly so, as having put a damper on political movements in England; yet, whereas it did frighten the governing classes, justifying in their eyes the policy of prosecution against some of the radicals, it also gave most radicals a heightened sense of responsibility about the role they were playing. Admittedly there were outbreaks of violence, especially after the close of the Napoleonic wars, but many of them appear to have been largely spontaneous, as in the case of the Luddites, and, although some were organized, the leadership was distinguished by amateurishness, as in the Cato Street plot and the Pentrich "revolution."[1] When one looks to the most prominent leaders in extra-Parliamentary politics one finds evidence of a firm commitment to peaceful methods. By 1831 when political unions came to play so important a part in the agitation for the Reform Bill, the Birmingham Political Union, which was a model for most of the others, always emphasized what was by now a standard theme in radical politics—its commitment to peaceful and legal means.[2]

1. R. J. White, *Waterloo to Peterloo* (London, Heinemann, 1957), pp. 162–75; Frank O. Darvall, *Popular Disturbances and Public Order in Regency England* (London, Oxford, 1934), pp. 174–75, 197.
2. C. M. Wakefield, *Life of Thomas Attwood* (London, 1885), p. 135. It is noteworthy that Place, the Radical and organizer of the National Political Union, played an important part in the development of police

Thus, throughout this period, even though the more nervous members of the governing classes dreaded revolution and saw evidence of it in public meetings and in radical journals, the leaders of the radical movement, with France in mind, rejected the role of conspirator or demagogue and thought of themselves as anything but revolutionaries.

There is no one of whom this was more true than James Mill. His desire for extensive reform informed all he did and thought, whether it was his journalism or his administrative activities on behalf of the East India Company, or even his *History of British India,* which, it has been argued, carried an esoteric critique of English society.[3] Even the education he gave to his son can be said to have had this purpose. Yet no Tory had a more discerning eye for and genuine horror of threats to the social order. He was a university student at Edinburgh from 1790 to 1793, but there is no evidence that he uttered a word of sympathy for the French Revolution. And while he referred to the French as a nation that had "dared to lift its eyes to liberty," he sharply condemned the result "when some hired ruffians in the metropolis were allowed to give law to the whole nation."[4] He expressed great distaste for Henry Hunt, the main speaker at the Peterloo meeting, whom he called "a demagogue . . . that appeals to the rabble." And his view that the spread of Hodgskin's economic beliefs "would be the subversion of civilized society" does not encourage a belief that he was irresponsible in his radicalism.[5] At the same time, however, he was a republican, an agnostic, and a democrat.

Wanting fundamental changes in the constitution, yet above all else anxious to avoid violence, Mill, like other radicals, turned to extra-Parliamentary politics. Here the traditional "rights" of public meeting and petition and the unanimous agreement that

---

tactics of mob control. Reith credits him with being "the inventor of the baton charge": Charles Reith, *British Police and the Democratic Ideal* (London, Oxford, 1943), p. 72.

3. D. Forbes, "James Mill and British India," *Cambridge Journal,* 5 (1951), 19–33.

4. "Sur la Souveraineté," *Edinburgh Review, 17* (1811), 409.

5. Mill to Brougham, Sept. 3, 1832, in Alexander Bain, *James Mill, A Biography* (London, 1882), p. 364.

liberty of the press was an established "principle" of the constitution gave some scope for action. Despite the risks attending the exercise of these rights, they gave some foundation to the belief that public opinion was not totally irrelevant to the deliberations of even an unreformed Parliament. This belief was encouraged by the Lockian tradition which influenced much popular political thought at this time. It is therefore not surprising that the Radicals turned to the press and public meetings as the lever of change. But unlike most other Radicals, who merely insisted that traditional rights be respected, Mill's response to the Radical's dilemma was not without novel features, a circumstance that allowed him to hope for more than ordinary influence during any future constitutional crisis.

While Mill was firmly attached to nonviolent methods, he was in a sense revolutionary in his political goals, for he sought a fundamental change in the constitution of government so that the legislature would be genuinely and fully representative of the people and not dominated by a small aristocracy. "The real object to be aimed at in the composition of a legislature," Mill said, "is to prevent the predominance of the interest of any individual, or of any class; because, if such interest predominates . . . it will be promoted at the expense of the community." Applying this principle to the British case, Mill held that "in the composition of the English legislature, the predominance of the aristocracy is so complete, that whatever they wish to do, they always have it in their power to do—whatever they wish to prevent, they always have it in their power to prevent." He therefore believed that "no change can, directly, be any improvement whatsoever in the British legislature, which does not substitute the predominance of the general interest to the existing predominance of a particular interest."[6] This meant that Mill was not satisfied with piecemeal reforms, nor with the Whigs, the party associated with the policy of small improvements introduced gradually. When certain members of the Whig opposition introduced bills providing for small "improvements" (redistricting, small increase in

6. James Mill, "Summary Review of the Conduct and Measures of the Seventh Imperial Parliament," in *Parliamentary History and Review* [for 1826] (1826), p. 781.

the electorate, redistribution of seats from the smallest boroughs to the counties and towns), Mill argued that such changes "would detract nothing from the power of the aristocracy, who would nominate just as many members after such a change, as before it." Thus he saw the Reform Bill as the first step, desirable only because it would inevitably bring still greater constitutional changes.[7]

Assuming the desirability of representative government, Mill turned to the question of how this fundamental change could be achieved. The difficulty, as he saw it, arose from his belief, which was fundamental to his psychological theory and at the foundation of his political speculations, that "rulers," like all persons, acted to maximize, and therefore perpetuate, their power. This belief prevented Mill from conceiving even the possibility of concessions being voluntarily granted by an oligarchy. Acting from selfish motives, which were the only ones Mill would acknowledge, an oligarchy would defend its superior position with force if necessary. Since Mill wished to achieve fundamental reforms without violence, it became necessary to devise means by which an oligarchy would be led to grant concessions out of self-interest.

In the absence of representation, there were only two alternatives: "they [the people] can only obtain any considerable ameliorations in their government by resistance, by applying physical force to their rulers, or, at least, by threats so likely to be followed by performance, as may frighten their rulers into compliance."[8]

---

7. Ibid., p. 782. The same holds for most of the other Benthamites. Roebuck: "Although the democrats were glad to receive the Bill at their [Whigs] hands, they . . . took it as an installment of justice—as . . . a stepping stone to further great improvements." Hume "supported the Reform Bill . . . with all its defects, because . . . the Government could not have carried out . . . any greater extent of reform": *Hansard, 36* (Jan. 31, 1837), 30; *46* (March 21, 1839), 1055. On the magnitude of the various changes for which the Reform Bills provided, see N. Gash, *Politics in the Age of Peel* (London, Longmans, 1953), chap. 3, 4; C. Seymour, *Electoral Reform in England and Wales* (New Haven, Yale, 1915), chap. 2–5.

8. James Mill, "Liberty of the Press," p. 18, in *Essays on Government, Jurisprudence, Liberty of the Press, and Law of Nations* (London, ca. 1825).

Since the use of physical force was to be avoided, Mill built his hopes on the second alternative, which he called "intellectual force."[9] Mill was proposing that revolution be threatened. He assumed that the threat would be sufficient and that it would not be necessary to carry it out. As it turned out, Mill was to have an opportunity to observe an event—the passing of the Reform Bill—which would put this assumption to a critical test.

Although Mill was advocating tactics that are often used in politics (the analogy of "brinkmanship" also comes to mind) and in bargaining situations generally, he was unusual for attempting to be explicit and in specifying the conditions under which these tactics would work.[10] The press was to be the means of making the threat of revolution an effective instrument of peaceful constitutional change. First of all, it was a means of stimulating criticism, of making discontent articulate, of enlarging the body of critics. "So true it is," Mill said, ". . . that the discontent of the people is the only means of removing the defects of vicious governments, that the freedom of the press, the main instrument of creating discontent, is . . . the greatest safeguard of the interests of mankind."[11] Therefore he felt that, "Nothing is more important than the frequent recounting of those evils [of bad government], which they who suffer them always know, but of which they lose the accurate and pungent sense, if the thought of them

9. "Liberty of the Press," *Edinburgh Review, 18* (1811), 104–05.

10. Various kinds of threats of civil disobedience were part of the radical tradition, but those who advocated them did not often calculate on nonviolent change as a consequence of their use. There was also a vague awareness that public opinion could in some way exert pressure, but the exact way in which this was achieved was not often made clear. For suggestions that come close to Mill's see: Jeremy Bentham, "To the Spanish People on Liberty of Public Discussion," in *Works of Jeremy Bentham,* ed. John Bowring, 2 (Edinburgh, 1843), 287; Thompson's letter of March 9, 1828, in L. G. Johnson, *Life of General T. Perronet Thompson 1783–1869* (London, Allen & Unwin, 1957), p. 137; and Matthew Arnold, *Culture and Anarchy,* ed. J. D. Wilson (Cambridge Univ. Press, 1932), p. 203, on the belief of some of his contemporaries that "obstinate governments" ought "wholesomely be frightened by a little disturbance, the good design in view, and the difficulty of overcoming opposition to it being considered."

11. "Liberty of the Press," p. 18, in *Essays.*

is not frequently and vividly renewed."[12] Unlike many of his Whig contemporaries, Mill was not simply saying that public opinion was a useful check on government; on the contrary, he thought that government "generally, and on all important occasions . . . may and does with security brave it." Public expression of discontent was only the first step, but in itself not sufficient, for the achievement of constitutional change without violence. For "resistance to have this effect," Mill said, it "must also be general. To be general, it must spring from a general conformity of opinion, and a general knowledge of that conformity." Public opinion, in other words, must appear to be unanimous as well as intense, and there must be a widespread belief that this is in fact the case. Only in these circumstances would the governing classes who were in a position to make concessions perceive its threatening character. As Mill put it, "defective institutions . . . will never be improved, unless the knowledge of those defects is diffused among the people, and excites among them a disapprobation which the rulers do not think it prudent to disregard." It was only the "force of a strong public feeling" to which the oligarchy was "destined to yield."[13]

In creating what was in fact a tactical doctrine for reformers, Mill seems to have been confident that there would be no violence —that the people in expressing discontent would not go too far and that, rather than risk disorder, the governing officials would prudently make concessions. He was assured in part by "the experience of history"; he invited comparison of "those countries which have enjoyed the most power of censure by the press; and those which have enjoyed the least:—in which," he asked, "has there appeared the greatest disposition to anarchy, and in which the least?" Looking to England, Holland, Switzerland, and the United States, on the one hand, Turkey and Italy, on the other, he sought to establish an association between a free press and order and between despotism and insurrection. But it was the example of France, where during the Revolution there were ac-

12. [James Mill,] *On the Ballot* (3d ed., London, 1830; with corrections and additions), pp. 12–13.
13. "Liberty of the Press," pp. 28–29, in *Essays;* "Summary Review," p. 778.

knowledged abuses by the press, that had to be explained. Looking on the abuses of the press "as the effect, not the cause of the public disorders," Mill decided that, "had real freedom of the press been enjoyed—had the honest men whom France contained been left a channel by which to lay their sentiments before the public—had a means been secured of instructing the people in the real nature of the delusions which were practiced upon them, the enormities of the revolution would have been confined within a narrow compass, and its termination would have been very different."[14] Mill felt confident in his position even without explaining away the anarchy that accompanied the French Revolution. "How absurd is it," he says, "because *one* experiment—that of France—has failed, to entertain a prejudice against all changes of government . . . when so many more have succeeded"; and he pointed to the revolts of the Swiss against Austria, the North Americans against Britain, and the British against the Stuarts, in which "no difficulty appears to have been experienced, in any of those instances, in restraining the excesses of popular violence."[15] When he turned to the actual circumstances of his own country—and he lived at a time when public disorder was anything but unusual— he could thus make light of the risk attending disorder. "What signify the irregularities of a mob, more than half composed, in the greater number of instances, of boys and women, and disturbing for a few hours or days a particular town?"[16] Mill could look not only to the experience of history for support, but to his rationalistic psychology as well. Assuming as he did that men were capable of rational calculation and that they were moved by the desire to minimize pain, he was able to

14. *Edinburgh Review, 18* (1811), 117–19.

15. "Emancipation of Spanish America," *Edinburgh Review, 13* (1809), 304. "In all questions of political change, there are two dangers, of an opposite direction, to be considered. The first is the danger of doing too little; the second that of doing too much. The first is by far the most common error; as timidity is a much more universal and powerful source of human misery than rashness; although the evils produced by the second, are much more simultaneous, and, for the moment, much more formidable": ibid., p. 303.

16. "Government," p. 32, in *Essays.*

assume that rulers would prudently make concessions in the face of public opinion that appeared to be sufficiently threatening.

Mill's tactics could of course have been used with any of the techniques of extra-Parliamentary politics, and Mill's friends did apply them in a variety of ways during the agitation for the Reform Bill. Mill himself mainly thought of them in connection with the press. He was aware of "the growing contrariety between the state of government, and the state of the public mind, in every country in Europe, and not least in England," and he felt that this would allow for a "considerable alteration at no very distant day in the mode of administering public affairs."[17] To this end Mill engaged in journalism and encouraged others to do the same. Even his apparently theoretical works, of which his essay "Government" is the most notable example, were in fact polemical writings dealing with immediate issues of his time.

Since the press could be effectively used as Mill wished only if it was available to like-minded Radicals, Mill understandably had a strong interest in the question of liberty of the press. He had written an analysis of the legal foundations of liberty of the press as early as 1811; he volunteered an article on the subject to the editor of the *Supplement* to the *Encyclopaedia Britannica,* for which he had already written the article "Government."[18]

17. *Parliamentary History and Review* [for 1826], p. 797. "That governments . . . can now turn back the tide of public opinion, it would require more than the blindness of bad governments, amid all that is passing around us, to believe": ibid., p. 798. Mill also observed that "The art of printing exists . . . information which it diffuses necessitates, not a change merely, but a perfect revolution in the art of governing mankind": *On the Ballot,* p. 4.

18. "There is," he wrote, "one article more . . . I shall be very glad to undertake. That is, Liberty of the Press, or Libel Law, whichever title you choose to range it under." And he added, "I think on that subject I could throw a good deal of light." This offer was made and its promise fulfilled between January and October of 1821: Mill to Macvey Napier, Jan. 3, 1821, in Macvey Napier, ed., *Selection from the Correspondence of the late Macvey Napier, Esq.* (London, 1879), p. 26. Mill later complained that he was not pleased with the article, apparently because he was obliged to compress his original draft; but, he wrote, "I still think that my doctrines are made out": Mill to Napier, Aug. 21, 1821: Napier Papers, Add. MSS 34,612, ff. 438–39.

This interest is also reflected in some of John Stuart Mill's earliest writings, which dealt with particular cases of prosecution as well as the general principle of a free press. Mill's concern was stimulated by his having witnessed, sometimes at close hand, efforts to intimidate Radical journalists. The law, as has been noted, made almost any kind of negative criticism of government vulnerable to prosecution. Mill had witnessed the way Bentham suppressed his *Art of Packing Special Juries,* written in 1809 and finally published in 1821. He knew Jonathan Wooler, editor of the *Black Dwarf,* who had been twice prosecuted and once convicted in 1817. With these and many other cases in mind Mill proposed a change in the law of libel. Thus his *Encyclopaedia* article, "Liberty of the Press," while giving scant attention to the description of facts that *Encyclopaedia* readers might have expected, took up the question of the limits it was "desirable" to place upon the press. And this normative inquiry was carried on in the context of his wish to allow the press to serve as a means of achieving fundamental but nonviolent change. His main emphasis was on a free press as a means of "removing the defects of vicious governments," and for this reason his essay "Liberty of the Press" should be seen as complementing his essay "Government," which analyzes such viciousness and proposes a remedy for it.[19]

Mill's approach to the subject was determined by his preoccupation with reforming government. After briefly disposing of individual rights in relation to the press, he turned to "the use of the press in speaking of the institutions and functionaries of governments" as the "main branch of the inquiry."[20] He sets up a fourfold classification of the statements the law might notice and, in seeing all of them as various kinds of "exhortation" to

19. "Liberty of the Press," p. 18, in *Essays,* where he refers his readers to his essay "Government" for a full explanation of "what is meant by a vicious government." On reading it Ricardo wrote to Mill, "The principles you lay down naturally follow from those which you had before established in your article on Government," Oct. 14, 1821, in *The Works and Correspondence of David Ricardo,* ed. Piero Sraffa with the collaboration of M. H. Dobb, 9 (Cambridge Univ. Press, 1952), 102.

20. "Liberty of the Press," pp. 4, 29, in *Essays.*

"resist" government, he reveals his central concern with fundamental change. Each of his four types of statement is examined to determine whether it should be permitted or made punishable.[21]

The only kind of statement that Mill would not allow in the press was an exhortation to use force "to resist the government in applying to the execution of the laws the physical power placed at its disposal by the laws" (a direct and detailed statement in his classification). Thus, for example, he would not allow distribution of a handbill that "may excite a mob to disturb the proceedings of a court of justice, to obstruct public officers in the execution of their duties, or even to disturb . . . the deliberations of the legislature itself." Mill justified this restraint on the press, first on the ground that such expressions, if allowed, "would render [the government] inadequate to the ends which it is provided to secure," and also for the reason that the conduct such expression encourages was "not that species of resistance which is necessary, in the last resort, to secure the people against the abuse of the powers of government."[22]

Apart from this one exception, Mill would not allow penalties for any other kind of statement. For one thing, he would permit a statement if it directly called for resistance, but in general terms, without directing men's attention to a particular act of government to be resisted. Statements of this kind (direct and general in his classification) call for "resistance to all the powers of government at once, either to withdraw them from the hands in which they have hitherto been deposited, or greatly to modify the terms upon which they are held." The purpose in either case would be "some great change in the government at large." By way of justification Mill indicated that such bold calls for extensive change would be either harmless or irresistible; harmless if consensus as to the need to resist does not exist, for "a mere exhortation, read in print, can have no effect which is worth regarding"; however, "if this consent exists in such perfection as

21. He saw political utterances as having two dimensions. They are either general or detailed and either direct (explicit) or indirect. Thus there are four categories: detailed and direct; general and direct; detailed and indirect; general and indirect.
22. "Liberty of the Press," pp. 14–15, in *Essays*.

to want nothing to begin action but an exhortation, nothing can prevent the exhortation; and forbidding it is useless."[23]

Direct (i.e. explicit) calls to resistance were of course uncommon, and it is in connection with the other kinds of statements that Mill's permissiveness was more important. These statements expressed censure and criticism—what Mill called "indirect exhortation to resistance." These could be either detailed or general, depending upon whether the comment was concerned with particular actions of government or with government in general. His rationale for allowing both kinds was the same; indirect comment (also called implied and constructive), he argued, contributed to "laying the grounds of dissatisfaction," and this was the source of resistance to bad government. Censure could thus be extended to the most general aspects of government and also to the decisions and actions of particular officials. Since Mill thought (as did the courts) that "all censure thrown either upon the institutions of government, or upon the conduct of any government functionaries, supreme or subordinate, has a tendency to produce resistance to the government," this provision would go far toward achieving the goal he had in mind. Mill's awareness of this is evident in his observation that "almost every thing which relates to the use of the press in matters of government, will be found to be involved" with this kind of comment.[24]

Mill makes other subordinate proposals that reveal his purpose to use the press as a means of bringing about fundamental change. One such proposal was that any belief or opinion that is not to be considered punishable for its substance ought not to be made so by the use of "passionate language" or "vehement expressions" or words "calculated to inflame," for there is, he contended, little

23. Ibid., pp. 14, 15, 17.
24. Ibid., pp. 17–18, 23–24. "The people ought to know, if possible, the real qualities of the actions of those who are entrusted with any share in the management of their affairs. This they have no chance of knowing, without the unlimited power of censure upon those actions, both in gross and detail": ibid., p. 24. Mill was so preoccupied with the need to eliminate oligarchical government that he thought undeserved praise worse than undeserved censure, for it gave security to bad government. He even suggested that it be made punishable: ibid., pp. 25–26.

difference in the consequences of passionate and calm modes of expression. He also claimed that in expressing moral approbation or disapprobation, language that is in some degree passionate is unavoidable, and that therefore passionate language cannot be forbidden without forbidding censure itself.[25] And it is censure that Mill wished to allow and even encourage.

Mill closes his essay with an argument that the boundaries proposed for liberty of the press be made applicable to questions of religion. While this is consistent with and perhaps even a reflection of his attitude to religion, the argument is above all political in character. It must be considered in relation to libel law and its enforcement. In common law, blasphemous libel was a criminal offence; it originally had been defined as a publication that promoted impiety and irreligion. It always had been relevant to politics, since religion was recognized to be a source of cleavage as well as consensus, but it was given special political significance during the early nineteenth century when prosecutions for blasphemous libel were directed to men whose political influence made them the object of official disapproval. This was only partly the result of the government's association of godlessness with radicalism and its belief that one encouraged the other; a more relevant consideration was probably the belief that juries would be offended more by atheism than democracy and therefore would more likely convict on a prosecution for blasphemy than for sedition. Mill certainly knew of the well-publicized trials in 1817 of William Hone, Radical editor of the *Reformist's Register,* and the several trials of Carlile and members of his family, in which the government prosecuted for blasphemous libel more often than for seditious libel. Although these tactics did not always succeed (Hone was acquitted three times), indictments (or informations) for blasphemy were generally more effective. It was not unreasonable then, for Mill, in view of his purpose, to seek to invalidate this means of suppressing the political influence of the press. He therefore noted that, "religious opinions can be made to embrace everything upon which the unlimited power of rulers . . . depend"; and he warned, "Permit any

25. Ibid., pp. 31–33.

man . . . to say what shall, and what shall not, be religious opinions, you make him despotic immediately."[26]

When Mill was developing these ideas, and in fact throughout his lifetime, both constitutional doctrine and the law were anything but favorable to his proposals. They were not adopted, nor could Mill have expected that they would be. Their significance lies in the way they reveal his view of the press as an instrument for provoking a constitutional crisis that might be resolved by the concession of fundamental reforms. The essay in which they appear was among the seven *Encyclopaedia* articles that were privately printed during the 1820's and which had a considerable influence on the small group of disciples that was forming at this time. While the more famous essay, "Government," was most influential among the younger disciples, many of whom entered the House of Commons in 1833, "Liberty of the Press" was capable of even greater appeal among those Radicals who, by preference or circumstances, chose, like Mill himself, to avoid the Parliamentary stage. It is thus in the conduct of men such as Place and Parkes that evidence of Mill's influence through this essay must be sought. Mill himself, of course, took an active part in the Reform Bill agitation, as several witnesses testify; and although the exact character of his activities is often uncertain, it is clear that he personally conveyed to his associates the tactical message to be found (though not systematically presented) in the essay.[27] The essay, then, was not necessarily the

26. Ibid., p. 34.

27. *The Amberley Papers. The Letters and Diaries of Lord and Lady Amberley,* ed. Bertrand and Patricia Russell, *1* (London, Hogarth, 1937), 369–70; Harriet Grote, *Life of George Grote* (London, 1873), p. 69; Mill to Albany Fonblanque, Oct. 25, 1831, in Mill-Taylor Collection, *49A,* 1 (British Library of Political and Economic Science). It clearly would have been imprudent for Mill systematically to present these tactics, for it would have invited charges of intimidation such as were in fact made in 1831–32; and it would have made it easier for anti-Reformers to claim that public opinion was artificially stimulated. For the fact that Mill admired the skillful use of the art of rhetoric and in fact practiced it, see John Stuart Mill, *Autobiography* (London, Oxford, 1958), pp. 36–37; Stillinger, ed., *Early Draft of J. S. Mill's Autobiography,* pp. 47, 61.

means by which men such as Parkes and Place or editors such as Fonblanque and John Black were exposed to Mill's tactical ideas, but it does reveal what tactical ideas Mill urged on those whose cooperation he sought. During 1831–32 several of Mill's friends played an important part in the organization of extra-Parliamentary support for the Reform Bill. Parkes and Place are the most notable examples, for they were deeply involved in all aspects of the agitation—writing in the press, writing important pamphlets, organizing meetings and street processions, and playing a large part in the organization and management of political unions. In these activities there are indications that they intended to mobilize public opinion in the manner recommended by James Mill.

The Art of Avoiding Revolution: The Whigs

The years 1830–32 provided the marked growth in public feeling that Mill's tactics required. Also, and this was equally necessary for his hopes, these years brought a government sensitive to the dangers of such public feelings, possibly even oversensitive to them. The Whig government that gained office in 1830 was well suited to play the role envisaged by Mill for the governing class. On the one hand, it was not without fear of anarchy; it revealed its nervousness in 1831 when, faced with rural disturbances, it prosecuted the Radical journalists Cobbett and Carlile, whose writings were thought to have encouraged the disorders. On the other hand, as it was strongly attached to the belief in government by consent, it used repressive measures with reluctance. When faced with a choice between governing, as Macaulay put it, either by the sword or by public opinion, the Whigs were disposed to choose the latter, so long as public opinion demanded changes that were in principle compatible with traditional institutions. Both their fear of anarchy and their belief in government by consent disposed them, when faced with loud and apparently angry demands of the public, to make concessions. To have to rule by the sword would increase the threat of revolution. Thus they thought of reform not in the manner of their Tory opponents, as the near-equivalent of revolution, but as the only alternative to it.[1]

Because of their antirevolutionary orientation, the Whigs adopted tactics complementary to Mill's, and they did so in a way that enhanced the influence of anyone following Mill's recommendations. Mill sought a fundamental change in the constitution, and he was willing to stimulate popular demand to the point at which it appeared to be revolutionary. On the other side, the Whigs above all sought to avoid revolution, and they were willing to concede a fundamental constitutional change to achieve this goal. Both were anxious to avoid violence and to facilitate peaceful change. But for the Whigs this was a primary goal, whereas for Mill it was to be made to appear secondary. Thus the Whigs, by making their determination to avoid violence so evident, were especially vulnerable to Mill's tactics.

There were, of course, numerous arguments that moved the Whigs to support reform. Without being democrats, their belief in representation was sufficiently ingrained that the more notorious of the rotten boroughs appeared anomalous, as did the lack of representation for the new industrial towns. They also sought to enhance the independent status of the House of Commons by introducing a basis of representation that would be somewhat independent of the largest holders of landed property who were, of course, represented in the Lords. But these arguments had been heard before. Now, in the face of agitation and many symptoms of unrest, the Whigs approached Parliamentary reform as a means of reducing discontents and the threat of revolution they held out. All other arguments for reform were subordinated to the Whig contention that reform was necessary in order to avoid revolution. It was not uncommon to draw analogies with 1789. Durham, one of the authors of the Reform Bill, for example, expressed the view that the French Revolution, as well as the

1. "Reform that you may preserve," Macaulay urged. Mackintosh said, "Repair is now the most likely means of preserving our fundamental institution": *Hansard, 4* (July 4, 1831), 679; *4* (June 21, 1831), 115. Bagehot said the Whigs "have a conservatism of their own": "The First Edinburgh Reviewers," in *The Works and Life of Walter Bagehot,* ed. Mrs. Russell Barrington, *2* (London, 1915), 66.

Revolution of 1641 and the separation of the North American colonies, "might all have been averted by timely and wise concession." Had this been done, he said, "the people would have been satisfied, the ancient institutions of the country ameliorated, the altar, the throne, and the aristocracy preserved from the horrible fate which afterwards befell them." But instead concession was refused, first under Turgot and then under Necker. "The nobility resisted, and the Revolution followed."[2] Lord Holland asked, "is [it] not much more dignified to yield before there is danger . . . than to concede after rebellion has raised its head?" The argument that concession was required in order to avoid revolution, that it is expedient to yield to necessity, appears to have been the decisive consideration in the Whig government's determination to see the Reform Bill passed.[3]

The Whig diagnosis of England's danger was based on an implied theory of revolution. Revolutions took place in a disordered society where there was a lack of balance or a disproportion between political institutions and social structure. This produced "intestine disorders" and ultimately revolution. "The great cause of revolutions," Macaulay said, "is this, that, while nations move onward, constitutions stand still," or in other words, "that the natural [i.e. social] distribution of power and the legal distribution of power have not corresponded with each other."[4] Lord

2. S. J. Reid, *Life and Letters of the First Earl of Durham, 1* (London, 1906), 282–83. Thus, while it is in part true, as commonly held, that the French Revolution discouraged reform during the early nineteenth century, it also had the opposite effect, for it helped justify the concession of reform as an alternative to revolution.

3. *Hansard, 7* (Oct. 5, 1831), 1327; M. G. Brock, "The Reform Act of 1832," in *Britain and The Netherlands,* ed. J. S. Bromley and E. H. Kossmann (London, Chatto and Windus, 1960), pp. 180–88. For skepticism about the concession theory, see D. C. Moore, "The Other Face of Reform," *Victorian Studies, 5* (1961), 8–9, 30–33.

4. Thomas B. Macaulay, *Speeches,* ed. G. M. Young (London, Oxford, 1952), pp. 25, 94. The object of the Bill was "to correct those monstrous disproportions and to bring the legal order of society into something like harmony with the natural order." And on another occasion Macaulay said, "There is a change in society," and therefore, "there must be a corresponding change in the government": ibid., pp. 83, 94.

Durham held the same view, that revolution resulted when those with social power were frustrated in their effort to gain a share of political power; the result of "continued exclusion must be a political convulsion . . . for the unnatural compression of great power by insufficient means, always ends not only in the annihilation of the feeble public bonds which restrain it, but in the destruction of all that is within the range of its explosion."[5] The precondition for revolution, then, was broad social and economic changes that led to a redistribution of "power" in society (i.e. wealth, influence, status); and the immediate cause was refusal by those who had access to the power of the state to alter the constitutional arrangements so as to allow "into the national councils every rising portion of the community."[6] The result will be a "change between confidence and distrust, affection and hatred . . . resistance must produce the very worst consequences, tending to destroy that harmony and goodwill among all classes of society, which are so essential in every well-governed state."[7]

This theory was placed in a historical context. Believing as they did that the source of danger lay in the framework of society, the historical causes were traced back to broad changes in the economic and social structure. Macaulay, it is not surprising to find, provided the most orderly explanation:[8] A "great revolution" had taken place, he said. "New forms of property came into existence. New portions of society rose into importance. . . . Towns shrank into villages. Villages swelled into cities larger than the London of the Plantagenets." However, "while the natural growth of society went on, the artificial polity continued unchanged." As a result there "came that pressure almost to bursting, the new wine in the old bottles, the new society under the old institutions." History provided many examples of the struggle between "the young energy of one class and the ancient privileges of another. . . . Such . . . is the struggle which the

5. *Hansard, 12* (April 13, 1832), 356.
6. Mackintosh, ibid., *4* (July 4, 1831), 682.
7. Durham, ibid., *12* (April 13, 1832), 362.
8. Macaulay, *Speeches,* pp. 8–9, 25. This interpretation is also to be found in speeches of other Whig spokesmen, for example in *Hansard:* Lansdowne, *4,* 131; Mackintosh, *4,* 682; Durham, *12,* 356–57.

middle classes in England are maintaining against an aristocracy of mere locality." If the middle class is granted "a place in the system, suited, not to its former weakness, but to its present power," then, "all is well." If it was refused, however, the future would be ominous.

The Whigs, although uneasy about the unrest that was all too evident in 1831, saw even more serious trouble on distant horizons. They were mainly concerned about the possibility of a revolution in the future—not in 1831 but in, say, 1851—or as it turned out, in 1842 and 1848. They thought the present unrest was under control for the time being, and that it would subside with the passing of the Reform Bill. When they acknowledged the extreme dissidence of men "who utterly distrust and despise all the institutions of the country,"[9] they thought it was confined to a small group that was dangerous only should its ideas spread. They also believed that the widespread discontent up to November, 1830 (when the Tories held office) had been reduced under Whig guidance. Before the Reform Bill was introduced, according to the Attorney-General, "the public mind was in a state of great turbulence and excitement," but the introduction of the Bill "tranquilized" it.[10] Macaulay noted that the inability of the King to proceed safely to the City in November 1830, and the incendiarism in the countryside were to be found under Tory rule.[11] This is not to say that throughout the year and a half of the Reform Bill struggle the Whigs were always confident about the short-run invulnerability of their society to revolution for, clearly, unrest was more evident at certain times than at others. Nor does this mean that the fear of imminent revolution had no part in the passage of the Bill. But they tended to see the unrest and the disturbances of 1830–32 as symptoms of revolution that could break out imminently but that was much more likely to occur, if not forestalled, in the more distant future.

Because they were primarily concerned with the threat of revolution in the foreseeable but not immediate future, the Whigs in 1831 thought of themselves as dealing with the moderate dis-

9. Jeffrey, ibid., *3* (March 4, 1831), 69.
10. Ibid., *11* (March 20, 1832), 575.
11. Ibid., *8* (Sept. 20, 1831), 310.

content that prevailed among a large section of the populace that was nevertheless still loyal and orderly. While on the surface less threatening than the ever-present, small, revolutionary group of the "desperate and dangerous" who "hate all law and authority," the relief of these moderate discontents was thought to be a means of establishing the groundwork for a society that could resist acute, revolutionary attack at some future time. Thus they focused their attention on the most numerous and important group that, because it was unrepresented in Parliament, felt "offended, alienated, and dissatisfied."[12] On the other hand, if discontents were not appeased they would grow into hostility, and then there would be "complete alienation of the people from their rulers."[13] Thus Lord Grey urged the Lords to "be wise in time."[14] Refusal to appease such feelings by passing the Reform Bill was thought to accentuate the difficulty by creating distrust of the aristocracy, especially since it was the House of Lords that created the main obstacle to its passage. "Distrust will beget distrust," Mackintosh warned. "The superior classes may, by their behavior at this critical moment, sow the seeds of lasting, and, perhaps, fatal discord."[15] The complaints and even the occasional disturbances were not the problem; they were but "the symptoms of a deep-rooted distemper" and the "proofs of the existence of a malady, liable to be called into convulsive action, by causes which, in the course of human affairs, must constantly occur."[16] Vulnerability to revolution in the future, therefore, was seen as the real danger. Sir James Graham put it differently: "When the waters of bitterness and strife had risen to a certain height, when the tide of discontent was full, a slight wave, raised by a passing gust, might, at a moment when it was least expected, overwhelm and swamp the vessel of State."[17] The goal of policy, therefore, was to in-

12. Jeffrey, ibid., *3* (March 4, 1831), 69. Grey saw the preponderant discontent as "ill feeling in the people toward the Government of the country": ibid., *7* (Oct. 3, 1831), 929.

13. Macaulay, ibid., *8* (Oct. 10, 1831), 390.

14. Ibid., *7* (Oct. 3, 1831), 965; also see ibid.: 967, 969.

15. Ibid., *4* (July 4, 1831), 689.

16. Ibid., *4* (July 4, 1831), 681–82.

17. Ibid., *3* (March 8, 1831), 230.

corporate the moderately disaffected into the constitution by granting political privileges to them in order "to teach them, that they, too, had a direct interest in supporting the institutions of the country."[18] While this was also seen as a matter of justice, the prudence of this policy was emphasized. To yield to demands for the Reform Bill would, Grey argued, have the effect of re-establishing the confidence of the disaffected in the government; this would then "embody the sound part of the community against the violent and disaffected, if such there be." Thus for Grey the Reform Bill was intended to provide "a ground on which a firm and safe stand might be made in defence of the principles of the constitution, if ever they should be really assailed." It was like "putting one's house in order to meet the coming storm."[19]

How was the Reform Bill to implement the Whigs' goal? Mainly by granting political privileges so that those who came to enjoy them would identify with the political order—by giving them, psychologically, a stake in the country. It was "one of the most invariable maxims of legislation," according to Mackintosh, "to bind to the Constitution, by the participation of legal privilege, all persons who have risen in wealth, in intelligence, in any of the legitimate sources of ascendancy over others."[20] These bene-fits were not to be derived only from those to whom the vote was to be extended. It was also thought that the Reform Bill would favorably affect the attitude of the unenfranchised to the constitu-tion, especially in towns (such as Birmingham and Manchester) that were to be represented for the first time. Macaulay appealed to Burke in support of his contention that the ordinarily unenfran-chised populace of an "unrepresented district is far more likely to be turbulent than [in] a represented district."[21] It was also

18. Lansdowne, ibid., *4* (June 21, 1831), 133.

19. Ibid., *8* (Oct. 7, 1831), 319; *7* (Oct. 3, 1831), 931, 935.

20. Ibid., *4* (July 4, 1831), 682. Macaulay argued (March 2, 1831) that the existing system drove "over to the side of revolution those whom we shut out from power. Is this a time when the cause of law and order can spare one of its natural allies?": *Speeches*, p. 5.

21. Macaulay, *Speeches*, p. 93. The passage actually reads, "a repre-sented district is far more likely to be turbulent than an unrepresented district." But this is clearly a reporting or printing error, for other pas-

intended that the Bill should eliminate at least some of the election practices that "work all respect for the Constitution out of the hearts of the people." Mackintosh referred to bribery of voters and to the sale of seats, and noted that such "disgusting scenes could not but uproot attachment to the government to which they seemed to pertain."[22] The elimination of nomination boroughs was to have taken Parliamentary seats off the market, and the reduction of members for many small boroughs was to have at least complicated the task of bribing voters. The existence of nomination boroughs was also objectionable because of the specific consequences it had for the public image of the aristocracy. The power of nomination, Lord Grey said, is "enjoyed only by a few, whilst the odium falls upon the whole body." By abolishing this power, a few wealthy individuals would have to sacrifice an advantage, but the peerage would be restored to its independent influence and its "high estimation in the public mind."[23]

Whig policy in 1831 was in many ways a reflection of general Whig political thought—its antiutopian character, its emphasis on prudential adjustment of institutions, its preoccupation with consent, and its concern with liberty of expression.[24] The Whig antipathy to utopian thinking was exemplified by Macaulay's famous attack on James Mill's "Essay on Government," and it was evident in their empirical approach to constitutional reform. They had few preconceived ideas as to what an ideal constitution was. "I rest my opinion," Macaulay said, "on no general theory of government." They were willing to shape the constitution in any one of many ways, depending on the particular circumstances of public feeling and public opinion. Macaulay indicates that he would approve of universal suffrage under certain

---

sages indicate that Macaulay was contending that representation reduces turbulence. For example, he says, "the people of represented London [will] be more orderly than the people of unrepresented London": ibid., pp. 93–94.

22. *Hansard, 4* (July 4, 1831), 679.

23. Ibid., *7* (Oct. 3, 1831), 954.

24. W. H. Auden, "Introduction," in *Selected Writings of Sydney Smith* (New York, Farrar, Straus, and Cudahy, 1956), pp. xvi–xviii.

circumstances.[25] This approach led Bagehot to suggest that it was not possible to "express theoretically the creed" of the Whig party. "In truth," he says, "Whiggism is not a creed, it is a character." Rather than be guided by "large theories and speculation," the Whig will have "a clear view of the next step."[26] This absence of preconceived ideas and the willingness to adjust to circumstances increased their susceptibility to tactics such as Mill's.

Their antiutopian approach meant they would attach greater importance to practical than to theoretical skills. They esteemed prudence as the most valuable political skill as, indeed, it would be for men who saw themselves as brokers of constitutional change, arranging a compromise between the inevitable demands from new classes and the established order that was destined to yield. The crucial question was, how much had to be yielded? And here prudence was necessary. What was needed was "a cool computation and calm comparison of the different degrees of safety and danger in the various systems open for our choice."[27] Such a comparison was to be based on the perception of "safety and danger" attending each alternative. Here, of course, judgments varied. "By what criterion," Jeffrey asked, "is a judgment to be formed? . . . This," he answered, "is truly a matter of feeling and observation; rather than of reasoning."[28] Grey argued that the most important thing, especially now, was a consideration of "the consequences likely to arise from the adoption or rejection of any given measure."[29] Among the causes of the ruin of the French aristocracy there was "no discernment of the signs of their time."[30] The Whigs claimed to possess this ability and they thought it "prudence of the highest order"—a quality that Sydney Smith defined as "the deliberate reflection of a wise man, who

25. *Speeches,* p. 3. Auden, in discussing Sydney Smith as an example of "English Liberalism at its best," emphasizes his antiutopianism. "He is never utopian or given to large generalizations but always attacks a specific abuse, and the reform he proposes is equally specific and always possible to realize": *Sydney Smith,* p. xvii.
26. "The First Edinburgh Reviewers," *Works of Walter Bagehot, 2,* 62.
27. Mackintosh, *Hansard, 4* (July 4, 1831), 691.
28. Ibid., *3* (March 4, 1831), 63.
29. Ibid., *3* (April 18, 1831), 1475.
30. Macaulay, ibid., *7* (Sept. 20, 1831), 309.

does not like what he is going to do, but likes still less the consequence of not doing it, and who of two evils chooses the least."[31]

Although the Whig politicians emphasized the prudential grounds for making concessions to the Reform Bill, their position was closely tied to the traditional Whig preoccupation with consent. Consent, of course, meant legitimacy, and not literal (i.e. democratic) consent. Phraseology had changed, however, and now, instead of referring to consent, one referred to public opinion. Public opinion, in this usage, represented feelings and sentiments that either could produce affection, attachment, identification, and ultimately loyalty to the political order, or could produce disaffection and alienation from it. The institutions of government were ineffective unless they were given legitimacy by "public opinion"; thus, "the law is nothing, nothing but a piece of paper printed by the King's printer . . . till public opinion breathes the breath of life into the dead letter." Therefore, when public opinion was opposed to institutional arrangements, assuming that it was unanimous and persistent, this meant that consent had been withdrawn. When it was quiescent, the established system continued to enjoy legitimacy. Therefore, in Macaulay's words, there were "only two ways in which societies can permanently be governed, by public opinion, and by the sword"; or, as Sir James Graham said, there were "but two modes of dealing with public opinion—either concession, or the suppression of it by force."[32] Government could be maintained by the bayonets of soldiers—for example, Ireland—but not free government. Thus reform, as the alternative to coercion, was made necessary by the withdrawal of consent.[33] It was symptoms of such withdrawal that perturbed Melbourne, who on other grounds was no enthusiast for reform. Political institutions, he

31. Sydney Smith, "Speech at Taunton," in *The Works of the Rev. Sydney Smith* (London, 1854), p. 563.

32. *Speeches*, pp. 59–60; *Hansard, 3* (March 8, 1831), 231.

33. Grey, ibid., *7* (Oct. 3, 1831), 931. Grey said, "No government can safely disregard public opinion; and least of all a Government, founded like this, on free principles": ibid., *7*, 957. And Melbourne considered "a reasonable deference to the will of the people distinctly expressed to be one of the conditions of the government of a free people": ibid., *12* (April 9, 1832), 45.

observed, "must be supported by authority, consent, reputation, and opinion."

> [But] if we find that the columns of that support are sapped and falling—if we find that, instead of authority, there is a disrespect for all authority—if we find that instead of *consensus* there is *dissensus*— . . . it is then our duty to look about us, and to consider the dangerous situation in which we are placed . . . that we may repair the edifice which is tottering and crumbling around us.[34]

Therefore, reform was to have the effect of restoring confidence, removing resentments, recovering consensus, by giving a sense of identification with the system to those who had been alienated from it—it would re-establish the legitimacy of the political order. The Whigs' great concern with consent meant that they would be willing to pay a high price for the assurance that it was not impaired. Since this assurance was gained by satisfying the demands of public opinion, here was still another source of that disposition to yield that would allow Mill's tactics to be used successfully.

Consent, then, was an indication of health in the political order. Ordinarily, however, one is assured of a healthy condition by the absence of symptoms of ill health. It was therefore important to allow free expression of discontent, for only by this means could assurance be gained that the legitimacy of the political order was being maintained. Thus in the Whig tradition the emphasis on liberty of expression was functionally important. During the Reform Bill agitation the government resisted most suggestions that it initiate prosecutions against the press and that it suppress the political unions responsible for the most notable public meetings. However, since the Whigs interpreted expressions of discontent and dissatisfaction as serious signs of weakness in the psychological foundations of the political order, and since they strongly believed that full opportunities for such expression ought to be maximized, this put a premium on the organized expression of discontent along the line proposed by James Mill.

34. Ibid., 7 (Oct. 4, 1831), 1177.

The Tory View

In contrast to the Whig view, the position of the Tories (and other Opposition groups) made it appear unlikely that they would be disposed to yield to the pressures of extra-Parliamentary politics. Yet in reality their attitudes were not so different from the Whig position.

Many of the prominent Opposition spokesmen held that Parliament was a deliberative body whose responsibilities required that it ignore pressures from without. The Earl of Mulgrave, for example, held "that we are not here to obey the dictates of the people."[1] To yield to the demands of a numerical majority was to submit to intimidation, and there was, Lord Wharncliffe said, "a system of intimidation" put into operation by the political unions, the press, and by members of the government.[2] The basic objection to the alleged intimidation was put by Peel. "It was the duty of the Representatives of the people not to be swayed by popular clamour, but to look prospectively to the future interests of the country. . . . If the minority were thus to give way to the majority, he was afraid that this would put an end to all discussion, and that such a deference to public opinion would only prevent them from performing faithfully those duties which they were bound to perform as Representatives of the people."[3] The antimajoritarian view that accompanied the argument on behalf of the deliberative character of Parliament was also evident in the definition of public opinion sometimes used by Tories. Croker said, "Public opinion is with us, and if opinion be the result of reflection and judgment, we are right"; but "if clamour be opinion," then, of course, the Whigs had its support.[4] By contending

1. *Hansard,* 7 (Oct. 3, 1831), 1009.

2. Ibid., 7 (Oct. 5, 1831), 1313. For other examples see ibid.: 1311; *4,* 109; *3,* 116.

3. Ibid., *4* (June 21, 1831), 188; also see ibid., 664.

4. Ibid., *8* (Oct. 10, 1831), 440. "There were two kinds of public opinion—one was . . . the clamour of an excited people; the other was that which resulted from the intelligence, the habits, the reflection, and the experience of settled society": ibid.

that public opinion was the opinion of the propertied, educated, and intelligent, the Tories were pointing to the illegitimacy and irrelevance of the opinions of the unenfranchised masses.

Holding such views, it would appear that the Opposition was not likely to be moved by the argument for concession to popular demands. There were, indeed, some extremists who throughout the period of agitation urged suppression of public meetings and associations and prosecutions of the press. But the Tory extremists, though numerous and prominent, did not adequately represent the Opposition, which was not so indifferent to public feelings as men like Croker and Ellenborough made it appear. The relevance of public opinion was implicitly acknowledged whenever the Whigs' assessment of its status was disputed. It was often denied that public opinion was as excited and demanding as the government and the press had described it. Wharncliffe argued that "the public Press had most grossly exaggerated the feeling which prevailed on the subject in London and its neighborhood." And Croker called the clamor fictitious.[5] Reports of the number of persons attending public meetings and the representative character of the signatories to a petition were disputed over and over again.[6] By quarreling over the facts that provided indications of the substance and intensity of public opinion, its relevance was acknowledged. The same implication can be drawn from the observation, frequently made from mid-1831 onward, that a "reaction" had set in against the enthusiasm for reform that was acknowledged to have existed earlier in the year.

The uncompromising attitude of some Tory spokesmen was misleading, for it came, in many cases, from a group of outspoken, rigidly traditional men who had also taken—and still retained—an uncompromising position with regard to Catholic Emancipation (Wetherell, Knatchbull, Winchilsea, Vyvyan, Lon-

5. Ibid., 7 (Oct. 5, 1831), 1314; 3 (March 4, 1831), 106. Related to this was the contention that public opinion favorable to the Bill existed, but that it was not genuine, as it had been artificially induced by the Whigs to serve their party cause: Londonderry, ibid., 4 (June 30, 1831), 495; Chandos, 3 (March 7, 1831), 116.

6. For example, W. Dunscombe, ibid., 3 (March 28, 1831), 1089–90; Londonderry and Eldon, 7 (Oct. 3, 1831), 921–23.

donderry). These men, who played a prominent part in Parliamentary debate, were still unwilling to forgive the leadership of their party for its stand on the Catholic question. Thus, when they suggested that the Opposition would never countenance concession made from prudential considerations, they hardly spoke for everyone who sat on their side, for the words and deeds of 1829 belied them. Reacting to the charge that the Reform Ministry, in pointing to dangers that would attend rejection of the Bill, were using threats and intimidation, Stanley read from one of Peel's speeches on the Catholic Relief Bill. "We have also had [Peel had said] the sad experience of that other and greater calamity, civil discord and bloodshed. Surely it is no unmanly fear that shudders at its recurrence . . . that looks out with anxiety for the alternatives by which civil war may be honourably averted."[7] And the Lords were reminded that since the Duke of Wellington had acknowledged the principle "that it is expedient to yield to necessity," he "ought to be the last man . . . to vote that it is dishonourable or unbecoming in us to yield to agitation."[8] What was implied in the policy of 1829 was finally made explicit by Peel. Using language that might have been Macaulay's or Mackintosh's, he stated (in early 1832) that, "If it could be shown that, whatever might be the abstract merits of a Constitution, the people were dissatisfied with it; that they had outgrown its original dimensions, that it was no longer applicable to the wants and interests of society; that the basis on which it rested was too narrow; that the public administration could not be carried on without constant suspicion on the part of the people, in such a case it became, no doubt, the duty of Parliament to devote its deliberate consideration to the means of effecting some

7. Ibid., *3* (March 4, 1831), 43–44. Furthermore, among the Opposition were the Waverers who based their position on the concession argument.

8. Shrewsbury, ibid., *12* (April 10, 1832), 122. Grey also reminded the Lords that Catholic Emancipation was introduced, not from conviction of its justice, but "upon the necessity of the case, and the expediency of yielding to popular opinion, when it could no longer be resisted without endangering the peace of the country": ibid., *7* (Oct. 3, 1831), 958. For other examples see ibid.: Lennard, *3,* 288; Russell, *3,* 1511; Mackintosh, *4,* 697; Brougham, *8,* 271; Macaulay, *8,* 395.

change." And admitting that these were the present circumstances, "it would have been difficult if not impossible for any administration to have been formed on the principle of resisting altogether Parliamentary Reform."[9]

Despite the extremity of some Tory rhetoric, therefore, the Tories were not without a Whig-like sensitivity to public opinion, at least as a symptom of instability. This was not yet, as it was for the Whigs, part of party tradition, and thus Tories were less ready to acknowledge and practice, let alone eulogize, prudential politics of this sort. But they were not entirely insensitive to the wisdom of Burke's maxim that a state "without the means of some change is without the means of its conservation," and thus to a degree they shared the Whigs' vulnerability to the "intimidation tactics" that James Mill advocated.

9. Ibid., *11* (March 22, 1832), 751–52. Although Peel was not indisposed to moderate constitutional reform and not insensitive to the concession argument, he was deliberately slower than the Whigs to acknowledge that popular discontent was sufficiently powerful to require concession. For this reason the Whigs felt that, although he conceded, he failed to do so in time: Gash, *Peel,* pp. 208, 251, 649, 671–72; J. A. Reynolds, *The Catholic Emancipation Crisis in Ireland* (New Haven, Yale, 1954), p. 167.

CHAPTER 3

The Language of Menace

James Mill spent most of his adult life under Tory governments that gave reformers little hope for immediate success. Yet in 1835, a year before his death, Mill had to "reflect with wonder" at the "shortness of the time in which the spirit of reform in this nation has grown to such a degree of strength." This, he said, "is perhaps the circumstance of the present period on which the future historian will dwell with the greatest astonishment."[1] Mill and his friends had some part in bringing this change about. Since Mill was sensitive to the potential influence of the press, which he called "the grand instrument for the diffusion of knowledge, or of error," he took every opportunity to urge his associates "to study the means of obtaining access to the public mind, through as many as possible of the periodical publications of the day."[2] Such advice was given to his colleagues in the Political Economy Club and to his young disciples, such as Grote, and of course to John Stuart Mill himself. This advice encouraged occasional publications, all of them polemical, by John Stuart Mill in the *Morning Chronicle,* the editor of which was a friend of the elder Mill's; it was the temptation that diverted Grote from both banking and scholarship; it moved John Stuart Mill to engage in the public debating on behalf of reform principles that he de-

1. "State of the Nation," *London Review, 1* (April, 1835), 3. The heightening of Mill's interest was such that he planned to attend the second reading in the House of Lords even though, he said, "I have not heard one debate these 20 years": Mill to Brougham, Sept. 15, 1831, in Brougham Papers.

2. Political Economy Club, *Minutes of Proceedings, 1821–1882, Roll of Members and Questions Discussed, 4* (London, 1882), 39.

scribed in his autobiography; it stimulated the enthusiasm and effort that went into establishing in 1824 the *Westminster Review,* a quarterly journal on behalf of Radical principles; and it led the younger disciples to plan ambitious publishing ventures all directed to the same purpose. There was the *Parliamentary History and Review,* an annual journal of commentary on Parliamentary debates, and the plan to establish a daily newspaper in 1829, which was given up only after Fonblanque, a Radical journalist and follower of Bentham's, became proprietor and editor of the prominent though not financially successful *Examiner.* These efforts, along with their pamphleteering, which included the reprinting and free distribution of James Mill's *Encyclopaedia* articles, were not without influence. One of the group, Roebuck, later estimated their impact:

> The important practical effect was not made evident by converting and bringing over large numbers of political partisans from one banner or class to another, or by making them renounce one appelation and adopt another; but it was shown by affecting the conclusions of all classes; and inducing them, while they retained their old distinctive names, to reason after a new fashion, and according to principles wholly different from those to which they had been previously accustomed.[3]

Even though they were responsible for only a small part of the combined efforts of Radicals and reformers of many types, these men did have a considerable influence on the movement for Parliamentary reform.

This Benthamite effect on public opinion, by way of stimulating discontent, formulating demands for change, and circulating arguments used by other reformers had its limits, however. First of all, James Mill and his associates were few in number. Francis Place and Joseph Parkes played the leading roles in this small group, and their importance was enhanced by reason of their wide range of associates among reformers in London and Bir-

---

3. J. A. Roebuck, *History of the Whig Ministry of 1830, to the Passing of the Reform Bill, 1* (London, 1852), 343–44.

mingham. Other names show up—Roebuck, Edward Gibbon Wakefield, Charles Buller, Joseph Hume, Grote, and William Tooke. But the moving figures were Parkes and Place.[4] Another limitation on their influence was the small size of the audience to which they directly appealed, for it was not nearly so large as that enjoyed by other Radicals, such as Cobbett, to take an example who probably provides the most unfavorable comparison. Furthermore, in seeking an audience they had to compete with such well-known Radicals as Cobbett, Attwood, Henry Hunt, and Hetherington, to say nothing of a broad range of "liberal" politicians. Mill himself recognized limitations; he had experienced frustration as a publicist up to the mid-twenties; and when he began to feel greater hope for change, seeing that "very moderate exertions will produce great results," he realized that this would not be the product of individual effort alone, but that great results take place "because it falls in with the current [toward good government] in which things are running of their own accord."[5]

Intimidation Tactics

If the few Benthamites were not a decisive influence on Parliamentary reform by way of arousing public feeling, and yet, as many historians claim, they had an important role in the passing of the Reform Bill, how was this achieved?

A clue is to be found in James Mill's tactical writings. Mill had argued that constitutional change could be peacefully achieved

4. Although he was sympathetic with the Reform cause, and even contributed £1 to the National Political Union, John Stuart Mill had little to do with active politics at this time. In October 1831, at the height of Reform excitement, he said he was "often surprised how little I really care about them. The time is not yet come when a calm and impartial person can intermeddle with advantage in the questions and contests of the day": Mill to Sterling, Oct. 20–22, 1831 in *The Letters of John Stuart Mill,* ed., H. S. R. Elliott, *1* (London, Longmans, 1910), 8; PCN, Set 63, *1,* f. 276.

5. Mill to Ricardo, Sept. 23, 1818: *Works and Correspondence of David Ricardo,* ed. P. Sraffa, *7,* 301.

by concessions from rulers, provided rulers saw that such concession was dictated by prudence; and this required that the ruler
see only the two alternatives—concession or revolution. Mill
visualized the ruler as conceding to a threat of revolution; for as
a rational being he would yield to the threat rather than follow
the more costly procedure of resisting it. If these tactics were to
be used successfully, it was necessary that the ruler really believe
that revolution threatened. However, it was not necessary that
those using these tactics shape the opinions and feelings of large
sections of the public; it was assumed that long-standing social
and economic developments disposed men to sign petitions, attend meetings, break windows, and perhaps even to burn palaces.
Once such dispositions existed, it became possible for a small
group of opportunely placed men to exploit them. Mill's tactics
required, in this situation, that public feelings be formulated and
interpreted in a portentous, even a threatening way, and that the
public, and especially the government, be persuaded that this appearance correspond to the reality. The emphasis was placed on
appearances. The professional reformer, like the public relations
man, dealt in images, and in his role as tactician, reality was his
concern only insofar as it was necessary to shape it to give plausibility to the image he was trying to create.[1]

This was the role Mill, Parkes, and Place sought to play during
the passing of the Reform Bill. They were mainly occupied in
journalism and public speaking, either directly or by encouraging
and organizing the efforts of others, in order to establish a widely
accepted image of a demanding, impatient, threatening public.
They were active in the two most prominent political associations
—the Birmingham Political Union and the National Political
Union—in order to give credence to the image they were trying

1. Butler probably refers to this when, denying that Reform excitement
was artificial, he noted that popular pressures were under the guidance
of the "agitators and agents" that are an inevitable part of any "concerted
democratic movement": *Reform Bill,* p. 275. It is necessary to question
Fraser's suggestion that Mill's view lacked sophistication and his statement that "James Mill and Francis Place [suggested] that [public opinion's]
remarkable progress was only the result of the self-generating powers of
reason fed with knowledge": "Public Petitioning," *History, 46* (1961), 200.

to shape. And they were energetic and ingenious in finding ways to communicate this image to the government. This kind of influence did not require that those exercising it be constantly before the public. Thus it is not surprising that Mill was known to have been active behind the scenes; as Mrs. Grote said, "no one would ever know what a moving power he had been at the time of the Reform Bill." And his son said, "he never cared about getting the credit of doing anything, as long as the thing itself was done, that he inspired everyone but [he] himself kept in the background."[2] Place, true to his reputation as a "wire-puller," was the moving force behind the National Political Union, though he rarely addressed public meetings and nominally held office as only one of the seventy-two members of the governing council. Similarly, Parkes shaped some of the critical policies of the Birmingham Political Union before he became a member, justifying, perhaps, Cobden's admiring characterization of him as one who "loves *management* . . . you condescend," Cobden told him, "to pull the wires which touch the secret springs of poor human nature [in order] to serve others."[3]

Mill's tactics were meant to bring concessions from men who feared the consequences of not conceding. In other words, they were meant to intimidate. In the article "Liberty of the Press" Mill spoke vaguely of "rulers." But, specifically, to whom were these tactics directed in 1831–32? While the King, his Ministers, the Lords, and Commons all shared in the exercise of power, Mill and his associates applied their intimidation tactics to the Ministers. They were, Mill noted, "the part of the legislature on

2. *Amberley Papers,* ed. B. and P. Russell, *1,* 370, Lady Amberley's diary, entry of Feb. 19, 1865. While Parkes' and Place's reform activities were known in official circles, Mill's were concealed. In contrast to the occasional allusions to Place that can be found in *Hansard,* Mill is rarely mentioned. He is named on one occasion for holding a doctrine of rent incompatible with the security of property and as "one of the class who in future [if the Reform Bill passes] are to be called upon to regulate our affairs": Vyvyan, *Hansard, 3* (March 21, 1831), 637–38. Of course, Mill does figure prominently as a witness before the committees considering the renewal of the East India Co. charter.

3. Cobden to Parkes, July 18, 1846: Add. MSS 43,664, ff. 13–14.

which public opinion acts with the greatest force."[4] Furthermore, given the conflict between Commons and Lords, it was only the Ministers, by taking the initiative in persuading the King to create Peers, who could assure passage of the Bill. If the Ministers failed to do this, since the King was reluctant to approve of creations, the Reform Bill would not pass. It appeared that if the reform cause was to succeed without creating Peers, it could do so only by the more extreme measure of removing the obstacle posed by the Lords. But since this would have challenged the very existence of the House of Lords, it most probably would have brought on civil strife—something Mill's tactics were designed to avoid. The goal, therefore, was to avoid failure on the one hand and violence on the other. Thus Parkes said that "support of that Ministry is our only chance for peaceable reform."[5] He stated the same dilemma in a different manner in a speech at Birmingham. "There were but two modes of carrying this measure—by constitutional means, or by means not strictly constitutional; in other words . . . by more peers or fewer."[6]

Parkes thought that, regardless of the Lords' opposition, the Reform Bill could pass: "only want of nerve in ministers can lose it ultimately, for by new peers they must carry it." But he was not often confident that the Ministers would have the required nerve. He thought a few of them (including Grey and Durham) and even the King *"honest* in the measure" but lacking "the moral courage or integrity to make the change required by the times." He also thought half the Cabinet were looking for an opportunity to compromise on reform so as to stay in office with Tory support.[7] His suspicion was justified, for the Ministers were in fact divided among themselves, with those favoring creations (except

4. "Summary Review," in *Parliamentary History and Review* (1826), p. 802; also see p. 784. However, they also tried to influence the composition of the House of Commons; when Parliament was dissolved in April 1831, they set up the Parliamentary Candidates Society and called for pledges of support for Reform from candidates as a way of enlarging the Reform majority.

5. Parkes to Grote, Oct. 26, 1831: Add. MSS 35,149, f. 117.

6. *Times,* Oct. 22, 1831, p. 1 (reporting meeting of Oct. 20).

7. Parkes to Grote, Oct. 4, 1831 and Oct. 26, 1831: Add. MSS 35,149, ff. 117, 177.

for Durham) even feeling uncertain about either the propriety or the effectiveness of the move. Their difficulty was accentuated by the hesitation and ambivalence of the King, who made clear his wish for settlement of the Reform question and his disapproval of creations, yet without refusing outright to allow them.[8] Considerable effort was expended, therefore, in trying to sustain Ministerial nerve. Parkes drew up and published a long brief defending the propriety and the legality of creating peers, in which the many precedents for such creations were described. In Parliament Joseph Hume taunted Ministers with "growing slack." In speech and pamphlet at Birmingham, Parkes, pointing to Tory precedents, asked, "Why, then, does the Premier hesitate?"[9] But above all the Ministers, by a variety of means, were encouraged to believe that creating peers was the only alternative to revolution.

The Ministers could assess the state of public feelings and thus the reality of the threat of revolution by their own observations, as well as by those of other members of Parliament who frequently commented on the disposition of the people. In addition —and most important—the government received intelligence through the Home Office. The Home Secretary received reports

8. Chester New, *Lord Durham* (Oxford, Clarendon, 1929), pp. 165–66; C. S. Parker, *Life and Letters of Sir James Graham 1792–1861, 1* (London, 1907), 133, 144; *The Letters of Sydney Smith,* ed. Nowell C. Smith, *2* (Oxford, Clarendon, 1953), 546, 553; *Early Correspondence of Lord John Russell,* ed. Rollo Russell, *2* (London, 1913), 29–31; Patterson, *Sir Francis Burdett, 2,* 598.

9. Hume, *Hansard, 6* (Aug. 27, 1831), 722; *Times,* Oct. 22, 1831, p. 1; *Birm. J.,* Feb. 25, 1832, p. 2; "Whig and Tory Creations of Peers," a broadside with a passage from *Political Union Register* for May, 1832, in PCN, Set 17, *3,* f. 162. Parkes' anonymously published pamphlet was *The Prerogative of Creating Peers* (London, 1832). Although it bears the date 1832, it was evidently printed and ready for distribution in early October 1831, for he sent six copies to Grote at that time: Jessie K. Buckley, *Joseph Parkes of Birmingham* (London, Methuen, 1926), p. 75. In March he reported a second printing and that, "Some members of the Cabinet are highly obliged by the argument. Lord Holland writes [that they will] take the proper steps (new Peers) to carry all. I *hope* they will have pluck enough to *do* this": Parkes to Sutton Sharpe, March 30, 1832, in Parkes Papers.

from magistrates, military officers responsible for the maintenance of public order, police officials (for the London area), and from citizens who were voicing complaints or expressing alarm. These sources varied greatly in reliability; frequently the magistrates, like many of the citizens who volunteered information, were excessively alarmist, whereas military and police officers' reports were more sober and realistic. Their variations in this regard only added to the difficulties the government faced when evaluating the evidence. There was also the press, which was filled with what was presented as accurate reports of public meetings, speeches, street mobs, processions, and riots, as well as estimates of "public opinion." Because of their concern with consent, the Whig government was especially disposed to attend to unofficial sources that might reveal discontentedness among the populace. Among these there was the group formed by Mill, Parkes, Place, and their associates, who communicated indirectly through the press and directly through correspondence, conversation, and deputations—special circumstances giving them unique opportunities to do this.

Francis Place had been active in Westminster politics for more than thirty years and was known as an effective election agent in the radical interest whose knowledge of extra-Parliamentary politics and acquaintance with local conditions was unrivaled. This circumstance, combined with his long acquaintance with many of the Radical leaders and journalists, qualified him, in the eyes of the Home Office, as an informative even if not unbiased judge of popular feeling. Thus Place, "from whom the Home Secretary constantly received information,"[10] was well situated

10. W. M. Torrens, *Memoirs of the Second Viscount Melbourne, 1* (London, 1878), 386, 391. Melbourne had once been a customer of Place's. Graham Wallas, *The Life of Francis Place* (London, 1908), p. 303, n. 2. Melbourne did not necessarily believe the reports that came from Place: *Lord Melbourne's Papers*, ed. L. C. Sanders (London, 1889), pp. 129–30. This is perhaps why Place also communicated with Tom Young, Melbourne's private secretary, to whom the Home Secretary referred when he said that, "Through him I am able to look down below; which for me is more important than all I can learn from all the fine gentlemen clerks about me": Torrens, *Melbourne*, p. 368. G. M. Trevelyan, *Lord Grey of the Reform Bill* (London, Longmans, 1920), pp. 286–87.

to influence the image of public opinion that Ministers, according to Mill's tactics, should hold. Place's opportunities were extended by the political position that had been achieved by John Cam Hobhouse, who had been Radical candidate for Westminster in 1818 and 1819, with Place serving as his election agent. By 1831 Hobhouse, now M.P. for Westminster, though still favorable to extensive reform, was associated with the Whigs, so here was another means by which Place could try to shape the Ministerial estimate of public feeling. The appointment of Hobhouse in January 1832, as Secretary for War gave even greater access to the Ministry. There were other circumstances that allowed access to government circles. James Mill had long known Brougham in connection with the *Edinburgh Review* and the Society for the Diffusion of Useful Knowledge, among other projects, and occasionally met him over Bentham's table; and now that Brougham was Lord Chancellor, Mill could draw on past friendship to justify audiences with him. To take another example, Grote, as a prominent city banker and a dogmatic adherent of James Mill, organized meetings among bankers and merchants and led a deputation carrying their petitions to Lord Grey.[11] Parkes, who enjoyed the reputation with Melbourne as the most talented of the Birmingham leaders, found the Ministers, in their desire to avoid prosecution of the Birmingham Political Union, seeking his help. In the course of these dealings Parkes also had opportunities to offer estimates of the state of public opinion. Althorp, describing changes in the Bill being contemplated by the Cabinet, asked Parkes what he thought would be the effect upon the feeling of the people; and he warned that he might "again trouble you, for from your position you can give me the best information as to the feelings of the Unionist Reformers and I feel great confidence in your judgment." Although it may have been accident rather than management, Ministers were also presented with estimates of public feelings originating with Parkes and Place, whose testimony was presented as from an impartial expert rather than from a partisan. For example, Melbourne had an informant in

11. [Harriet Grote] *Brief Retrospect of the Events of 1831–2* (London, 1878), pp. 9–11.

whom he evidently had confidence, who reported Parkes' estimate of public reactions. It would occasionally happen that the source of such estimates was not identified, as when Burdett wrote to Grey in order to inform him what the public outside the political unions was thinking. He therefore quoted at length a letter "from a man of a good deal of influence amongst the middle class of people"—a man who in fact was Place.[12] Finally, access to Lord Melbourne, who as Home Secretary had responsibility for evaluating the threat to public order, was also gained through acquaintance with Melbourne's private secretary, Tom Young, on whom Melbourne relied for information. Young, according to Parkes, was "in reality a Rad. tho by profession and gratitude a Melbourne-ite," and thus Parkes would send an alarmist letter to Place, instructing him to pass it to Young, who "will shew it [to] Lord Melbourne."[13]

The effort of Mill and his friends to shape the governing classes' image of public feeling also involved the press. While the Ministers were aware of the venality of some editors, this did not invalidate the belief that the press was in some sense a reflection of public opinion. Although the views expressed in the independent newspapers were assumed to be those of the editor and proprietor, attributions of fact were less clearly a reflection of editorial policy. Therefore, press reports of attendance at public meetings, enthusiasm displayed there, and disposition of the public toward the Bill, while subject to misrepresentation, and especially exaggeration, could not be automatically discounted.

12. Althorp to Parkes, Nov. 6, 1831 and Nov. 18, 1831, in Parkes Papers; Buckley, *Parkes,* pp. 85–86. The passage quoted by Burdett (with small alterations) was from Place to Burdett, Oct. 19, 1831: Add. MSS 35,149, ff. 101–02. Grey Papers: Melbourne to Grey, Nov. 18, 1831; Burdett to Grey, Oct. 24, 1831; also see Durham's Minute to Grey, n.d. but ca. Oct. 15, 1831; Parkes to Durham, May 14, 1832. Parkes' letter of May 14 apparently was written so that it could be sent to Grey, for Parkes said he was with Durham until 2 A.M. on the day it was written, thus making written communication unnecessary: Parkes to Grote, May 14, 1832, Add. MSS 27,794, f. 10.

13. Parkes to Durham, Aug. 7, 1836, Lambton Papers. Parkes to Place: PCN, Set 17, *3,* f. 155 (on back of a placard).

Furthermore, the press had at this time a political importance it has since lost. Politics, and especially Parliamentary politics, was given the most prominent place in the paper. Its importance was enhanced by the near-monopoly of the press in the day-to-day (or week-to-week) communication of news. In view of its importance the Benthamites did not neglect the press. It presented seemingly independent evidence of public feeling that was scrutinized not only by Ministers but also by the Opposition. Here too Mill and his friends had opportunities that gave them an influence far beyond what their meager numbers might lead one to expect. The *Examiner,* a prominent weekly, was owned and edited by Albany Fonblanque, at this time an enthusiast for all Benthamite reforms and a close acquaintance of the other disciples; his sub-editor, Edwin Chadwick, had been Bentham's secretary. The *Morning Chronicle,* a prominent and widely read daily that supported the government, was edited by John Black, who was an old acquaintance of Mill's.[14] Later in the 1830's Place recollected that "many times have I and Mill laid our heads together to find inducements for Johnny Black either to do what was right and honest, or to refrain from doing what was wrong and dishonest, and pleased enough he was to consult with us either together or separately."[15]

The *Spectator* was edited by Rintoul, who was also an associate of several Benthamites, with whom he shared political views. Parkes, with Joshua Scholefield, was proprietor of the *Birmingham Journal.* And most important, Parkes corrected the reports of the meetings and other activities of the Birmingham Political Union before they appeared in the *Birmingham Journal,* and he wrote the reports that appeared in the *Times* and the *Morning*

14. John Stuart Mill records in his *Autobiography* that Black was "a particular friend of my father, imbued with many of his and Bentham's ideas, which he reproduced in his articles." The *Morning Chronicle,* according to Mill, "became to a considerable extent a vehicle of the opinions of the Utilitarian Radicals." Fonblanque wrote for the *Chronicle* before going to the *Examiner.* During Grey's Ministry, according to Mill, the *Examiner* became "the principal representative, in the newspaper press, of Radical opinions": *Autobiography,* pp. 74–75, 146–47.

15. Place to Parkes, Jan. 18, 1838: Add. MSS 35,151, f. 70b.

Chronicle.[16] Furthermore, the significance of Millite influence was enhanced by the way the papers subject to it dominated the London press; in addition, these were the sources from which articles were most frequently taken for reprinting by provincial papers. There were but two Tory papers of any prominence at this time (*Morning Post* and *Standard*), and they were unsatisfactory even to their Tory patrons.[17]

Wholesome Terror

While it is difficult to know how newspaper reports were used and evaluated, it is clear that the Radicals' accounts of the state

16. Asa Briggs, *Press and Public in Early Nineteenth-Century Birmingham,* Dugdale Society Occasional Papers, No. 8 (Oxford, 1949), pp. 10–11; "Complete Set of the Press Reports of the Public Meetings of the Birmingham Political Union," Birmingham Reference Library, Birmingham Collection, 442,194–442,211 (Parkes' copy). Parkes did not report for the *Times* at certain periods in 1832 when they sent their own reporters. He reported for the *Morning Chronicle* throughout the Reform Bill period. Usually he would send the same report to each paper; for example, see *Times* and *Morning Chronicle* for Oct. 5, 1831, reporting meeting of Oct. 3. It was in reference to this meeting that he said "two or three of us were up most of the night, and again at 6 this morning to get the report composed and fit to go to town which at half past seven we accomplished by sending it off to the Times and the Chronicle": Parkes to Grote, Oct. 4, 1831, Add. MSS 35,149, f. 77. Grote in reply said, "It is of immense moment that you were there to draw up the proper account of it, and to guide it": Grote to Parkes, Oct. 6, 1831, Add. MSS 46,691, unfoliated. The official history of the *Times* acknowledged "the help of practical workers like Parkes and Hone.": *History of the Times, 1* (London, 1935), 276. Briggs states that the *Journal* became the most celebrated of Birmingham newspapers at this time. Because it printed in full the news of the big political meetings and demonstrations it became a widely used source of information outside Birmingham. Parkes bought the paper in February 1832, and became editor, apparently in March: *Press and Public,* pp. 8–11, 17.

17. For example, see *Scotsman,* Oct. 15, 1831, p. 3; Oct. 29, 1831, p. 2; quoting the *Morn. Chr.* on public feeling in London and on the Birmingham Political Union. There were other Tory papers, like the *Albion* and *John Bull.* Certain Tory papers (*Courier* and *Sun*) switched sides and supported the Whigs when they came into office in November 1830: A. Aspinall, *Politics and the Press* (London, Home and Van Thal, 1949), pp. 241–43, 247–48, 330–40, 468–75.

of public feeling were widely read. Descriptions of Birmingham Political Union meetings, edited by Parkes, were read in Parliament where, for example, Lord Wharncliffe complained that "the language of threat and intimidation" had been used before 150,000 persons—a language that pointed "to the employment of menaces and of physical force with a view to overawe the deliberations" of the House of Lords.[1] On another occasion Wharncliffe observed that they "were now accustomed to hear daily the language of Revolution," and he reported that on opening the latest issue of the *Westminster Review* he found inserted among the fly-leaves a slip which said, "The question of Reform or Revolution is rapidly approaching its solution in Great Britain. The honest part of the Radicals have done their duty in endeavouring to promote the first, and are quite ready to take their parts in the other." Wharncliffe claimed that "similar language was addressed to them every morning when the public newspapers were placed on their tables."[2] The Ministers were exposed to the same reports, and although they had an opportunity to check press reports against other sources of information, they were far from independent of the press for intelligence, especially since many of the magistrates, from whom they might have requested verification, sent alarmist reports that did not allow for a critical evaluation of press accounts.[3]

As a result of their successful infiltration of the press, evidence of the Radicals' use of the "language of menace" can be found in several of the leading papers of the metropolis. While Mill's

1. *Hansard, 7* (Oct. 5, 1831), 1311. There are other examples of complaint about intimidation accompanied by descriptions of union meetings or quotations from Radical speeches. Col. Trench quoted a Mr. Hill (Matthew Davenport?) as saying there was "an audacious opposition . . . who resist all Reform, till it comes in the shape of revolution." A solicitor, Mr. Tooke (Thomas Tooke, Jr.?), was quoted as saying, "the enemies of [reform] were those men, against whom the voice of that meeting, and, if necessary, their arms should be raised": ibid., *3* (March 9, 1831), 252.

2. Ibid., *7* (Oct. 3, 1831), 984.

3. The Home Office occasionally called for provincial papers. For example, it ordered a Manchester paper in February, 1832: H.O. 41/11, f. 92. It also used the *Times'* account of a London meeting: Phillipps to Maule, Nov. 30, 1831, H.O. 49/7, f. 439.

disciples probably were familiar with the "threat theory" underlying the article "Liberty of the Press," James Mill did not spare effort in emphasizing its relevance to immediate events.[4] Albany Fonblanque, whose enthusiasm for Benthamism was sufficiently great that he named a son after his mentor, was urged by Mill to publish accounts of public feeling that would be in accordance with the "threat theory." "The people," he wrote to Fonblanque, "to be in the best state, should appear to be ready and impatient to break out into action, without actually breaking out. The Press, which is our only instrument, has at this moment the most delicate and the most exalted functions to discharge that any power has yet had to perform in this country. It has at once to raise the waves and to calm them; to say, like the Lord, 'Hitherto shalt thou go and no further.' " Then, anticipating the effect, he went on to say, "With such words ringing in their ears, Ministers cannot waver if they would." Since he calculated that the people's enemies would "give up nothing but in fear of worse following," Mill sought to create the appearance of impending revolution in order to extort concessions.[5]

4. Some of them reveal in their writings that they had been exposed to James Mill's tactical doctrines, which is to be expected in view of Mill's intellectual leadership of the Benthamite Radicals. Charles Buller, for example, in language very similar to Mill's, observes that, "Concessions are always extorted from rulers, if not by force, by such a fear of it as renders its use unnecessary"; and, "Constitutional improvements must always be gained by unconstitutional means." Applying these maxims to England, he said "that the aristocracy have the greatest interest in preventing a civil war; and that property and life are worth preserving, even by the sacrifice of their political power": C. Buller, *On the Necessity of a Radical Reform* (London, 1831), pp. 6–7, 22–23, 25. Grote argued, "Until public opinion attains an height and unanimity, which the holder of an unjust privilege no longer dares to disregard, no person of common sense will even hope for a voluntary sacrifice of his gains": Grote, *Statement of the Question of Parliamentary Reform* (London, 1821), pp. 3–4.

5. James Mill to Albany Fonblanque, Oct. 25, 1831: Mill-Taylor Collection, *49A*, 1, British Library of Political and Economic Science. This letter is incorrectly attributed to J. S. Mill in *The Life and Labours of Albany Fonblanque*, ed. E. B. de Fonblanque (London, 1874), pp. 29–30; see *Journal of Political Economy, 51* (1943), 470, n. 1.

Fonblanque's leading articles—editorials that were heavily interwoven with descriptions of the state of public feeling—satisfied Mill's dictum that the people "should appear to be ready and impatient to break out in outrage." "We sincerely believe," he wrote in September 1831, prior to the Lords' rejection of the (second) Bill, "that the North would be in insurrection instantly upon the news of the defeat of the Bill."[6] In October, after the Lords' rejection of the second Bill and after the riots at Nottingham and Derby (which fell far short of insurrection but still were ominous), Fonblanque again sought to create an image of a hardly restrained disposition to violence. He complained that other newspapers had "represented the public feeling but imperfectly." They referred, it is true, to "warmth of feeling" and "strong sentiments," but to underestimate in this manner Fonblanque thought "extremely mischievous, as it creates a false security on the part of the anti-reformers." He reminded his readers that the laboring classes were without "deliberative habits" and therefore were "prone to express their feelings by acts"; but he insisted that this violent disposition had spread to the ordinarily peaceful and timid middle classes who, on the present occasion, showed "determination . . . to obtain their rights by force, should their peaceable demands be rejected."[7] And again, after the introduction of the third Bill, following the Lords' rejection of the second one in October, he asserted that, should the Lords again oppose reform, "The public excitement will again burst out. . . . The Lords dared the indignation of the Country . . . and had their triumph . . . one more such triumph would be their doom."[8]

The same dire predictions are to be found in the *Morning Chronicle,* edited by Mill's friend John Black. While the Lords were still considering the second Bill the *Morning Chronicle* urged its readers to be prepared for the worst.

6. *Exam.,* Sept. 25, 1831, p. 609. This issue was the first to be published after the second Reform Bill passed its reading in the House of Commons.

7. Ibid., Oct. 16, 1831, p. 668; Oct. 23, 1831, p. 681. "To government, we say, 'Strike fearlessly,' or another power may strike wildly. Safety is now in boldness": ibid., Oct. 9, 1831, p. 641.

8. Ibid., Jan. 1, 1832, p. 1.

It is of immense consequence that the army of the people should now be such as to dispel the illusion which some Peers may entertain, that this is a question with regard to which the people may be safely opposed. . . . Let it never be forgotten that power is with the people, and that the people have merely to resolve, and their purpose is effected. This every sensible Peer must know.[9]

The *Chronicle* also quoted the *Examiner* where Fonblanque's words are a paraphrase of James Mill's: "Nothing but fear will act upon these infatuated persons." And, finally, the Peers were warned that the people had "knowledge of the means of combining with effect," and that care should be taken not to "force the people to become too intimately acquainted with the secret of their own strength." In the same vein a fortnight later the paper warned, "If the Anti-Reformers will not yield to reason, perhaps the following plain facts will startle them." These were, as certain consequences of rejection, a prolonged agitation, stagnation of trade, and continued public discussion of fundamental principles of government "by opposite classes in a state of angry excitement"; among the probable consequences was a refusal to pay taxes or tithes, a run on the banks, strikes, political association, swing, and hatred of the peerage.[10]

Parkes adopted the same tactics. During early October 1831, after the second Bill had passed in the Commons and before the vote on it in the Lords, the Birmingham Union organized a mass meeting to be held October 3. Parkes stated his position two days earlier in a speech that he knew would be reported widely, and certainly in the *Times*. Should the Lords throw out the Bill, he said, "the question of the utility of an hereditary peerage would infallibly arise." For his own part, he professed moderation; but

9. *Morn. Chr.*, Sept. 19, 1831: PCN, Set 17, 2, ff. 206–07.
10. Ibid., Sept. 19, 1831; Oct. 6, 1831, at ff. 206–07, 247. Also see *Morn. Chr.*, Oct. 26, 1831, pp. 1, 2, and Oct. 13, 1831, p. 4, where the "best informed man in Birmingham" is quoted as saying that "indignation here approaches to madness." The *Times* warned, "interpose one further obstacle . . . convulsion in our political system . . . must inevitably follow": Oct. 15, 1831, p. 3. Again, "The people must obtain their rights by concession, or *will* take them by force": ibid., Nov. 21, 1831, p. 2.

there were the irrational impulses of the populace, and he "did not blind himself to the perils of the crisis. . . . if anarchy occurred, its horrors in this country would far exceed any ever recorded." As if to place this observation in the desired perspective he reminded his audience of the French Revolution, drawing an analogy between it and the present situation. Turgot, "like Lord Grey, attempted by timely reforms to save his country from anarchy and revolution. But a blind and infatuated aristocracy prevailed. . . . Turgot was driven from office. The revolution followed, with all its consequent horrors and evils."[11] The report on the meeting of October 3, 1831, that appeared in the *Times,* and which was probably by Parkes, was not written in a manner calculated to assuage fears of disorder. There were said to have been more than 100,000 at the meeting: "Moderately speaking," said the *Times,* "the numbers could not possibly fall much short of that amount." The crowds covered twelve acres of rising land. The meeting was called "for the purpose of demonstrating to the House of Lords that the public enthusiasm in favor of the Reform Bill is not abated." It was reported that "the inhabitants looked up to the meeting . . . as the one which would most effectively develop the state of public feeling; and in this they were not mistaken." The reporter seems to have been trying to convey an impression that the crowd was in a state of barely restrained excitement. "There never was, we may safely assert, any previous occasion upon which such a deep and universal excitement pervaded the public mind of Birmingham and its neighborhood."[12]

Mill's advice that the press should make the people "appear to be ready and impatient to break out into action, without actually breaking out," was closely followed by the *Birmingham Journal*

11. Ibid., Oct. 3, 1831, p. 5.
12. Ibid., Oct. 5, 1831, p. 4. The same article appeared in the *Birm. J.,* Oct. 8, 1831, p. 3; and in the *Scotsman,* Oct. 12, 1831, p. 8. Also see his speech to a county meeting at Warwick on Nov. 8, 1831. He said the Bill must be carried either "constitutionally or unconstitutionally," otherwise there would be chaos, confusion, tumult, anarchy, deluge, and "God forbid that the passions of the people should be let loose . . . scenes would occur beggaring all former revolutions in general ruin and suffering": *Birm. J.,* Nov. 12, 1831, p. 4.

in an article, "State of Public Feeling in Birmingham," which also most probably was written or inspired by Parkes, and which was reprinted in the *Morning Chronicle*. "The state of public feeling" was reported to be "in the highest degree feverish and excited, yet . . . up to the present time, no material outrage or breaking of the public peace has been committed." There were, it is true, some broken windows and a scuffle between a man and the police, but with these exceptions, "we have to relate the occurrence of no act of aggression occasioned by political feelings." In the absence of anything more serious, it was ominously reported that many persons were robbed of their newspapers by idle vagabonds who infested the streets "for that purpose, or indeed, that were ready to become actors in any other affair of a mischievous nature."[13] Supported with reports such as this, the *Chronicle,* while urging its readers to agitate, at the same time warned that, "in agitating a whole nation, who can say that the desired point may not sometimes be passed? Let us, therefore, guard against accidents."[14]

The placards, pamphlets, and journals of the Birmingham and the National (i.e. London) Political Unions over which Parkes and Place, respectively, had a dominant influence, attempted to create the same image of an impatient, turbulent populace about to commit violence. The printed Report of the Committee that established the National Political Union claimed as a justification for such an association "the convulsion which may on a sudden be produced in the metropolis, and in the country."[15] And the *Political Union Register* (Birmingham) argued that delay of reform was "endangering the very existence of society."[16] The unions claimed they were the only barrier between order and

13. A grocer's windows were broken, he suffering for the political opinions of his predecessor. But elsewhere, nearly 200 panes were broken, "without respect to the political feelings of the residents": *Birm. J.,* Oct. 15, 1831, p. 3; *Morn. Chr.,* Oct. 17, 1831, p. 2.

14. Ibid., Oct. 26, 1831, p. 2.

15. "Report of a Committee appointed by an Adjourned Public Meeting of Delegates and Representatives . . . October 14, 1831, to consider the best means of forming a Union or Association" (London, 1831), p. 3.

16. "Monthly Retrospect, Addressed particularly to Political Unions," *Political Union Register, 1* (March, 1832), 39.

chaos. "Nothing but the establishment of *Political Unions* has prevented us from becoming the victims of the dreadful catastrophe to which the state of things was hurrying us. . . . They have acted as safety valves to prevent a dreadful explosion . . . the prospect which they have held out of an immediate *peaceful* change, has withheld the people from those acts of violence into which nature would have urged them, if Political Unions had not cheered the dark horizon of their fading hopes."[17]

It was not only the few Millite Radicals who directed the alarmist message to the Ministers. The backbench support led by Lord Ebrington, which was constantly stimulated by Hume and O'Connell, presented similar arguments, as did newspapers not directly influenced by the Radicals. Thus the Radicals had allies in Thomas Barnes of the *Times* and in certain radically inclined Whigs, such as the Whip, Edward Ellice, and Hobhouse and Durham, who for their own reasons were anxious to push the Ministers to extremes. However, while there were many gloomy and nervous forecasts of the consequences of failure to pass the Reform Bill, it was the Millite Radicals and the editors inspired by them who continuously and systematically emphasized the imminence of violent revolution.

The unique character of the warnings held out by journalists and speakers whose rhetoric was in accord with Mill's recommendation is somewhat obscured by their similarity to statements made by the Whig Ministers who also claimed that the Reform Bill was necessary to avoid revolution. The Whigs, like their Radical supporters, urged passage of the Bill mainly on prudential grounds; both claimed to fear the consequences of the Bill's failure to pass; and both indicated that the consequences would be disruption, anarchy, revolution. Whereas the Radicals forecast violence as an immediate consequence, the Whigs, in most cases, saw revolution as a possible long-run consequence. As has been noted, for them the risk of revolution was in the far future, and the risk would be increased if reforms were not granted in time to incorporate the middle classes into the constitution. The words describing this concern often were the same

17. Ibid., p. 3.

as those used by the Radicals, but this was a similarity that concealed gross differences. In contrast to the forecasts made by Place, Fonblanque, Parkes, and Black, Lord Grey said: "Although I do not state that the rejection of the measure will lead to a civil war—I trust it will not produce any such effect—but still I cannot conceal . . . my apprehension, that the result of its rejection will be most dangerous to the best interests of the country."[18] Even Macaulay, who went farther than most of his Parliamentary colleagues, saw as the immediate consequence of the Bill's rejection "the same kind of resistance which was offered to the late Government, three years ago, by the people of Ireland—a resistance by no means amounting to rebellion—a resistance rarely amounting to any crime defined by the law—but a resistance nevertheless which is quite sufficient to obstruct the course of justice, to disturb the pursuits of industry, and to prevent the accumulation of wealth."[19] These observations are in clear contrast to the statement of Mill's associate, Joseph Hume, that "the country was in imminent danger, and the peace of the country was likely to be interrupted most unnecessarily."[20] Even though their interest as politicians seeking to retain office must have encouraged exaggeration, the Whigs nonetheless used a rhetoric much more temperate than the Radicals'. This does not mean they were immune from fear of violence or even imminent revolution. There were times when such fears were experienced, and the Ministers lived among persons who certainly were frightened. But they were disposed to locate the greatest danger

18. *Hansard, 7* (Oct. 3, 1831), 967.

19. Ibid., *8* (Oct. 10, 1831), 394. In September 1831, when the Millite Radicals were sounding alarms, Macaulay said the present calmness of the people was not the "calmness of indifference. It is the calmness of confident hope": ibid. (Sept. 20, 1831), 307–08. Whereas the Radicals used the term "convulsion" to refer to a violent upheaval, Macaulay said the very long-run social and economic changes that made reform desirable was one of "the great convulsions of society": ibid. (Oct. 10, 1831), 394. On the other hand, Macaulay occasionally sounded alarmist, but this was by no means typical. For example, in March 1832 he warned that "disorder and excitement would immediately spread" if the Bill failed: ibid., *11* (March 19, 1832), 462.

20. Ibid., *12* (May 11, 1832), 884.

in the foreseeable but still distant future. At the same time, they were capable of feeling nervous about the immediate danger; and the Radicals, already helped by the Whigs' long-run concern, sought to give immediacy to the Ministers' sense of danger.

Among the efforts of the Radicals to substantiate the image of a turbulent and impatient populace was the dispatch to Ministers of deputations professing to represent genuine public feeling. The most notable of these was the one organized and led by Francis Place. During the weeks following the Lords' rejection of the second Bill he was concerned that the Ministers, reluctant to create peers, would become less resolute and attempt to achieve an accord with the Lords by sacrificing some features of the second Bill. Place was also concerned that the Ministers might be encouraged along this line by certain signs of public indifference which could be observed, especially in London, along with sporadic outbreaks of rioting, such as occurred at Nottingham and Derby. In response to this situation he took part in the organization of the Procession of October 12, the purpose of which was to give the anti-reformers a feeling of "salutary fear"; the same purpose informed his efforts at this time to organize the National Political Union. Allegations of apathy had been made frequently in the press and in Parliament. In these circumstances, a long delay before a new Reform Bill (the third) was introduced could allow for confirmation of such claims. If there is a recess of three months, he asked, "may it not happen that one after another the expectations of the people will subside, while the expectations of the enemy will increase."[21] Place wished to avoid even the risk that this would happen, and he therefore agitated for a short prorogation on the publicly stated ground that public

21. Bowyer to Place, Oct. 14, 1831; Place to Grote, Oct. 16, 1831; Place said, "You will see also that the compromise you feared has taken place," Place to Parkes, Oct. 13, 1831; all in Add. MSS 35,149, ff. 89–92, 99. Palmerston discerned that "those out of the Cabinet who are most clamorous for an immediate meeting [of Parliament] are so because they see that it would prevent negotiation with the moderate party": Palmerston to Melbourne, Nov. 20, 1831, in Sanders, *Melbourne*, p. 142. The *Morning Chronicle* defensively commented on "fallacious assertions that have been made—that the people are getting lukewarm about Reform": Oct. 26, 1831, in PCN, Set 17, *2*, f. 399.

excitement, if left in a state of uncertainty, was dangerous, and a declaration of intentions by the government was necessary to reduce its intensity to a level compatible with the maintenance of public order.

It was in these circumstances that he led the deputation that called on the Prime Minister (October 12) to urge upon him the dangers of delay in introducing again a Reform Bill unscathed by compromise. Again the most forceful language was used, and it may have been made more forceful for being used against the background of the procession that had taken place this same day, to say nothing of the riots which had broken out at Derby and Nottingham. The deputation, claiming intimate knowledge as well as influence in the several parishes in which its members resided, expressed astonishment about the rumor that Parliament was not to assemble until after Christmas. It argued that if the Bill was not reintroduced after a short prorogation, not to exceed seven days, and the necessary means (i.e. creation of peers) provided for its passage, "this country will inevitably be plunged into all the horrors of a violent revolution."[22] Not content with this, Place then arranged for the *Morning Chronicle* to report what the deputation had "ascertained," namely, that the government planned a long delay before introducing a new Bill, that it was unlikely that peers would be created, and that the new Bill would be altered in order to assure its passage. The report was skillfully written to convey the impression that the government held these views, without directly attributing them to the Prime Minister's actual words. This report, which made its way to other papers, was not in accord with Grey's account of the interview. In his version nothing was said on his part about the time that would elapse before Parliament was reconvened. Place, in effect, confirmed this, for it is evident from subsequent explanations that

22. "The opinion generally is, that the peace of the country can only be maintained by a short prorogation, attended with some indications to show that the success of the Reform Bill is certain": "[Memorial] To the Right Honourable Earl Grey," Add. MSS 35,149, ff. 88b–89. The *Times* took up this line, "The country cannot—ought not to be kept in its present feverish state": Oct. 13, 1831, p. 3; Oct. 18, 1831, p. 3; also see *Birm. J.*, Oct. 8, 1831, p. 4.

his report was based on an "inference" from the Minister's words but not on any "expressions" that were actually used. (The implications drawn, Place said, were "as correct as any inference from mere reasoning can be.") After seeking to intimidate Grey during the interview, evidently Place then sought to stimulate alarm or anger among reformers and at the same time to provoke the government into denying that it contemplated a long delay, thus forcing its hand.[23] While this appears to have been Place's intention, it is difficult to determine the extent of his success. He had asked that Parliament be prorogued for only seven days (from October 20). It was generally believed, so Peel claimed, that Parliament would not meet again before Christmas. When it convened on December 6 the Tories argued that, since government was accepting advice from a Radical deputation "headed by a tailor and an apothecary," it was "swayed by the dictates of the mob and of the Press."[24]

The wish to spread an alarmist view of the state of public feeling is evident in occasional writings of peripheral members of the Radical group. Edward Gibbon Wakefield, for example,

23. *Hansard, 8* (Oct. 17, 1831), 851; Place to Editor of *Morning Chronicle,* Oct. 19, 1831, published Oct. 20 (quoted from Cobbett's *Political Register,* Oct. 22, 1831, col. 193–94 and 216–20). Also see col. 195–205, 268–69, and "State of the Government," *Quarterly Review, 46* (Nov. 1831), 292–95. Without defending the truth of his letter to the *Morning Chronicle,* Place equivocally said, "I think I have acted as I ought to have done for the public service": Place to Burdett, Oct. 19, 1831, Add. MSS 35,149, f. 101. Cf. Place's observation, appearing in his narrative of these events written in 1835, "It is easy to govern the people of England by reason,— not by deception": Add. MSS 27,790, f. 51.

24. Dawson, *Hansard, 9* (Dec. 7, 1831), 109; Peel, ibid. (Dec. 6, 1831), 73–74. Wharncliffe had been told that Parliament had been convened in case its support was necessary for further measures (in addition to the Proclamation of Nov. 22) against the unions. But Wellington thought "the unions and the press insisted upon it, and they could not be resisted . . . Who ever heard of assembling Parliament and having nothing for them to do? Nobody, but the mob and Mr. Place the tailor!": *Despatches, 8,* 157–58. Also see Croker, *Hansard, 9,* 49. Halevy saw it as a reflection of the deputation's influence: *Triumph of Reform,* p. 41; also see H. Ferguson, "The Birmingham Political Union and the Government, 1831–32," *Victorian Studies, 3* (1960), 269–71. The apothecary was John Constantine Carpue.

skillfully alludes to the violent disposition of the populace and hints at the relevance of such feelings to the Reform Bill struggle in writings that ostensibly are not even political in character. Such writings were not critically important in the passing of the Reform Bill; though they may have contributed to the atmosphere of anxiety about the social order that weakened opposition to the Bill. However, they do indicate the intentions of the group working with Parkes and Place. In one of the pamphlets Wakefield published late in 1831, *Swing Unmasked,* he analyzed the rural incendiarism that was so frequent during the previous winter, and which persisted into the winter of 1831–32. Incendiarism was not an expression of political discontent, and Wakefield, in his own analysis, looks to nonpolitical causes—i.e. poverty among the peasantry made worse by the effects of the Poor Laws. Wakefield, however, argued that political excitement connected with the Reform Bill accentuated the problem, which he saw as an example of the way, "during periods of great political excitement, the weak . . . devised new and secret modes of injuring the powerful."[25] Such allusions could only aggravate anxieties

---

25. *Swing Unmasked; or, the Causes of Rural Incendiarism* (London, 1831), pp. 5, 8–11, 46. Wakefield addressed public meetings of the National Political Union and worked with the Benthamite Radicals during the decade that followed. His uncle, Daniel Wakefield, was a member of the Council of the National Political Union, and his father, Edward Wakefield, was a close friend of James Mill's. The *Morning Chronicle* commended Wakefield's pamphlet and attempted to use its argument to support the Reform Bill. "The very fact of the prevalence of incendiarism . . . supposes on the part of the people a great want of the means for obtaining in a proper manner redress for the grievances under which they labor": PCN, Set 21, f. 232. Also see Place's anonymous pamphlet, *An Essay on the State of the Country, in respect of the condition and conduct of the Husbandry Labourers, and to the Consequences Likely to Result Therefrom* (Feb. 26, 1831); while apparently dealing with agricultural disturbances, Place played upon fears of revolution by connecting the rural disorders with the possibility of an economic "standstill." He described at length the likelihood of refusals to pay taxes, the stoppage of trade, and the refusal to take Bank of England notes. All this alluded to financial panic, a theme familiar in Place's rhetoric, and to the dissolution of government and the possibility that "the very bonds of society will be in danger of being burst asunder": ibid., pp. 13–15.

about the foundations of society. The effort to encourage alarm-
ism, however, is revealed still more clearly in another of his pamphlets, *Householders in Danger from the Populace,* published in
1831 after the Bristol riots. Here he sought to exploit the fears
generated by the events at Bristol, where a mob burned public
buildings and terrorized the town for two days before finally being subdued by the military. He wrote:

> All history proves that great political changes . . . are liable
> to numerous accidents; that the general tendency of such
> accidents is, by disturbing the course of transition, to con-
> vert peaceful changes into revolution; and . . . the chances
> of mischievous accidents must be in proportion to the delay
> which takes place in consummating a political change. A
> specimen of the kind of accidents . . . has been lately ex-
> hibited at Bristol. . . . if events similar . . . should occur
> at the capital . . . who will say that we should escape a
> revolution?

With this possibility put to his readers, Wakefield then described
the populace in terms calculated to give greater likelihood to
that possibility. The populace, by which he meant "enemies of
the protective laws by which society is upheld," consists of three
groups—"common thieves"; "the Rabble," who are "impover-
ished persons" who would not "neglect an opportunity to enjoy
other men's goods by force"; and "Desperadoes," a term he uses
in reference to the Rotunda Radicals. Wakefield acknowledged
that the thieves and the rabble were apolitical, but as a large,
fierce, irresponsible minority they would welcome an opportunity
for "plunder" that an accident might provide. He thought these
groups had become hopeful for such an opportunity to "sack the
town" since the Lords had rejected the second Reform Bill. Their
leaders "were fully aware of the utility of barricades . . . various
histories of the Three Days in Paris had been greedily read by
them." The third group, the Desperadoes, was described as
being few in number and in some cases benevolent in intention,
but they were "fanatics." "I mistake them," Wakefield said, "if
they would not destroy the existing race of men, in order to re-
place it with another which would condemn the institution of

property." In order to protect against the danger, Wakefield suggested that householders arm themselves, a proposal also made by Hume who in Parliament suggested the need for a "Burgher Guard." Similar suggestions as to the necessity of a "national guard" had been made by Place, by Fonblanque in the *Examiner,* and it was a call soon to be taken up by some of the political unions.[26] While anyone could be alarmed by Wakefield's lurid descriptions and by the sense of immediate danger that he tried to convey, the government would have reason to be concerned not only with the evil he described but also with the remedy he proposed.

Political Unions: The Appearance of Unanimity

Among the conditions that had to be satisfied before a government would yield to a threatening populace, James Mill had specified that there had to be unanimity in the demands made by the populace and there had to be general awareness of this, especially among the governing class. This was realistic, for the more general the demand, the more pressing it would appear, and for the Whigs this had additional importance arising from their belief that legitimacy was gained by consent. In order to give credence to the image of a discontented populace that was unanimous in its demands and in its determination neither to relax nor compromise, Parkes and Place and their associates at-

26. *Hansard, 4* (June 27, 1831), 396; *Householders in Danger from the Populace* (London, 1831), passim. Place also predicted the formation of a "national guard" in *An Essay on the State of the Country,* p. 14; *Exam.,* Oct. 16, 1831, pp. 665–66. The Radical Colonel De Lacy Evans provides another example of one whose words appear to have been deliberately alarmist. He reportedly said that 10,000 men were prepared to march on London if Ministers were defeated. In the House he announced that if a government "were formed to coerce British feeling and govern the country by the sword, he would be one of the first men to draw a sword against it." He also said it "was the opinion of many, that there was no alternative between the success of the Reform Bill and a revolution, in case of its failure." *Hansard, 3* (March 7, 1831), 118; *7* (Oct. 4, 1831), 1210; *8* (Oct. 10, 1831), 449. On Evans' association with Place, see Wallas, *Place,* p. 304; and A. Aspinall, ed., *Three Early Nineteenth Century Diaries* (London, Williams and Norgate, 1952), pp. 278, 284–86.

tempted to use a new kind of political association—the political union.

This new form of extra-Parliamentary organization emerged just prior to the Reform Bill agitation and assisted the Radicals in their attempt to achieve the appearance of unanimity in popular support for the Reform Bill and in popular determination to have nothing less than the "whole Bill." The first Political Union appeared at Birmingham in 1830. It was the largest and most influential of the unions as well as a model for many that followed. The object of the Birmingham Political Union was to "collect and organize the peaceful expression of the Public Opinion, so as to bring it to act upon the legislative functions in a just, legal, and effectual way."[1] The Union claimed to be exercising the traditional constitutional rights of petitioning and assembling public meetings. However, its greatest influence was not based on the exercise of these rights alone, but on its claim that it expressed the opinions, grievances, and demands of a vast majority of the populace in a given locality. In order to give plausibility to this claim the leaders of the Union sought to establish a mass membership for the organization, to assemble immensely large meetings, and to submit petitions signed by tens of thousands of persons. There were precedents for some of the Union's activities. During the agitations of 1816–19 and during the late eighteenth century as well there had been large meetings and petitions signed by large numbers of persons. But the novelty of the Birmingham Political Union (which it shared with the Catholic Association on which in part it was modeled)[2] consisted of its claim to have mobilized the opinions of large masses of men who previously, it was assumed, had been politically quiescent. This suggested that the populace would now have a permanent concern with political questions, unlike earlier generations when engagement in extra-Parliamentary political activities had been casual and tem-

1. "Objects, Rules, and Regulations of the Birmingham Political Union," Jan. 25, 1830. The Union had antecedents in Birmingham politics of 1819 and the early 1820's: Bain, *James Mill*, p. 439.

2. James A. Reynolds, *Catholic Emancipation Crisis*, pp. 164, 173–75; *Report of the Proceedings of the Great Meeting of the Inhabitants of the Midland Districts, held . . . May 7, 1832* (Birmingham, 1832), p. 4.

porary. The apparent ease with which the Union at Birmingham convened large public meetings suggested that a change had taken place. The growth of the new towns and of the metropolis itself provided the urban environment necessary for such extra-Parliamentary organization, just as discontent and the spread of democratic sentiments in the face of oligarchic institutions encouraged it.

What allowed the unions to be used as evidence of unanimity in public opinion was, first of all, their composition in terms of social class. They aspired to be "popular," to include men of all ranks, and they particularly sought to recruit "the Lower and Middle Classes of People." There is no theme more common in the literature published by the unions than their claim to represent the common interests of these two classes that included the overwhelming majority of the increasingly large nonrural populace. At the same time they were not explicitly antiaristocratic, and their rhetoric did not neglect the agricultural classes; but the main emphasis was on the classes that dominated the social setting of the industrial towns. It was not merely aspiration or rhetoric to speak of the "lower and middle classes of the people," at least not in Birmingham. The particular circumstances of economic organization, religious background, and social structure combined in an unusual way to produce a situation in which class conflict was attenuated and the disparate character of economic interests was obscured. Among other things, in Birmingham there was a prevalence of small workshops rather than factories, and this encouraged close contact between masters and men and meant that they shared a vulnerability to distress. As a result, class cleavages were not so sharply defined as they were in other industrial towns, and it was possible to talk of the middle and working classes as if they in fact had shared interests and similar political opinions.[3] Though circumstances elsewhere were not congenial to the kind of organization developed by the Birming-

3. A. Briggs, "The Background of the Parliamentary Reform Movement in Three English Cities (1830–2)," *Cambridge Historical Journal, 10* (1952), 297–98. Also see T. R. Tholfsen, "The Artisan and the Culture of Early Victorian Birmingham," *University of Birmingham Historical Journal, 4* (1954), 146.

ham Political Union, other unions were thought of as similar in structure and composition to the "parent" union at Birmingham, and evidence of diverse aims was obscured. As a result, the claim, and in some cases the fact, of multiclass composition, combined with very large numbers attending meetings—in the tens of thousands at Birmingham—made it possible to represent union meetings as evidence of unanimity among the public. Another circumstance lent itself to the development of this appearance of unanimity. Large meetings, without the technological means of allowing a speaker to be effectively heard and of course without the possibility of discussion, could be controlled by an autocratic chairman, for almost any resolution that expressed with rough accuracy the feelings of most of the audience was supported by applause and acclamation. This was especially true for large, open-air meetings where it was particularly difficult to allow for amendments of proposals put to the meeting—indeed, as Place has reported, they would hardly be audible for half those present.[4] The unanimous endorsement of resolutions put before such meetings might be achieved with relative ease.

There was another aspect of the unions that added to their tactical value. The reformers, and not least James Mill, sought peaceful change, and the unions were well adapted to this purpose. Unlike the somewhat reckless approach of certain leading radicals of an earlier period, the men who established the political unions were nearly obsessive in their disapproval of violence. Insistence on legality was almost as emphatic in the rhetoric of the union leaders as their claim to be representative across class lines. Members were enjoined to "bear in mind that the strength of . . . [the union] consists in the Peace, *Order, Unity,* and Legality of our proceedings; and to consider all persons as enemies who shall, in any way, invite or promote violence, discord,

---

4. Wallas, *Place,* p. 282. Attwood also used the circumstances of a crowd to evoke expressions of apparent unanimity. "I see that you are all of one mind on this great subject. (*Cheers*) Answer me then, had not you all rather die than live the slaves of Boroughmongers? (*All, All!*) We are told indeed of apathy and indifference in the public mind": *Report of the Great Meeting, Birmingham, May 7, 1832,* p. 4.

or division, or any illegal or doubtful measures."[5] However, while the unions claimed to preserve the public peace, their very orderliness made them seem formidable for still another reason, for it suggested to some that they had a concealed military organization; but even discounting this, the speed and orderliness with which their meetings disbanded suggested an obedience to leadership that at least was susceptible to organization on military lines. This added to their intimidating appearance. Furthermore, their emphasis on the necessity of using peaceful means took the form of exhortations to the rank and file for self-restraint; whether or not such restraint was required, these exhortations also served to suggest the possibility of popular violence.[6]

The significance attached by James Mill and his associates to the appearance of unanimity in public opinion is revealed in their attempt to organize a union in London that could claim to represent metropolitan opinion and serve as well as a central body to coordinate the actions of political unions throughout the country. The National Political Union, as it was named, took shape under the leadership of Francis Place, a long-time associate of James Mill and a disciple of Bentham, who had recently retired as master tailor so as to give full attention to his political activities, which included organizing pressure groups, serving as

5. "Regulations of the Birmingham Political Union," Jan. 25, 1830. Apart from tactical considerations, there was an additional reason for the Benthamites to look with favor on political unions of the Birmingham type. This derives from the emphasis in Benthamism on the need for legislation to be based on the "universal" or whole interest of "the People" in contrast to the "sinister interests" of any segment of the populace; this required that political organizations, to be legitimate, represent the whole or "popular" interest and that they not exclude any segment of the populace. The unions that emphasized union of middle and working classes clearly qualified for their approval.

6. This rhetoric, skillfully combining allusions to potential physical force while at the same time calling for the maintenance of law and order, is exemplified in Attwood's speech of May 7, 1832, and in the address of the Council of the Birmingham Political Union published after the Lords' rejection of the Bill: *Times,* Oct. 10, 1831, p. 4; Henry Jephson, *The Platform. Its Rise & Progress,* 2 (London, 1892), 121. Even the proposals for arming the unions were justified on the ground that this would protect order and property in the face of popular unrest.

an election agent in Westminster, and pamphleteering on behalf of his particular version of Radicalism, an activity that provoked Parkes into calling him an "Intellectual Incendiary."[7] His union was begun in mid-October, 1831, after the Lords' rejection of the second Reform Bill, when it became "clear . . . that the aristocracy would not spontaneously renounce their power." The purpose of the Union was "to give a definite form to public opinion, to create an organ through which that opinion could be efficiently transmitted"; the intention of the organizers "was to put the wishes of the people at large in organized array; to give them, by union, so imposing an appearance, that denial of their demands should be hopeless, and direct oppression dangerous."[8] It was begun at this particular time in response to claims that a "reaction" in public opinion had begun, and that the enthusiasm for the Reform Bill that was evident earlier in the year was no longer to be found. "The cry of a re-action in the popular opinion was raised by the enemies of Reform. These infatuated opponents to good government had mistaken, or pretended to mistake, the silent and dangerous dissatisfaction of the people for an apathy towards the measure of Reform."[9] In November 1831, a placard asked, "Shall we the people of England, anxious for Reform, remain in our houses instead of meeting, proclaim our sentiments, and thus afford the Boroughmongers a pretext for saying that we are not of one mind. . . . Shall we by our supineness, suffer the bigots to fire other Bristols?"[10] Thus it was to

7. Parkes to Place, Oct. 15, 1831, Add. MSS 35,149, f. 97.

8. No. 8. National Political Union, *Report of the Council to the First Annual General Meeting . . . February 2, 1832*, p. 1; *Proceedings of the Second Annual Meeting of the National Political Union . . . February 4, 1833*, p. 3. "When Union is called for in politics, the meaning is, that one party should unite against another party that is united; so that, in this sense, Union is a congregation of physical power": *Union. A Prospectus of a New Publication*, p. 1. The proposal for a union was made on Oct. 15, an organizational meeting was held on Oct. 19, and a public meeting on Oct. 31: Wallas, *Place*, pp. 279–81; Harriet Martineau, *A History of the Thirty Years' Peace*, 2 (London, 1877), 453.

9. No. 8. NPU, *Report of the Council, Feb. 2, 1832*, p. 2.

10. A placard, n.d., but in Place's hand, "National Political Union, 16 Nov. 1831. Proposed to the Council and adopted": PCN, Set 17, *3*, f. 13f.

produce evidence of continued public concern for the Bill after
its defeat in the Lords. It was also to demonstrate general agreement as to what was being demanded. A placard announced that
"Reformers, nearly to a man, have been unanimous in their acceptance of the Ministerial Measure" and that there had been a
"rejection of all other plans and theories."[11] But in fact Place's
Union was being challenged by advocates of universal suffrage
who joined the Tories in claiming that the public was indifferent
to the Reform Bill. Since these extreme Radicals claimed to represent working-class opinion, they seriously disturbed the image
of unanimity that Parkes and Place (and the Whigs too) were
seeking to maintain.

The challenge to the National Political Union came from
Radical politicians and journalists who organized the National
Union of the Working Classes. They appear to have concentrated their efforts in Manchester and London. The most prominent of the group at this time was Henry Hunt, who was to have
addressed the crowd at Peterloo and now was Member of Parliament for Preston; but they were also led by Thomas Wakley
(M.P. for Finsbury), William Benbow (author of *Grand National
Holiday*), as well as by Henry Hetherington, William Lovett, and
John Cleave, who were to become prominent in the Chartist
movement. Their program in 1831 anticipated Chartism in its
advocacy of universal suffrage, annual parliaments, the secret
ballot, and abolition of property qualifications for members of
Parliament.[12] Inspired by the writings of Robert Owen, Thomas
Hodgskin, and William Thompson, they were critical of the institution of private property and of the middle classes as one of its
main beneficiaries. With these views they opposed the Reform
Bill as a measure that enfranchised the middle classes to the
exclusion of the working class, and they urged the working classes
to withhold their support for the measure. These views were put
before the public at meetings in Manchester and London, and in
the *Poor Man's Guardian* (claiming a circulation of 3,000), in
which it was asserted that the Reform Bill "is a measure in which

11. No. 3. NPU, a placard, Nov. 16, 1831.
12. *The Objects and Laws of the National Union of the Working
Classes and Others*, p. 5: in H.O. 64/18; Linton, *James Watson*, pp. 40–42.

you [the working classes] have no interest . . . it is purely a question between the aristocracy and the *middle*-money getting-classes, and which, so far from being intended for your benefit, is brought forward . . . to completely block up the narrow passage, which leads to your redemption."[13] Similar views were put to Parliament by Henry Hunt, who persistently claimed that because the Reform Bill brought no advantage to the working classes they were indifferent to its fate. In late August of 1831 he noted that "public feeling towards the Bill . . . had greatly changed. The people felt much cooler towards the measure. It was now, in fact, a dead letter." And he challenged supporters of the Bill to call public meetings to test public reaction.[14] In October, after the Lords' rejection, he reported that at a meeting he had attended there were seven persons favorable to the Bill and two thousand against it. He did admit that "in some parts of the country, and about the metropolis" there was "great excitement"; but, he asked, "did that justify the Government in asserting that the nation was unanimous in their support?"[15] Hunt's claims thus pointed to the possibility of apathy and the absence of general agreement among the people.

This was a challenge that Place could not easily ignore. Hunt, it is true, was the only prominent spokesman of the so-called working-class Radicals in Parliament; but he spoke often and attracted attention, and since his claims coincided with some of the Tory arguments, his argument was given additional prominence by the Opposition which, of course, delighted in Hunt's claims. This was so evident that when twitted about his "new allies," Hunt rose to say "he was misrepresented to have con-

13. Henry Hetherington, the editor, also noted that Lord Grey "was obliged to talk of 'justice,' etc., and of *'natural rights,'* both of which are the grounds on which we stand": *Poor Man's Guardian,* Oct. 15, 1831, p. 121.

14. *Hansard, 6* (Aug. 30, 1831), 871–72.

15. Ibid., *8* (Oct. 12, 1831), 636. At a Manchester meeting of April 7, 1831, he had described the Bill as a "trick of the Whigs": Bouverie to Phillipps, April 10, 1831, H.O. 40/29. Also see *Birm. J.,* Nov. 5, 1831, p. 2, for a hostile report of another Manchester speech (Nov. 1) expressing similar views.

tracted a political alliance" with the Tory party.[16] And even though the National Union of Working Classes was a small and factionally divided organization, it was a militant group, and its claim to represent the interests of the working classes, if believed, would have taken the steam out of a device that was designed to put pressure on the government. It was therefore with resolution and unscrupulousness that Place moved to silence the Huntite Radicals.

The working-class Radicals in London—Cleave, Hetherington, Lovett, Benbow, Watson—knew that Place's organization was being set up to support the Whigs in carrying the Reform Bill. In any case, looking on Place and his friends as intruders in working-class political organization, they deemed it necessary to attend the public meeting called by Place for 31 October. On arrival they were asked into the committee room where Place, filled with suspicion, inquired as to their intentions. Lovett explained that, "as they [Place and his committee] were about to appeal for the support of the working classes, I should deem it my duty to move an amendment for extending the suffrage to persons of that class."[17] The ensuing meeting, which was moved out of doors in order to accommodate the 20,000 said to be in attendance, witnessed the proposal by Lovett and Cleave of an amendment for universal male suffrage, accompanied by the accusation that the purpose of the National Political Union was to conceal an effort by "the middle classes . . . to make them [i.e. working class] the tools of their purposes."[18] Lovett and Cleave, according to the press, were "listened to with impatience and finally

16. *Hansard, 4,* 205, 958; *6,* 873.

17. W. Lovett, *The Life and Struggles of William Lovett, in his pursuit of Bread, Knowledge, and Freedom* (London, 1876), p. 75. Lovett reports that Roebuck urged the amendment be adopted, but this seems unlikely, especially in view of the fact that Roebuck was later proposed for the Council of the Union by Place: National Political Union Balloting Lists, PCN, Set 17, *3,* 108a–108d; also see Add. MSS 27,791, ff. 74, 78.

18. Wallas, *Place,* p. 282. The *Poor Man's Guardian,* Nov. 5, 1831, p. 145, reported the attendance of 6,000 to 7,000, and *Exam.* (Nov. 6, 1831, p. 709) upwards of 15,000. The Home Secretary's intelligence estimated that 3,000 were present: Melbourne to Brougham, Oct. 31, 1831, in Brougham Papers, 20,386.

howled down."[19] Lovett, however, offers an account that makes the howling down appear anything but spontaneous. "The Committee and their friends," he reports, "knowing of our intention to propose an amendment, so arranged themselves that they drowned by their noise and clamour every effort that Mr. Cleave and myself made in proposing our amendment to the meeting." Lovett was "interrupted by hisses and loud cries of 'off,' " and the hostility was such that he "was barely allowed to propose . . . an amendment [for universal suffrage]." Cleave "was opposed and insulted as much as Mr. Lovett, and Scotch-economy-Hume demanded of him 'for what mischief he was there,' " and then "the uproar became so great that he was obliged to retire."[20] This was the meeting about which Place had been apprehensive that any amendment offered might pass by the acclamation of a large crowd that could neither hear very well nor make distinctions such as Place did between two proposals, both for reform, but one for the Bill and the other for universal suffrage.[21] In this case he appears to have guarded against such an eventuality by placing his claque near the immoderates so they could quickly give the cue for a hostile response to the crowds beyond.

This success was not an end of Place's difficulties, for an amendment proposing that half the Council be made up of workingmen was offered by Wakley, and after a procedural wrangle and much confusion it was carried. This upset of Place's intentions, which was blamed on Burdett's mismanagement as Chairman of the meeting, meant that the Council, which was to consist

19. Jephson, *Platform*, 2, 109.

20. Lovett, *Life and Struggles*, p. 75. The *Poor Man's Guardian,* Nov. 5, 1831, p. 146. It also observed that "had you witnessed the disgraceful manner in which the very mention of you [working classes] was received—had you beheld two of your most worthy advocates and fellow working-men, Mr. Lovett and Mr. Cleave, insulted, denied a hearing, and reproached as belonging to your 'gang'—you could no longer hesitate as to withdrawing from your enemies the confidence you so blindly repose in them." The *Times'* report indicates that Lovett was interrupted by hostile observations six times and Cleave four times, each during very brief speeches: Nov. 1, 1831, pp. 3–4.

21. Wallas, *Place,* p. 282.

of seventy-two members, was to be elected from two lists of candidates, one working class and the other "not of the working classes."[22] This opened the door for the immoderate Rotundaites to sit on the powerful Council. Previous to this the organizing committee, which probably would have become the Council when the Union was formally established, was packed with sympathizers such as W. J. Fox, John Taylor, and Roebuck. When faced with the need to have workingmen on the Council, Place acted to exclude the Rotunda Radicals so as to preserve the Union as an all-inclusive, representative body united in a demand for moderate reform such as offered by the Bill. In doing this he again showed himself both adroit and ruthless. Applicants for membership were screened, and respectable-appearing workingmen were interviewed; if they were opposed to the Rotundaites, they were invited to be nominees for the Council and asked to name others who might qualify. Such men were then interviewed and inquiries were addressed to their employers and neighbors. If they passed the test, they were invited to join the Union "with a view to their being elected to the Council." By this means, Place reduced the number of positions available to the Rotunda Radicals. In fact, Place avoided an election at this time by gaining

22. "Resolutions Passed at a Public Meeting Held in Lincoln's Inn Fields . . . for the purpose of forming a National Political Union" (Nov. 2, 1831) (a placard). Buller blamed Wakley's success on Burdett's "weakness": *Life of Sir William Napier,* ed. H. A. Bruce, *1* (London, 1864), 362. Seven asterisks are used instead of Burdett's name, but since he chaired the meeting he is clearly meant. He urged the crowd to give Cleave a hearing, and after Wakley proposed his amendment he recognized a Rotundaite (Savage) who seconded and then another person (Thelwall) who supported Wakley; if Burdett knew Thelwall's position, he did not take it into account: *Times,* Nov. 1, 1831, p. 4. The *Poor Man's Guardian,* Nov. 5, 1831, p. 146, was surprised by Wakley's initial success in carrying his motion for equal representation for the working classes. "We can hardly reconcile, we must confess, the carrying of the last motion, with the insulting manner in which the very mention of you [working class] had been previously received: however, such as it is, it is a point gained, and we urge you to elect . . . such persons for members as have been proved your able friends." Place later spoke of Wakley as one of a group of "fluent speakers all favourites of the working people in whose prejudices they not only participated but fostered": Place to Brougham, July 1, 1837, in Brougham Papers.

the Union's consent to the appointment of a temporary Council until an election could be held, as provided by the rules, in February. This arrangement was made within the subcommittee that governed the Union between its organizational meeting (October 31) and its first general meeting on November 10 when the Council was formally appointed. There were three Rotunda men (Wakley, Cleave, Lovett) on this subcommittee of thirteen. Therefore, had they opposed the arrangement they would have failed. But on November 9, when the list was first proposed within the subcommittee, no Rotunda men were even present. Next day at the general meeting of members, a small group of Rotundaites appeared, but they were howled down when one of them, Osborne, proposed adding four of his associates to the list of approved names. The poor representation of the Rotunda Radicals in part reflects the demoralization resulting from their having been intimidated by the Home Secretary into canceling a large, open-air meeting that had been scheduled for November 7, at the very time Place was arranging to exclude them from the Council of his Union. In the end, only one known Rotundaite, William Lovett, was given a place in the Council.[23]

Place consolidated his position still further in February, 1832, when the first election to the Council was held, and he did this in spite of the effort to assert themselves made by the Rotunda men at that time. Despite complicated changes in the rules governing the method of nominating and establishing eligibility of candidates that Place introduced in anticipation of the election, nineteen Rotundaites managed to gain places on the ballot, eleven on the working-class list and eight on the nonworking-class list.[24] But the number of nominations made by Rotunda men was un-

23. "Minutes of NPU meetings," PCN, Set 63, *1*, ff. 8, 40–42; Add. MSS 27,791, ff. 70, 74, 87; *Scotsman*, Nov. 16, 1831, p. 4; No. 1. NPU, pp. 1–2; Wallas, *Place*, p. 283.

24. No. 6. NPU, *Objects and Rules of the National Political Union . . . adopted at a General Meeting . . . Dec. 1, 1831* (London, 1832), p. 8, sec. 4, especially rules 1, 2, 4, 7. It is assumed that the names crossed out on Place's sample ballot (in PCN, Set 17, *3*, f. 108) are all Rotundaites.

necessarily restricted, either from their own naïveté or from having been misled by Place, for every Rotundaite made at most only one nomination to each of the two lists, and only two of them made as many as two nominations to the two lists together. In contrast, Place's lieutenants felt no such restraint; Detroisier, for example, nominated ten persons and Perry nine. (Place shrewdly confined himself to two, one of them Roebuck.)[25] As a result, the Rotunda men had eleven candidates on a list of forty-eight working-class nominees; and eight on a list of forty-seven nominees on the nonworking-class list. Since each voter was to select thirty-six from each of the two lists, this facilitated the exclusion of the Rotunda candidates. That Place had this goal clearly in mind is indicated by a comment he made on a sample ballot: "List made by me and agreed to by several in the hope of excluding the dishonest men who would destroy the Union—viz. Augero, Grady, Lovett, Cleave, Dias Santos, Fall, Hunt [John, not Henry the M.P.]." All of these—among the most prominent of the Rotunda candidates—failed, and only four out of their nineteen candidates succeeded, one gaining a place on the working-class half of the Council and three on the nonworking-class half.[26] By these means Place secured "honest, sensible, well-intentioned men," for the Council; since these men had "the confidence of their fellow-workmen," Place felt there was "a certainty that their fellow-

25. NPU Balloting List, PCN, Set 63, *2,* f. 23. That this is the list for the Feb. 1832 election is indicated by the fact that the results written on it by Place agree with the results given in the Minutes for Feb. 7, 1832, in PCN, Set 63, *1,* ff. 87–88; the Balloting List inserted at f. 86 is for the election of Feb. 1833, the results of which appear at ff. 209–10. Dias Santos and Carpenter each made two nominations.

26. PCN, Set 17, *3,* f. 108; Set 63, *1,* ff. 87–88. Wakley, Potter, and Savage were successful, being 27th, 34th, and 36th respectively, out of 36. However, Wakley had quarreled with the Rotundaites, so his success is not necessarily theirs. In addition, William Carpenter, editor of the *Political Magazine* and formerly a Rotundaite, was 28th, but he too had fallen out with his former associates; he publicly attacked Hunt and announced that, while still for universal suffrage, he wished to see the Reform Bill passed: Carpenter to Editor, in *Times,* Oct. 15, 1831, p. 5.

workmen would vote for them."[27] Thus Place fulfilled his goal of making the Union an organization for all "real" reformers.[28]

Meanwhile, in view of their failure to change the program endorsed by the National Political Union and their exclusion from its Council, the immoderates, hostile in any case, became embittered in their isolation and frequently abused Place and his associates as "false Whigs" and as "aristocratical."[29] While Place could only be pleased with his success, he must have been grieved by the accusation that his union was the tool of the Whigs and the middle classes. This is reflected in his protest that gave an account of his life as a starving journeyman, his record, once he became an employer, of paying the highest wages, and of his efforts to bring about repeal of the laws against combination of workingmen. He gave this explanation in order to show "that I really am, what I pretend to be, the ardent and active friend of the working classes."[30]

At the same time, the rival organization, the National Union of Working Classes, while immensely important as one of the seeds from which Chartism grew, was, thanks to Lord Melbourne, not to mar the appearance of unanimity Place was about to achieve. Having announced a public meeting of this rival body, Lovett and his associates were advised by Melbourne that the

27. Wallas, *Place*, pp. 283–84.

28. This might be compared with Place's activities in connection with the 1824 Committee on the Combination Laws, for which, according to George, the evidence was "carefully staged and prepared by Place 'to show the evils of the Combination Laws' ": M. Dorothy George, "The Combination Laws," *Economic History Review*, 6 (1935), 174.

29. Wallas, *Place*, p. 283. G. J. Holyoake, compiler, *The Life and Character of Henry Hetherington* (London, 1849), not paginated. The following words are attributed to Place as Chairman of the Council in a fictional and playful account of its first meeting (presumably after the election of Feb. 1832): "I am very glad the members of the Union have made as good a choice as they could from such a list as was offered them; and I hope this Council will be good boys, and behave as well as the last . . . [with] good sense and docility." NPU, "First Meeting of the New Council" (not in Place's handwriting; but Place wrote in the names of speakers, including his own as chairman; he also added a title, and presumably identified the author: "Mr. Churchill's Wit"), PCN, Set 17, *3*, f. 109b.

30. Wallas, *Place*, p. 199.

government considered it seditious and that, if held, they would be subject to prosecution, possibly for treason. By this move they were effectively intimidated, leaving the field to Place's Union. The working-class Radicals continued to hold informal meetings at the Rotunda, but their publicity was confined to a few fugitive newspapers that were unstamped and therefore illegal, whereas Place's Union was covered by such papers as the *Examiner,* the *Morning Chronicle,* and the *Times.* Thus, despite the evidence of dissent offered by the Rotunda Radicals, and despite the fact, admitted by Place, that middle-class persons were reluctant to join after the success of Wakley's motion,[31] Place tried to perpetuate the image of the political union as an organization consisting of both middle and working classes; even after the meeting of October 31, where the disagreement of the working-class spokesmen was expressed, he continued to emphasize cooperation and harmony across class lines.

This is not a Union of the Working Classes, nor of the Middle Classes, nor of any other class, but of all Reformers, of the masses and of the millions.

The *National Political Union* is essentially a Union of the People, and is the first instance on record of the nation breaking through the trammels of class, to associate for the common interest.[32]

---

31. Ibid., p. 284. Place noted, "We have upon our books many of the first names which London offers among the middle classes. . . . In time the dread of taking part in new modes of proceeding will disappear from among the great body of the middle classes, and they will then . . . join in this great work of national amelioration." Place then explicitly acknowledged that "the members of the middle classes have exhibited *their* distrust by silence and apathy": No. 8.   NPU, *Report of the Council, Feb. 2, 1832,* p. 4. Tocqueville, during his visit in 1833, noted the prevalent suspicion of the working classes among middle-class persons: *Journey to England and Ireland,* Eng. tr. G. Lawrence and K. P. Mayer, ed. J. P. Mayer (London, Faber, 1958), pp. 45, 70, 73. Also see Buller to Sir William Napier, Nov. 4, 1831: *Life of Sir William Napier,* ed. Bruce, *1,* 362–63.

32. "Resolutions Passed at a Public Meeting, Oct. 31, 1831" (a placard), Nov. 2, 1831.

After this brief struggle the National Political Union, like its great associate in Birmingham, was in a position to serve its tactical purpose. An indication of Place's success can be found by comparing London with Manchester, where there were two unions that rarely ceased to quarrel. A meeting was organized by moderates in Manchester on October 12, 1831, in order to protest the Lords' rejection of the Bill. But the meeting was dominated by unionists urging universal suffrage. The Borough-reeve who initially chaired the meeting walked out, and when another moderate, Thomas Potter, took the chair, he found himself unable to control the meeting or to direct its proceedings in a manner congenial to his own views, with the result that he "refused to sign those resolutions, which were carried against the higher union by the lower one"—a circumstance for which "the latter have threatened him with their vengeance." The "lower" union finally captured the hustings, and the pro-Reform Bill *Manchester Guardian,* in response to the subsequent proceedings, said the resolutions and addresses "have no claim whatever to be construed as the act of the *'inhabitants of Manchester.'* " This led General Bouverie, who was responsible for aiding the civil authorities in maintaining public order in the Northern District, to observe in his report to the Home Office that "there is not much real mischief to be apprehended from the Unions whilst things continue in this state."[33] The circumstances in London could have allowed the formation of a similar judgment. The critical difference lay in the way Place managed to organize the expression of certain opinions while stifling the expression of others.

Place's efforts to sustain an appearance of unanimity in Lon-

33. Foster to Melbourne, Oct. 12, Nov. 27, 1831, H.O. 52/13; Bouverie to Phillipps, Oct. 20, 1831, H.O. 40/29; *Absalom Watkin, Extracts From His Journal, 1814–1856,* ed. A. E. Watkin (London, 1920), pp. 153–55; *Manchester Guardian,* Oct. 15, 1831, p. 4; Oct. 22, 1831, p. 3. The *Manchester Guardian* called the members of the "lower" union "Huntites." The Huntite union had a majority at a Preston meeting of 1,500 on Oct. 14, 1831. The disunity in Manchester did not prevent the *Times* from asserting, "There is but one voice in the town, and all differences on minor points are abandoned": Oct. 10, 1831, p. 4.

don were paralleled by Joseph Hume (who was a member of
Place's Union) in Parliament. There he attempted to meet Hunt's
argument that the working class was interested only in universal
suffrage and that, since it had nothing to gain from the Reform
Bill, it was indifferent to it. Hume insisted that the Bill "would
benefit every individual in the country, not even excepting the
7,000,000 [i.e. the working classes] of whom the hon. member
for Preston [Hunt] had spoken"; and he contended that "the
feeling of the people . . . was unparalleled in unanimity in the
history of England."[34] In order to sustain this image Hume, with
Daniel O'Connell, discouraged Radical politicians arriving from
the country from presenting petitions for universal suffrage.[35]
And in response to applications made by Radicals throughout
the country he was said to have issued "instructions" in which
he "expressly enjoined all applicants to make no objections to the
plan of Reform, but to take it as it was, so that there might be
no doubt of its success."[36] Unanimity was also attributed to a
broad range of Radical politicians whose views, it was presumed,
were roughly correlated with the wishes of their followers. Sir
Francis Burdett, who chaired the first meeting of the National
Political Union, affirmed in Parliament the "unanimity which prevailed amongst the Reformers" with regard to the Bill; this, he
said, "was the best proof that those persons were not actuated
by . . . wild and visionary schemes . . . ascribed to them."[37]

34. *Hansard, 4* (July 8, 1831), 957; *8* (Oct. 12, 1831), 627.
35. Ibid., *4* (July 8, 1831), 957, 964.
36. Ibid., *3* (March 25, 1831), 945–46. Hume acknowledged this: ibid.,
p. 946. It was also said that he issued a "circular" intended to silence the
expression of dissent from the Reform Bill among other Radicals: Mahon,
ibid., *4* (June 21, 1831), 196.
37. Ibid., *3* (March 15, 1831), 449–50. Burdett also noted that Jeremy
Bentham had signed the petition that had been presented; this, he said,
"was at once a guarantee of the soundness of the measure, and of the
uprightness of those who proposed it." O'Connell also noted that certain
petitioners "declared themselves Radical Reformers, and yet were decidedly favorable to the Bill": ibid., *5* (Aug. 8, 1831), 927. The reform movement at this time was said to have consisted of four elements that were
personified by Burdett, Cobbett, Hunt, and Carlile, as the reformers "who
have been before the public the greatest number of years." And it was

The fact of the matter, however, is probably to be found in an early draft of a placard under consideration by the National Political Union; it contained the following statement: "Reformers are now scattered, separated, and for the most part unknown to each other." Where this passage appeared there is a note in Place's handwriting: "This paragraph to be omitted."[38]

Political unions were not confined to Birmingham, Manchester, and London. They are mentioned in connection with other places —at Bristol, Sheffield, Leicester, Newcastle, Glasgow, and Edinburgh, among others. But in many cases it is difficult to determine how large and viable these organizations were—a difficulty sometimes experienced by the Home Secretary as well.[39] Both Place and the leaders of the Birmingham Union encouraged the establishment of unions elsewhere. At Birmingham it was claimed that during a three-week period the Union had received fifty applications for copies of its rules on which other unions were to be formed.[40] Most of these other political unions appear to have

---

noted that all but Hunt supported the Bill, and Hunt's opposition was discounted as arising from "his fear of deviating from a consistency": *Union. Prospectus of a New Publication* (n.d. but ca. Oct.–Nov. 1831), pp. 2, 6, and passim.

38. "National Political Union," a placard, PCN, Set 17, *3*, f. 12e.

39. Political unions are also reported at Bath, Fairfield, Yeovil, Bilston, Darlaston, Wolverhampton, Kidderminster, Coventry, Warwick, Nottingham, Radford, Shepton-Mallet, Walsall, and Norwich, among other places. The Northern Political Union, led by Charles Attwood, was founded at Newcastle in June 1831. Although it was able to claim a large constituency if miners attended its meetings, on other occasions it had a meager following. For example, 50,000 were reported at its Oct. 17, 1831, meeting; 3,000 on Sept. 8, 1831. On April 18, 1832, it adopted a petition before fewer than 2,000 at an indoor meeting, though it claimed that others were turned away: *Newc. Cour.,* Oct. 22, 1831, p. 2; Sykes, *Local Records, 2,* 313–15; Charles Attwood to Durham, April 19, 1832, Lambton Papers.

40. *Birm. J.,* Nov. 5, 1831, p. 3; *Times,* Nov. 18, 1831, p. 3 (Hume's letter); Grote, *Life of George Grote,* p. 69. The National Political Union aspired "to form district unions throughout the country" and offered information and other aid for this purpose. NPU (Nov. 3, 1831), pp. 1–2: "Rules suggested for the formation of Branch Unions" (a placard), PCN, Set 63, *1,* f. 32.

been rather meager, although there are scattered reports of significantly large meetings sponsored by a few of them.[41] However, they rarely matched the Birmingham model either in size or in apparent vigor which explains, perhaps, why the Birmingham leaders described their town as "the Barometer of the Reform feeling throughout the kingdom"; and why Fonblanque attempted to show that Birmingham, "with all its might, is but a part, and a small part, of this united people, and its voice is but a breathing of the common spirit. Its language is but a sample of the general sentiment."[42]

The importance that Parkes and Place attached to political unions as instruments for creating the appearance of unanimity is revealed in their response to the Royal Proclamation, issued November 22, 1831, declaring certain kinds of political associations to be illegal and warning the people of the penalties attached to joining them. The Proclamation was directed against political unions that had proposed to organize in a quasi-military fashion, "with various divisions and subdivisions, under leaders with a gradation of ranks and authority, and distinguished by certain badges, and subject to the general control and direction of a superior Committee or Council."[43] It was just such organization that had been proposed to the Birmingham Political Union. At the weekly meeting of the Council on November 2 it was suggested (by Mr. Charles Jones) that a "National Guard" be

41. For example, at Walsall the Union was said to have members in "the hundreds"; at Leicester the Union initially had 800 and later reached 4,466: C. Porter to E. J. Littleton, M.P., Nov. 24 (?), 1831, H.O. 40/29. A. T. Patterson, *Radical Leicester, A History of Leicester 1780–1850* (Leicester, University College, 1954), pp. 187–88.

42. *Exam.,* Oct. 9, 1831, p. 641; *Report of the Proceedings of the Great Meeting of the Inhabitants of the Midland Districts, held at Birmingham, May 7, 1832,* pp. 6–7. It is tempting to refer to "the unions" on the assumption that they flourished in all the places that were said to have them; see H. Ferguson, "The Birmingham Political Union and the Government, 1831–32," *Victorian Studies, 3* (1960), 264, 266, including reference to them at a period (March 1831) before most of them were even established. See p. 88 above and p. 127 below.

43. *Annual Register for 1831,* Chr., pp. 186–87. It was signed Nov. 21, published Nov. 22.

formed in order "to preserve the peace of the town." His plan
was to divide the members into "sectional bodies" which would
enable the union "to act as an efficient body of Police." There
were to be seven districts, each to be identified by a distinctive
color as well as number. Each of these was to comprehend a
hierarchical organization made up of units of ten, led by a
"Tything man"; ten of these were to form into a unit led by a
"Constable of a Hundred"; five such groups, in turn, were responsible to a "Marshal of a sub-Division." All of the Marshals in
any one of the seven districts were subordinated to a member of
the Council of the Union who was to be called an Alderman.
Each person was to be identified by the color of his district as
well as by a number. Apart from administrative duties, obligations were to suppress riot or tumult.[44] The plan did not mention
firearms, but there were allusions to them in the discussion of it,
including opposition to their adoption. The newspaper report of
the first meeting at which this plan was proposed alludes to arms
without specifying what they were to be. If an anonymous letter
sent to the Home Secretary is to be believed, the Council planned
raising a subscription to purchase muskets for the "lower
classes."[45]

The plan was never implemented; in fact, it never was adopted,
for when, after two weeks with a committee, it was formally presented to the Council, it was decided to print and circulate it
throughout the country in order to determine what public reaction
to it would be. Even though the plan was frustrated by anticipation of the effect of the Proclamation, the discussion of it had
the effect, which may have been intended, of creating alarm
among Ministers about the possibility of armed and organized
insurrection. The evidence is mixed, but the possibility that the
proposal (or the exploitation of it once it was put forward) was
another example of the "language of menace" ought not be dis-
missed, even though the proposal, like others put forward in
November, was defended as a precaution required by the example
of the Bristol riots. Proposals for such a "national guard" had

44. *Birm. J.,* Nov. 5, 1831, p. 3; Nov. 12, 1831, p. 3; Nov. 19, 1831,
p. 4.
45. A letter signed "Truth" to Melbourne, Nov. 3, 1831: H.O. 40/29.

been made before the rioting at Bristol, and the particular proposal made at Birmingham was contemplated before the news of
rioting could have arrived from Bristol. The Union certainly
could not have afforded arms, for rarely if ever was it without
financial difficulties (and Melbourne was aware of this). That at
least some of the Birmingham leaders were mainly interested in
stimulating the anxieties of the governing classes is also suggested by the fact that soon after the Union's compliance with
the Proclamation was made evident, it was announced that
Mr. John Portlock, a gunmaker, was unanimously elected to the
Union's governing Council, where he joined another gunmaker,
Charles Jones, who had originally proposed the plan of organization.[46]

The government must have agreed to the issuing of this Proclamation with considerable reluctance, for, even though it had
divided feelings about political unions, apprehension was combined with the realization, at least among some of the Ministers,
that the unions, and especially the one at Birmingham, were useful to the government in its dealings with the King and with Parliament. For the government, since it frequently referred to the
unanimity among the people, was grateful for the evidence the
unions provided, both in their rhetoric and by their large meetings.
Thus Grey, in writing to the King's secretary about the extent to
which public opinion supported the Bill, expressed the view that
"there never was a sentiment so general, or rather so nearly universal, as that which now prevails," and in evidence he referred

46. *Birm. J.*, Dec. 3, 1831, p. 3, reporting Nov. 29 meeting of Council.
Ferguson suggests it was "merely a feint in the political warfare": *Victorian Studies, 3* (1960), 268–69. On financial difficulties of the Union,
see Melbourne to Grey, Nov. 18, 1831, Grey Papers; Broughton, *Recollections, 4,* 164; Parkes to Place, May 2, 1832, Add. MSS 27,792, ff. 305–
06. Proposals for an armed national guard appeared in *Morn. Chr.*,
Oct. 26, 1831, p. 2; also in Place, *An Essay on the State of the Country*
(Feb. 26, 1831), p. 14, and in *Exam.*, Oct. 16, 1831, p. 666. If in fact the
Council was not considering the adoption of arms, the anonymous letter
signed "Truth" can be seen as part of the effort to create alarm. The
Birm. J., Oct. 29, 1831, p. 2, protested against "the absurd and foolish
project," indicating a dispute within the Union. *Wrightson and Webb's
Directory of Birmingham* (1835).

to "the meetings in all parts of the country, the members and description of the persons attending them, and the unanimity of their decisions."[47] In May the Lord Chancellor presented a petition agreed to at a meeting of the Birmingham Political Union attended "in numbers unexampled," reportedly 200,000.[48] Yet, as the Proclamation noted, the government could not tolerate a power "acting independently of the Civil Magistrates"; a citizen, subject to serve as a constable, might face conflicting demands of magistrate and political union; it was "subversive of the authority with which we are invested . . . for the protection of the public peace." However, so great was the government's (or at least some of its members') interest in the evidence that the unions provided that, just prior to the issuing of the Proclamation, Althorp asked Parkes to warn his colleagues at Birmingham of the risks of prosecution that would attend any adoption of the quasi-military plans attributed to them. "We shall be obliged," Althorp wrote, "to take some steps to prevent him [Attwood] from having a regularly organized force at his command," and this, he said, "will bring us into conflict with the Unions perhaps throughout the Country."[49]

Parkes' intercession at Birmingham at Althorp's request was successful. The proposed form of organization was formally rejected. The Union was not prosecuted, but Parkes and Place feared the effect of the Proclamation on the willingness of the populace to join the unions or to attend their meetings. Place promptly arranged that four of his colleagues on the Council in

47. Jephson, *Platform, 2,* 81. Grey on Oct. 3, 1831, presented petitions from various places—Manchester, Davenport, Glasgow, and from the "Northern Political Union of Birmingham," signed by 30,000: *Hansard, 7,* 925. Also see ibid., *3* (April 18, 1831), 1476; *7* (Oct. 3, 1831), 958–59.

48. Ibid., *12* (May 9, 1832), 760.

49. Althorp to Parkes, Nov. 18, 1831: Parkes Papers. An account of Parkes' intervention at the formal, open meeting of the Council can be found in *Birm. J.,* Nov. 26, 1831, p. 4. Melbourne tried to achieve the same object through an informant (a Mr. Lawly, not Sir Francis Lawley, M.P. for Warwickshire) who had access to Attwood: Melbourne to Grey, Nov. 18, 1831, Grey Papers. Grey told the King that such efforts were to be made: Grey to Taylor, Nov. 18, 1831; *Correspondence of Grey and William IV, 1* (London, 1867), 425.

London write a letter to several of the most important papers in which objection was made to "misstatements" that had been made with regard to the Proclamation which, they said, "*does not apply* to the National Political Union nor to the great majority of unions now in existence."[50] In the *Times* a leader commended this letter to the readers' attention, and this was followed two days later by an additional leader and a report of Parkes' speech at Birmingham on the subject.[51] Place reinforced this publicity with a pamphlet in which he argued that members of the few large unions could assist in the organization of other unions so long as the new unions were not made part of a national organization.[52] All this was in accord with Parkes' dictum that "it is of great importance that it should not get abroad that the Proclamation *puts down* Unions."[53] It was, indeed, important that the unions survive for, while there were those in the government who welcomed the unions and those who were tempted to suppress them, it was Melbourne's moderate and realistic view that prevailed. He saw them as unimportant in themselves and significant

50. To the Editor of the *Times, Morning Chronicle, Morning Herald, Morning Advertiser,* from H. B. Churchill, R. H. Franks, H. Powell, and D. M. Redman, Members of the Council, Nov. 22, 1831. The letter, including the names of the signatories, is in Place's handwriting: PCN, Set 63, *1,* f. 53.

51. *Times,* Nov. 22, 1831, p. 2; Nov. 23, 1831, p. 2; Nov. 25, 1831, p. 2.

52. It pointed out that the laws did "not prohibit any Union from recommending the establishment of other Unions. They do not prohibit any Union from sending instructions to any body of persons for the formation of other Unions. . . . from appointing delegates to meet persons desirous of forming Unions, and assisting to conduct their proceedings *to the moment the Union is formed": Political Unions Not Contrary to Law. The King's Proclamation Examined, in an Address, by the National Political Union* (1831), p. 15.

53. Parkes to Place, Nov. 23, 1831: PCN, Set 17, *3,* f. 32. Parkes also said the Proclamation "will only attract attention to Association. Also it is good for agitation." An endorsement in Place's hand indicates that Place had "already written a paper on the law to show the legality of Unions, and it is in wide circulation." This evidently refers to a placard, "Laws relating to Political Associations," proposed to the Council by Place on Nov. 16, in anticipation of the Proclamation: PCN, Set 17, *3,* ff. 12d, 12g. It appeared in the *Times,* Nov. 19, 1831, p. 5, and the *Scotsman,* Nov. 23, 1831, p. 2.

only as symptoms of public feeling. So long as they were viewed in this manner they might have the kind of influence that was intended for them by Parkes and Place.[54]

"What remains except the ultima ratio?"—Grote

During the five months following the Proclamation the fate of the Bill remained uncertain. The Unions in Birmingham and London carried on despite the Proclamation. Agitation in favor of the Bill was made more ominous as the result of the riots in October—at Nottingham, Derby, and Bristol. On the other hand, opponents of the Bill claimed that there was public indifference and pointed to poorly attended meetings and a general relaxation in Radical activities. Meanwhile a new Bill (the third) was introduced on December 12, 1831 (Parliament having convened on December 6). The Cabinet deliberated as to the creation of Peers, but arrived at no determination to insist that the King authorize this. During April and May the Bill reached its critical stage. After it passed the Commons and just prior to the Lords' vote, Parkes, like others addressing Union meetings, used menacing language. At Birmingham, before a crowd reported to consist of 200,000 persons, he confessed to "mingled feelings of hope and fear"—with fear predominating. For the fate of the Bill was in doubt, and many young men "are resolved to enrol themselves in your ranks, and to stick by you in the breach." Then Parkes exclaimed, "God forbid that I should excite you to the dernier resort of a civil and physical contention for your liberties as Englishmen, or that I should seek to influence British Noblemen by any unworthy or false terror of revolution." On the other hand, he felt it necessary to "solemnly warn" and "implore" the House of Lords "not to force the Reformers to a civil contest," and he

---

54. For various ministerial views of the unions see *The Correspondence of Earl Grey and William IV,* ed. Henry Earl Grey, *2* (London, 1867), 467–75; Aspinall, ed., *Three Early Nineteenth Century Diaries,* pp. 270–72; Jephson, *Platform, 2,* 112–15. Wellington hoped that the Proclamation would separate the government from their Radical supporters, but Place's interpretation of it, and its wide acceptance, clearly frustrated this hope: Wellington, *Despatches, 8,* 80, 99–100.

said, in addition and for good measure, that if the Bill was rejected again, "the Unions will be trebled and quadrupled in numbers."[1] But a majority in the Lords, apparently unmoved by such language, again defeated the Bill, having passed amendments that led the government to resign.

The government resigned on May 8, 1832. For eleven days it was uncertain as to who would be the next Prime Minister. There were several possible outcomes, among which three alternatives appeared probable. Initially, the Duke of Wellington attempted to form a government committed to introduce a Reform Bill providing much the same kind of changes as the Bill just defeated. A second alternative was for Grey to return, with the King's authority to create Peers in order to overcome opposition in the Lords. (When he did resume office it was with the King's assurance that he could create a sufficient number of Peers should it become necessary.) A third possibility was a compromise Bill imposed on the country by the Tories or accepted on behalf of the reformers by a Whig government. Only the second of these alternatives, which they had been promoting for more than a year, was palatable to Parkes, Place, and Mill. Even a Tory government committed to the Whigs' Bill was not satisfactory, for a Tory government would not have been trusted to push such a bill through. In addition, it was not the terms of the Bill that attracted their support so much as the hope that its passage would give momentum to the reform movement, which of course was not likely if the Tories were in office.[2]

As it turned out, after Wellington failed to form a government, the Whigs returned to office and passed the Bill without creating

1. *Report of the Great Meeting . . . held at Birmingham, May 7, 1832,* pp. 5, 7, 8.

2. Le Marchant, who had been Brougham's private secretary, reported that a deputation, including Mill, thought it expedient to support "any new Government even of Tories, on the condition of carrying the Bill." But this can hardly have been Mill's opinion, for Le Marchant reports that, as leader of this deputation, Mill "represented to him [the Lord Chancellor] the risk of serious disturbances throughout the country in the event of a change of Ministry": D. Le Marchant, *Life of Althorp* (London, 1876), p. 420.

peers, for once the Tories discovered that the King had given authority to create peers should it become necessary, the Bill's success was made certain, and Tory lords in sufficient number stayed away in order to avoid defeat by this means. As a result, Parkes and Place never faced a Tory government, nor a Whig government determined to pass a compromise Bill. It is thus not possible to know how they would have reacted in either of those circumstances. Perhaps they themselves did not know. Mill had assumed that it would never be necessary to face the dilemma of choosing between reform and civil peace. He had been confident that concessions would be made from considerations of prudence.[3] He had not specified what was to be done in case a government (or, as now, the House of Lords) was obstinate or underestimated the threat of resistance. Already during the previous October Grote felt "that we now have no choice between the evils of tumult and violence on one hand, and the loss of Reform on the other"—the very dilemma Mill's tactics were designed to avoid. Grote also had noted that "the language of menace" had been "repeated with the thinnest possible varnish, to satiety; and what remains," he asked, "except the ultima ratio?"[4] Now in May 1832, the same question arose, but they narrowly avoided having to answer it. They claimed, after the episode was ended and the Bill secured, that (as Place said to Hobhouse) "there would, positively, have been a rising if Wellington had recovered power";[5] and Parkes told Mrs. Grote that, "if we had been overreached this week by the Borough-mongers, I and two friends

---

3. They assumed that by creating peers the opposition could be overcome, either in a vote or, as it turned out, by the threat of creating peers. Thus Mill wrote to Brougham (Sept. 15, 1831, in Brougham Papers) that in conversation the opinion had been expressed that the creation of peers would be a death blow to the peerage. "Very well, said I, and if the peerage will so have it, who is to blame? What I want the Ministry to do—is to give out—fairly to proclaim—that they will *not* be defeated by the Lords; that will do—the Lords are not wanting in that kind of wisdom which is called *sapere sibi*. . . . If they know you are determined; they will know what it is proper for them to do."

4. Grote to Parkes, Oct. 29, 1831, in Grote, *Posthumous Papers*, p. 42.

5. Broughton, *Recollections*, 4, 234.

should have *made* the Revolution, whatever the cost," and, he added, "I *think* we could have prevented anarchy, and set all right in two days."[6]

What might they have done? Place, who could have been the best informant, destroyed his correspondence connected with these transactions, but later he claimed that military officers had been contacted and their support enlisted, though who most of them were and what military action they were to engage in remains uncertain.

Place also claimed that barricades were to be set up in Birmingham, and "other towns were to follow the example." Families of Tory lords were to be seized as "hostages for the conduct of the Duke towards reformers." He also hoped that the army, even if it had remained loyal to a Tory government, was not sufficiently large to uphold the authority of government all over the kingdom at the same time. Thus, demonstrations in London were to be organized in order to confine a large part of the army in the metropolis, preventing it from moving elsewhere.[7] These may have been the tactics Parkes referred to when he said, "I *think* we could have prevented anarchy and set all right in two days." To the painter, Benjamin Haydon, Parkes also said that had the Duke come in, there would have been an attempt to arrest the Birmingham leaders, "and then the people would have fought it out."[8] These observations suggest they might really have attempted to organize resistance, and while some observers have thought such a suggestion ridiculous, it is worth noting that Mr. F. C. Mather has suggested, in connection with a similar plan considered during the Chartist disturbances in 1842, that had there been "a truly general rising affecting several widely separated regions at once, it would probably not have been possible

6. Parkes to Mrs. Grote, May 18, 1832, in Grote, *Life of George Grote,* pp. 79–80.

7. Add. MSS 27,793, ff. 99–100, 141–42; Wallas, *Place,* pp. 294, 308, 317–19; Trevelyan, *Lord Grey,* pp. 346–47; Buckley, *Parkes,* pp. 108–09, 195–96.

8. *Life of Benjamin Robert Haydon, Historical Painter, from his Autobiography and Journals,* ed. Tom Taylor, 2 (London, 1853), 341.

to supply troops to put it down—at least not for a considerable time."[9] There was also a severe shortage of troops in 1832.

On the other hand, it is very uncertain whether Parkes, Place, and their associates commanded sufficient obedience to allow them to organize uprisings. Judged by Parkes' estimate during the previous November, when popular excitement was even greater, it seems unlikely; at that time he thought that if a "Tory juste milieu" government came in, he would have to be satisfied with "a half measure," for "there is *not* sufficient virtue in even the best part of the people to resist and to enforce their rights."[10] Furthermore, it should be remembered that, while Parkes and his associates often sounded militant, their accounts of actual plans for resistance came after the crisis was resolved, except for those "leaks" to persons like Tom Young and Hobhouse who presumably were supposed to have passed the information on to Ministers.[11] For example, Place spoke freely to Young, the

9. The suggestion is ridiculed by F. W. Haydon, ed., *Benjamin R. Haydon, Correspondence and Table-Talk, 2* (London, 1876), 343, n. H. Ferguson, "The Birmingham Political Union and the Government, 1831–32," *Victorian Studies, 3* (1960), 274. F. C. Mather, *Public Order in the Age of the Chartists* (Manchester Univ. Press, 1959), p. 164. The officer commanding the troops stationed at Birmingham in May 1832 reported that he would be unable to successfully resist attack in the event of insurrection. He was not predicting insurrection nor was he suggesting that his troops were unreliable: Aspinall, ed., *Three Diaries*, p. 258.

10. Parkes to Grote, Nov. 28, 1831 (copy in Place's hand and mistakenly signed by "Francis Place"): Add. MSS 35,149, ff. 128–29. In the same letter Parkes also said (in contrast to the confident statement to Mrs. Grote, see n. 6 above), "It is possible that we may be able to bring about a Revolution; but it would be through the *worst* of the people. I know every leader of the Union. I know they do not mean to lead the people, and will not."

11. Among the statements made after the crisis was resolved was Roebuck's that, "not only was the question of insurrection gravely mooted, but steps were actually about to be taken for the purpose of organizing an armed resistance": *History of the Whig Ministry, 2,* 311. Fonblanque said that, had the people "been put on trial, we speak advisedly, when we say that every populous town would have been a fortress held by the people, and for the people, against an oligarchical government": *Exam.,* May 20, 1832, p. 321. Also see *Report of the Proceedings of the Public Meeting of the Inhabitants of Birmingham, May 16, 1832,* pp. 5–7. Cf. Butler, *Reform Bill,* pp. 418–21.

radically inclined private secretary to Lord Melbourne, about the plans. Young reported that Place "talked big to me and felt assured of success. The run upon the banks and the barricading of the populous towns would have brought matters to a crisis and a week they—the Reformers—thought would have finished the business." Place also told Young that agitation in London would have prevented the soldiers there from moving to other towns where military forces were not large enough to resist insurrections. Young had also been asked by Parkes for a frank with which to send a letter asking Napier to take command at Birmingham. Of course, Parkes could have easily acquired a frank from any one of a dozen persons, yet he asked Young and, like Place, revealed plans of insurrection to the private secretary of the person mainly responsible for internal security. The letter to Napier, if written, was never sent, and the Home Secretary, rather than Napier, most probably was the person for whom all these communications were intended.[12] However, it is impossible to be certain about what they would have done, for the situation that might have called for organized resistance was narrowly avoided.[13]

The situation they did face was different. For about seven days there was the possibility of a Tory government, until the Duke

12. Young to Napier, June 25, 1832, in Buckley, *Parkes*, pp. 195–96. Napier said he would not have "cooperate[d] in arms with a Birmingham attorney and a London Tailor against the Duke of Wellington": *Life of General Sir William Napier*, ed. H. H. Bruce, *2*, 274. Other military officers whose names appear were Lt. Col. George De Lacy Evans, Gen. Johnstone, and Maj. Revell. In Oct. 1831, John Stuart Mill thought Napier was ready to lead a movement of armed resistance: *Letters of John Stuart Mill*, ed. Elliot, *1*, 7. Parkes was also said to have given an account of revolutionary plans to Durham so that it would be passed to the Cabinet: New, *Durham*, p. 180.

13. For whatever it may tell of Parkes' determination, we have his judgment of Papineau during the Canadian rebellion, about whom he said, "I don't much respect the *Bolters* in revolutions they have mainly caused": Parkes to Roebuck, Feb. 5, 1843, Public Archives of Canada, Roebuck Papers, *14*, 10. On the other hand, in 1833 Place, in a different context, considered the question whether "it were possible [to] produce civil war in the land," or even whether "a commotion could take place," and decided that "happily it is not [possible]": Place to Parkes, Dec. 7, 1833, Add. MSS 35,149, f. 244. In 1837, with regard to his wish for an

gave up his commission on May 15. Then, for about four more days there was uncertainty as to whether the King would assure Grey that peers could be created if necessary. It was a period of great uncertainty, calling for a continued application of intimidation tactics. These tactics were directed, as before, at the Whigs so as to keep them resolute—so they would not visualize compromise as a peaceful alternative. If the backbench support to the government did not waver, it would be impossible for the Tories to gain a majority in the House of Commons. And if the Ministers remained firm, the King, without the alternative of a Tory government, would have to yield on the question of creating peers.

To achieve this end things were done which were meant to persuade the Ministers (and the backbenches and the King) that a Tory government would bring a risk of economic chaos and civil disorder. The famous run on the Bank was organized; rumors were spread of a march on London by the Birmingham Political Union and, in connection with this, allusions were made to the arming of the populace; and predictions of imminent violence, in the event of failure, were made with greater urgency and foreboding than heretofore. As Place said, "Neither argument, nor threat, nor prediction of evil consequences was spared." There also was talk—although the Millite Radicals do not appear to have been connected with it—of refusing to pay taxes and that the House of Commons would stop supplies.[14]

Unlike certain other of their tactics, organizing the run on the Bank required public participation if it was not to be seen as an empty threat. Placards were displayed in London with the famous motto for which Parkes and Place were jointly responsible: "To stop the Duke, go for Gold." It was intended that Bank of Eng-

---

extension of the suffrage, he said, "I have patience, I learned it long since and have continually practiced it, yet I have acquired with many a character for rashness, and men believe I am rash without being able to cite the acts of rashness I have committed. I can wait for the changes which I know must come": Place to Brougham, July 1, 1837, in Brougham Papers.

14. Add. MSS 27,792, f. 40. For threats to stop supplies and to refuse payment of taxes, see *Hansard, 12* (May 11, 1832), 876, 879–80; (May 17, 1832), 1034.

land notes would be presented in exchange for gold coin, and it was hoped that the drain on the Bank's reserves would be sufficiently great to generate fears that Bank notes would not be accepted for coin, so that the notes would cease to circulate. They were playing on fear of financial panic.[15]

There was a response to the call. For about a week large numbers of persons presented notes at the Bank, so many that a former governor of the Bank said that he "certainly never saw the hall of the Bank, for many years I have gone through it, except in 1825, so crowded with applicants tendering their notes."[16] It is difficult to determine what classes of the population presented notes and why they did it. It is fairly clear that the demand for currency was confined to the metropolis.[17] The witnesses before the Parliamentary Committee on the Bank Charter, which met in late 1832, did not agree as to the motives. Some, like N. M. Rothschild, thought the wish to distress the government was not important, but that a fear of revolution sent people to

15. G. J. Holyoake, *Sixty Years of an Agitator's Life, 1* (London, 1893), 219–20. Place said the placards were sent to other towns as well: Wallas, *Place*, p. 310. Parkes had alluded to such a run in speeches at Birmingham, and during the previous October Place appealed to fear of financial panic: Place to Hobhouse, Oct. 11, 1831, Add. MSS 35,149, f. 84b. Lovett also suggested "the propriety of [the working classes] withdrawing their monies now invested in the Savings Banks and Benefit Societies," as a protest against their exclusion from the suffrage: Lovett to the Editor, *Morn. Chr.,* Nov. 11, 1831, p. 3. During the Irish agitation, O'Connell called for a run on the banks in Ireland: James W. Gilbert, "The History of Banking in Ireland," in *The History and Principles of Banking* (London, 1866), pp. 228–29; Reynolds, *Catholic Emancipation Crisis,* pp. 151–52.

16. "Report from the Committee of Secrecy on the Bank of England Charter; with the Minutes of Evidence. . . . (Aug. 11, 1832)": *PP,* 1831–32 (772), VI, question 4981 (John B. Richards). Henry Hunt, who came around to supporting the Bill in May 1832, said he had been kept waiting three quarters of an hour before he could get a ten-pound note changed: *Hansard, 12* (May 14, 1832), 972.

17. Richards "was surprised that there was so little application from the Country Bankers." "Report . . . on the Bank of England Charter," *PP,* ques. 4981. Vincent Stuckey, a country banker, "was assured our house did not find it necessary to have a single sovereign from the Bank of England": ibid., ques. 1064.

the Bank;[18] others, however, such as V. Stuckey, T. Attwood, and J. Horsley Palmer, thought it the result of both political motives and apprehension about the value of paper money. It was, in Attwood's words, a result of "political men" saying "we will do all the mischief we can by the legal means in our power" combined with the fact "that every man was alarmed [with the] thought that society was going to break up" and that he should "have a few sovereigns for protection, thinking that the Bank notes would be worth nothing in a general stoppage."[19] Apparently many of the notes presented were five and ten pound notes, and thus it was not the very poorest classes who took part in the run; on the other hand, there were some observers who thought that many of the holders of the notes "were persons in the lower classes of life."[20] Altogether the amount drawn during this period was £1,600,000, whereas the Bank held between three and four million in gold coin.[21] This represented larger withdrawals than were usual, and it was thought to be serious

18. Ibid., ques. 4938–4940.

19. Ibid., ques. 5613; Palmer, ques. 743–744; Stuckey, ques. 1060, 1062; also see *Hansard, 12,* 979. Cf. Ferguson who states that, "Experts believed the demand was a consequence of Uncertainty, not the product of a specific political aim, such as Place's": "Birmingham Political Union and the Government," *Victorian Studies, 3* (1960), p. 273, n. 40. While the experts testifying in 1832 did not think an exclusively political aim operated, they did not exclude political considerations in their analysis. Another expert, without explaining his reasoning, thought the political character of the demand was "proved from the trifling nature of the applications from the country banks": John Francis, *History of the Bank of England, 2* (3d ed., London, 1848), 67.

20. "Report . . . on the Bank of England Charter," *PP,* ques. 4663; also ques. 4710–4711, 5613. Henry Vizetelly observed that "the 'sovereign people' lacked the necessary notes": *Glances Back Through Seventy Years, 1* (London, 1893), 79. There were appeals to working people to withdraw their deposits from savings banks: "Reports of the Principal Staffordshire Reform Meetings . . . 14th of May, 1832," p. 11; *Report of the Proceedings of the Public Meeting, Birmingham, May 16, 1832,* p. 5.

21. "Report . . . on the Bank of England Charter," ques. 2678 (G. Warde Norman). The Governor of the Bank, J. Horsley Palmer, said the £1,600,000 was issued over "a week or ten days," and he indicated that the figure could be adjusted to two million pounds in view of the April dividend that was not returned: ibid., ques. 745.

without yet being critical when on May 16 the drain eased after it became clear that Wellington had failed to form a government.

But how serious was it? Witnesses before the Parliamentary Committee, while agreeing that this "political discredit," as they called it, was dangerous, did not agree as to the extent or immediacy of the danger. One of those who minimized its seriousness, while acknowledging that "there was a great degree of political discredit, which is always a period of some anxiety," at the same time insisted that the effect "would not have been very material, if it had continued only a week longer; it must have continued a considerable period more than that, to have placed the Bank in danger."[22] On the other hand, J. Horsley Palmer said that "continuance of the political discredit might have drained every sovereign from the Bank of England."[23]

The public did not know the extent to which withdrawals were made or the magnitude of the Bank's reserves. The press presented what at best could be an informed estimate of the extent of the run, but which also could have been deliberate distortion of what it believed were the facts. On May 15 the *Times* reported that withdrawals, mainly in amounts from £20 to £100, were increasing, but had not reached a critical level. "It does not appear, however, that the run has as yet reached an extent which can justly create alarm." About one million pounds had been withdrawn, an amount, according to the *Times,* not one tenth of the gold stored in the Bank, and the warning was given that,

22. Ibid., ques. 2675–2676 (Norman). By way of explanation he added that, "The sacrifices entailed on those demanding gold for notes would have increased with the daily reduction in the latter, while the impulse given to the import of Treasure from abroad would have augmented": ibid., ques. 2676.

23. Ibid., ques. 740–741. Concern may have been accentuated by there having been "a diminution of little short of seven millions [in coin and bullion] since June, 1830." Tooke ascribed this to stagnation in trade arising from revolution in France in 1830 and other continental disturbances; a renewed drain from Ireland; renewed imports of foreign corn; and "chiefly [to] the political disquiet and distrust which prevailed in this country from the first agitation of the reform question in November, 1830, to the final passing of the bill in the spring of 1832": Thomas Tooke, *A History of Prices,* 2 (London, 1838), 219.

"if some step is not taken to allay the popular ferment," the supply might be exhausted. On May 16 it showed greater concern; while gold reserves were holding up, it reported, "The gold in the Bank will be exhausted in a week if a Tory Ministry is appointed in the face of the obstinate determination against it on the part of the people."[24] The *Morning Chronicle* reported that before noon on May 15, more than a million in sovereigns and half-sovereigns were exchanged at the Bank for notes, and that, "according to some, since the end of last week, one fourth of the whole amount of gold in the Bank has passed into the hands of the public."[25] Grote—who was a close associate of Parkes and Place as well as a banker—told the Committee that if a "conspiracy" was attempted for political purposes, "exaggerated reports . . . would of course be current under such a state of things."[26] However, if the *Times* and the *Morning Chronicle* in this case intended exaggeration they failed, for their statements underestimated the magnitude of withdrawals of gold coin and overestimated the Bank's reserves.[27]

Meanwhile rumors of a march on London were being spread. Already in April a complaint was made in Parliament that the publishers of one of the "leading Radical Journals" were not prosecuted for a statement "to the effect that if their Lordships evinced any intention of rejecting the Bill . . . 100,000 men were

24. *Times,* May 15, 1832, p. 3; May 16, 1832, p. 3.
25. *Morn. Chr.,* May 16, 1832, p. 3.
26. "Report . . . on the Bank of England Charter," *PP,* ques. 4683.
27. According to Norman the amount withdrawn was £1,600,000, whereas the amount of coined gold in the Bank on May 1 was "between three and four millions." Even taking the larger figure (four million), the withdrawals amounted to 40 per cent of the reserve in gold currency; whereas the *Times* estimated them at less than 10 per cent, and the *Morning Chronicle* at 25 per cent. The figure of 40 per cent takes into account gold coin held by the Bank, but not the bullion it had. Norman did not give the figure for this, but during the previous months bullion was held in amounts ranging from 15 to 33 per cent of the value of gold coin. Again, assumed that in May the reserve of bullion was at the higher level, the withdrawals still would have been about 30 per cent of the amount of coin plus bullion. This figure remains larger than the papers estimated it to be.

to march up and compel their assent to it."[28] Attwood also alluded to this possibility in a speech on May 7, the day before the Whigs resigned. The marchers were said to have planned an encampment on Hampstead Heath, where they were to remain till the Bill was passed.[29] It is doubtful that such a march would have taken place or, indeed, that it was ever planned. Place, in referring to Birmingham in his account of what would have been done had the Tories established a government, makes no reference to a march on London, but states that barricades were to be established in Birmingham. In the Council of the Union at Birmingham there was too much timidity for such a march; according to Frederick Hill, who was attending its meetings, the general feeling was for a lawful solution and for avoiding violence unless they were attacked by a Tory government.[30] Furthermore, it seems very unlikely that large numbers of men could have been drawn away from work and home for a political purpose. Despite the legendary character of this planned march, it is difficult to believe that any of the leaders of the reform movement ever expected it to take place. Yet apparently the rumor was believed, at least by some persons, among them Alexander Somerville.[31]

28. Wynford, *Hansard, 12* (April 13, 1832), 345.

29. Jephson, *Platform, 2,* 121; *Report of the Proceedings of the Great Meeting . . . Birmingham, May 7, 1832,* p. 4. There had been an allusion to a march on London early in the reform agitation by Col. De Lacy Evans. He said "10,000 men [were] ready to march up to London from [Sussex] . . . if Ministers were defeated": *Hansard, 3* (March 7, 1831), 118. His statement was repeated and discussed in the press and in the House of Commons.

30. Frederick Hill, *An Autobiography* (London, 1893), p. 92.

31. Alexander Somerville, *The Autobiography of a Working Man,* ed. J. Carswell (London, Turnstile, 1950), p. 157. Vizetelly in his memoirs says the Birmingham Political Union "indulged in some very tall talk, threatening, amongst other things, to send up to London in support of Ministers a couple of armies 'as' good as the one which fought at Waterloo. . . . The strange thing was that many sensible middle class people . . . actually believed in this swagger; and I remember how, for several days, the mail coach from Birmingham used to be surrounded on its arrival . . . and the guard beset with inquiries, one of which was whether the provincial armies had started on their march": Vizetelly, *Glances Back,*

There were also allusions to the use of arms. A petition urging reinstatement of the Grey Ministry and drawn up for approval by the Birmingham Political Union referred to the part of the Bill of Rights that provides for holding arms, and observed that "this great right will be put in force generally, and that the whole of the people of England will think it necessary to have arms for their defense, in order that they may be prepared for any circumstance which may arise."[32] Parkes, speaking to the meeting that endorsed this petition, remarked that "If the laws were broken for the purpose of aiding the efforts of their enemies, the laws might be broken for the purpose of supporting and protecting the rights of the People."[33]

At the same time the populace was described as being anxious to fall in line with any plans for resistance. The Birmingham petition claimed that passage of the Bill by the Whigs was the only alternative to revolution. Only by passing the Bill, unmutilated, could they give safety to the lives and property of all; this was the only way by which "the just and sacred Rights of Englishmen can be recovered . . . except by means that will break up the fabric of society, and endanger the fortunes and lives of millions."[34] Parkes, with two others, was to deliver the petition

---

1, 75–76. There are other references to the march, but it is difficult to determine whether they are based on accurate memories of the rumor in 1832 or the development of a legend about it in later years; see Joseph McCabe, *Life and Letters of George Jacob Holyoake, 1* (London, Watts, 1908), 22; *Memoirs of the Life and Adventures of Colonel Maceroni, 2* (London, 1838), 468; J. M. Ludlow and Lloyd Jones, *Progress of the Working Class 1832–1867* (London, 1867), p. 22.

32. *Report of the Public Meeting, Birmingham, May 10, 1832,* pp. 4–5; also reported in the *Times,* May 11, 1832, p. 3; but a letter from Attwood in the *Times,* May 14, 1832, p. 2, stating the substance of the petition, does not mention arms.

33. *Report of the Public Meeting, Birmingham, May 10, 1832,* p. 5. An article in the *Morn. Chr.,* May 16, 1832, p. 4, presumably by Parkes, reports that the Birmingham "streets are filled with people who talk loudly of 'arms.' " There is very little reference to arming in the *Times, Morning Chronicle,* and *Examiner* between May 7 and 19.

34. *Report of the Public Meeting, Birmingham, May 10, 1832,* pp. 4–5. In Parliament, O'Connell, professing himself to be a Radical, said, "The spirit of revolution was abroad; and if it were allowed to pass a certain

to O'Connell for presentation in Parliament. While in London for this purpose he undoubtedly spoke the language of menace to all he saw. One such person, Le Marchant, Brougham's private secretary, noted in his diary (May 15) that Parkes told him "it was with extreme difficulty that the people could be kept from coming to extremities."[35] James Mill himself at this time gave up the obscurity he preferred in order to lead a deputation to his friend Lord Brougham. Le Marchant reported the deputation to have been in a state of "great alarm" and Mill as having "represented to him the risk of serious disturbances throughout the country in the event of a change of Ministry." Referring to the "lower classes," Mill also said, "We must recollect, after all, they are our masters." Le Marchant also noted that the "thoughts of the deputation seemed absorbed in their fears of a popular outbreak."[36] Meanwhile in the House of Commons Hume and Burdett gave the same warning with, it is true, a nervousness shared by many others but in tones somewhat more urgent and filled with even greater foreboding. Hume "never felt greater anxiety to address a few words to the House." The recent events gave him alarm—not "merely politically, but commercially, and with a view to every social tie in the country."[37] And Sir Francis Burdett reported that what he had witnessed at the Crown and Anchor (where the Council of the National Political Union met) "was calculated to remove the doubts of the most sceptical Anti-Reformer. The people of this country were so intensely fixed upon having their favourite measure, that nothing short of madness could dream of longer withholding it."[38]

_____

stage, it would be difficult to check it. . . . Let but a single week elapse," he warned, "and revolution and the utter destruction of the beautiful fabric around us might be the consequence": *Hansard, 12* (May 14, 1832), 973.

35. Aspinall, ed., *Three Early Nineteenth Century Diaries*, p. 258.

36. Le Marchant, *Life of Althorp*, p. 420. This probably was the deputation referred to by Bain as "headed by Mill; the purpose being to strengthen [Brougham's] hands in the great contest. . . . Having mislaid the document, I cannot supply the exact date or terms of the address": Bain, *James Mill*, p. 363.

37. *Hansard, 12* (May 14, 1832), 967.

38. Ibid., *12* (May 11, 1832), 893.

One other example of their use of the language of menace concerns the later part of the "days of May"—after the Tories gave up trying to form a government but before Grey finally received satisfactory assurances from the King that peers could be created if necessary. On May 18, Place had a request from Hobhouse for a letter "telling him all the facts I could, and giving him my opinion of the state of feeling among the people, as far as I could, and my view of prospective results." The letter, which was wanted for use at a Cabinet meeting, noted that:

> [at the] moment it was known that Earl Grey had been sent for [May 15], the *demand for gold ceased*. . . . We cannot, however, go on thus *beyond to-day*. If doubt remains until tomorrow, alarm will commence again, and panic will follow. . . . Lists containing the names, addresses, etc., of all persons in every part of the country likely to be useful have been made. . . . Means have been devised to placard towns and villages, to circulate hand-bills, and to assemble the people. So many men of known character, civil and *military,* have entered heartily into the scheme. . . . If the Duke come into power now, we shall be unable longer to "hold to the laws"; break them we must, be the consequences whatever they may. . . . Towns will be barricaded, new municipal arrangements will be made by the inhabitants. . . . Let the Duke take office as Premier, and we shall have a commotion in the nature of a civil war, with money at our command . . . in less than five days we shall have the soldiers with us.[39]

After the Bill passed, the Benthamite Radicals were pleased to think that their varied efforts to agitate and to interpret public opinion had had a large influence on the course of events. Place thought that the run on the Bank and the threat of its being renewed and extended to savings banks and provincial banks was especially influential in the Duke's decision to step down, and in the King's final and reluctant decision to allow that peers be

---

39. Wallas, *Place,* pp. 315–16. Despite all its allusions to violence the letter is remarkably unclear. The prudent Place does not indicate what "the scheme" is into which so many had heartily entered.

created if necessary.[40] It was widely believed at the time, even in official circles, that a convulsion or insurrection might have taken place had the Duke formed a government, and that passions and discontents were such that widespread civil disorders were only narrowly avoided.[41] The fact that this belief was held and acknowledged made it easier for the Benthamite Radicals to think that they had played an important part. While it is uncertain as to how influential they were, it is clear that they visualized themselves as playing the role of interpreter of public feelings, and as doing so in a manner that would stimulate the fear of popular uprising in the minds of the governing class so as to encourage its prudent members to concede reform as the only alternative to revolution.

40. Ibid., pp. 315, 319, 321. Grote, as a City banker, thought the call for a run on the Bank irresponsible and publicly disassociated himself from it. But after the Duke gave up, Place wrote to Grote of "a great man"—Hobhouse—who came in, "saw the placard, and said, that is the settler, that has finished it." Place went on, "I told you it would send the country to the Bank of England, and send the Bank of England to the Palace of St. James and 'Stop the Duke.' It has done its duty well": Place to Grote, May 15, 1832, Add. MSS 35,149, f. 144. Also see Buckley, *Parkes*, p. 109.

41. Broughton, *Recollections, 4,* 185; Aspinall, ed., *Three Early Nineteenth Century Diaries,* pp. 246, 251, 255, 258, 263–64; *Cabinet Annual Register . . . 1832,* pp. 28–29. There was a disposition in any case to believe that disorders were likely; see Houghton, *Victorian Frame of Mind,* pp. 54–58.

CHAPTER 4

The Threat of Revolution: Rhetoric or Reality?

It was commonly held by nineteenth-century historians (and some of their present-day successors as well) that there was a revolutionary situation in 1831–32, and that timely concessions forestalled the outbreak of revolutionary violence. W. N. Molesworth, for example, writing about public feeling in October 1831, after the Lords' rejection of the Bill, said that a "stirring word thrown among the multitude at that moment might have produced a revolution." Spencer Walpole contended that the Lords' rejection "brought the country to the verge of civil war." Sir Frederick Pollock claimed that in 1832 "a large part of the English people were of opinion that the difference between an unreformed and a reformed Parliament *was* worth a civil war; and it was the knowledge of their opinion and of their readiness in extremity to act on it that then narrowly saved the State." And Dicey has noted that while "the inflexibility of French constitutions has provoked revolution, the flexibility of English institutions has, once at least [in 1832], saved them from violent overthrow."[1] These conclusions have made the fable concerning Mrs. Partington and the Atlantic Ocean, which Sydney Smith so effectively used, the source of a convenient metaphor. Popular demand for reform was compared to the rising tide; it might be temporarily diverted, as political agitation was after Peterloo but, in Spencer Walpole's words, "the waters rose again. . . . It was in vain that the governing classes attempted to repair the breach, which was continually increasing. A child might as well hope to arrest the tide with its sand-castle. . . . The force of a mighty nation swept

1. Spencer Walpole, *Life of Lord John Russell, 1* (London, 1889), 172; Sir Frederick Pollock, *An Introduction to the History of the Science of Politics* (London, 1919), pp. 95–96; A. V. Dicey, *Law of the Constitution* (4th ed., 1893), p. 122.

away the legislators who fancied they had power to control it."[2]

These observers were not thinking of revolution merely as a sudden and far-reaching change in the constitution; they referred to the deep feelings of anger and resentment that bring men to the threshold of violent action. This view has persisted. The editors of the most recent edition of the *Greville Memoirs* note that by May 18, 1832, "the country was on the brink of revolution." Cole and Postgate say that in October 1831 "it became manifest . . . that nothing less than the Bill would now avail to prevent revolution." This assumption is also made when it is said that in 1832 (as in 1829) Peel and Wellington "established the tradition that that which can no longer be defended except at the cost of civil strife, must be surrendered."[3] Some modern historians avoid the term *revolution* without avoiding the question

2. Spencer Walpole, *A History of England from the Conclusion of the Great War in 1815, 3* (London, 1890), 215.

3. Lytton Strachey and Roger Fulford, eds., *The Greville Memoirs, 2,* 296, n. 1; G. D. H. Cole and Raymond Postgate, *The Common People, 1746–1938* (London, Methuen, 1938), p. 248; A. Aspinall and E. A. Smith, eds., *English Historical Documents, 1783–1832* (London, Eyre and Spottiswoode, 1959), p. 55. A recently published text states that "October 1831 was the month when England came closest to violent revolution. . . . a wave of outbreaks swept the country . . . it was clear that lasting peace depended on the successful passage of the Bill." And, "It was thus [in May when Wellington failed to form a government] that revolution was averted": Anthony Wood, *Nineteenth Century Britain 1815–1914* (London, Longmans, 1960), pp. 83–85. Hobsbawm asserts that, while there was no violent revolution, "there was, nevertheless, a good deal of revolutionary feeling in large parts of the country, particularly during the bleak half-century from the middle 1790's to the late 1840's." He indicates that the years immediately preceding 1832 were particularly dangerous because the ruling class came close to losing control of the political situation. "It is conceivable that something like a 'revolutionary situation' might have developed had the Unreformed Parliament not been wise enough to yield peacefully": E. J. Hobsbawm, "Methodism and the Threat of Revolution in Britain," *History Today* (Feb. 1957), p. 116. Also see David Cecil, *Melbourne* (London, Reprint Society, 1955), p. 181; Halevy, *Triumph of Reform,* p. 41; Asa Briggs, *The Age of Improvement* (London, Longmans, 1960), p. 259; David Thomson, *Equality* (Cambridge Univ. Press, 1949), p. 67; Feiling, *Second Tory Party,* pp. 390, 394–95. For a presentation of two sides of the question, see E. L. Woodward, *The Age of Reform 1815–1870* (2d ed., Oxford, Clarendon, 1962), pp. 83–86.

raised by its use. The Reform Bill is explained as a response to the "force" or "pressure" of public opinion. But this implies that concession was made from a fear of the consequences of not yielding, for it was not a democratic age and most politicians, even liberal Whigs, were not likely to respond to the "pressure" of public opinion only from a belief in the legitimacy of its demands (though occasionally these were acknowledged). In the absence of such belief, the pressure of public opinion had its source in threats of resistance, which were not necessarily explicit, but which were not entirely concealed either.[4] To explain an event only by referring to such pressures leaves unanswered questions about the state of public opinion and public feelings. How realistic was the estimate of the pressure or the threat in response to which concessions were made? Many historical interpretations have been greatly influenced by rhetoric that was widely used in 1831–32. The historical judgment in which the country is seen as having been in a revolutionary situation accepts the diagnosis of imminent revolution that was used at the time in order to justify concession. It may, indeed, be a correct judgment. But since that diagnosis could have been called forth by polemical considerations and therefore might not have been based on an analysis of the actual conditions, its validity as a historical judgment should be examined.

The belief that the threat of revolution was real is especially worthy of scrutiny in view of the fact that some of those who voiced the threat in 1831–32 clearly intended it as rhetoric. James Mill in outlining tactics for the achievement of fundamental constitutional changes by peaceful means had argued that concessions would be made provided the governing classes saw revolution as the only alternative to such concessions. The success of such tactics, then, depended on the image of public feelings held by those in a position to make the concessions. Concessions would be granted, Mill said, from a fear of the consequences of withholding them. The crucial thing was to stimulate

4. Aspinall and Smith refer to "the irresistible pressure" of public opinion without which the Reform Bill could hardly have been carried: *English Historical Documents, 1783–1832*, p. 45. But what made it irresistible?

fear. How it was done was less important. Of course, fear is not the result of rhetoric alone, nor did Mill assume that rhetoric alone would be sufficient. But he did not exclude the use of rhetoric in a way that would stimulate greater fear than was justified by the actual circumstances. Thus in advising the editor of the *Examiner* in 1831 Mill said the people "should appear to be ready and impatient to break out into outrage, *without actually breaking out.*" That Mill would allow misrepresentation is even more clear from his observations concerning "the rule of veracity" in political situations. While it is important, Mill says, that men be able to confide in one another and that therefore truth not be violated, "There are circumstances, however, in which another man is not entitled to the truth"; these circumstances "create a radical distinction" and "constitute a class by themselves" and are "subject to rules altogether different." The circumstances in which men are not to be told the truth are "when they would make a bad use of it." Thus one does not give "information to a villain which he will employ in forwarding his villainous ends. Wrong information, for the prevention of evil, and, in certain circumstances, for the promotion of good, has rarely been classed among forbidden means by any set of men, civilized or barbarian." Mill gives other examples. Is it justified to mislead a ruffian pursuing his victim? or for a physician to reassure a patient in the utmost danger? Then, turning to politics, Mill argued that never does "wrong information" serve to prevent so much evil "as when it is conducive to the prevention of misrule. In no instance is any man less entitled to right information, than when he would employ it for the perpetuation of misrule." In these circumstances wrong information is "not a breach of morality, but on the contrary a meritorious act."[5]

5. [James Mill] "The Ballot," *Westminster Review, 13* (July 1830), 33–34. Mill made these observations in a discussion of the secret ballot. But the argument is cast in general terms applicable to the circumstances of 1831–32, for the goal then was to overcome misrule, and this justifies for Mill a violation of the rule of veracity. In addition to the perhaps normal exaggeration of their campaigning, they appear to have fabricated evidence as well. Parkes thanked Place for "your 'anonymous' letters to me," which, he added, the Union "soaked in." Parkes to Place, Oct. 15, Oct. 24, 1831, Add. MSS 35,149, ff. 97–97b, 115–16.

Not only did Mill's doctrine allow for deliberate misrepresentation, but his associates, when looking back on the events of 1831–32, show that they at least thought of themselves as having practiced deception. There is John Arthur Roebuck writing in later years about the passing of the Reform Bill. Though in 1831 Roebuck had not yet begun his long and stormy career in Parliament, he was at the time a close observer of the extra-Parliamentary agitation in London, serving as a member of the Council of the National Political Union where he earned Place's commendation as one of the more clever, efficient, and active workers.[6] In an anonymous article published in 1848 Roebuck confessed that public feeling was often described, not as it was, but as it was meant to appear. He acknowledged the existence of genuine excitement: "Yet," he said, "to attain our end, much was said that no one really believed; much was done that no one would like to own. . . . often, when there was no danger, the cry of alarm was raised to keep the House of Lords and the aristocracy generally in what was termed a state of wholesome terror. When the Bill proceeded with ease . . . a grave calm was preserved in our demeanour and writings . . . when its provisions were threatened . . . black clouds rose obedient to our call, as regularly as on the stage at the scene-shifter's command; our language grew violent, we stormed, we threatened and prophesied, and, like some other prophets, we were determined to accomplish our own predictions. Processions, meetings, harangues, revolutionary resolutions, banners, mobs, assemblages both by night and day, all like a furious hurricane, swept over the face of the political waters." In contrast to the "noisy orators who appeared important," those "who pulled the strings in this strange puppet-show were cool-headed, *retiring,* sagacious, determined men." They "avoided publicity," but they were, as one always found in such situations, the "one or two ruling minds, to the public unknown."[7]

6. Torrens, *Melbourne, 1,* 389–90; Place to Mrs. Grote, Jan. 8, 1836: Add. MSS 35,144, f. 357.
7. "Some Chapters of the Life of an Old Politician," *Bentley's Miscellany, 23* (1848), 521–22. These men behind the scenes "use the others as their instruments . . . so it was . . . in London or Birmingham; the noisy men of note were not the real actors and managers in those scenes,

Roebuck offered one example of the way in which "wholesome terror" was fabricated and applied. Roebuck recalled a deputation to Grey, and most of the details indicate that it was the one led by Place on the night of October 12, 1831 (see page 69). The situation at this time was uncertain; the second Bill, after passing in the Commons, had again been defeated in the Lords. Since Grey was reluctant to create peers, yet unable to pass the Bill without doing so, Place felt that, in the absence of strong public pressure the Whigs might give up the Bill, or at least compromise on its provisions. Hints in Ministers' speeches and rumors about Cabinet deliberations confirmed this.[8] Thus Place organized the deputation that urged Grey to avoid a long delay, on the grounds that public feeling would not tolerate any evidence of lack of resolution by the Ministry. Recalling the preparation for the deputation, Roebuck attributes these words to one of those present (doubtless Place):

> *We must frighten them.* . . . No reality we can create will be sufficient for our purpose. We must work on Lord Grey's imagination. We must pretend to be frightened ourselves. We must send him a parcel of London shopkeepers,—men who are, many of them really frightened,—who will tell him they cannot answer for the safety of the city if the just demands of the people are trifled with.[9]

Roebuck's *History of the Whig Ministry of 1830,* which was published in 1852, shows no change in interpretation. Alluding to Parkes, Place, and Mill, he attributes considerable influence to

---

as was made plain after the passing of the Reform Bill. Men who had swelled into importance by the agitation [an allusion to Attwood] . . . were by popular acclaim sent into the House of Commons. There, dependent on their own ability only, they quickly fell from their high estate . . . serving as a puzzle . . . to those who were ignorant of the secret history of the agitation." For the identification of Roebuck as author of this article, see *A List of the Principal Publications issued from New Burlington Street during the Year 1848* (London, Richard Bentley, 1897), not paginated.

8. Wallas, *Place,* pp. 276–78.

9. *Bentley's Miscellany, 23,* 523.

"a most active committee, sitting in London" that manipulated "secret machinery."[10] In describing public opinion in May 1832, when Wellington was trying to form a Cabinet, Roebuck claims that "what appeared to be the spontaneous result of popular feeling, was, in fact, brought about by the incessant labours of a few industrious and shrewd partisans, forming a secret, but very active and efficient committee in London."[11] Without denying the existence of genuine excitement, Roebuck does suggest that any belief that the people generally were in a revolutionary posture was the result of exaggeration and misrepresentation about the extent and intensity of public feelings.

The Benthamite Radicals were exposed to a doctrine that allowed for the deliberate misrepresentation of reality; in their dealings with the government they intended (as will be shown presently) to misrepresent; and when they looked back on these dealings they saw themselves as having done this. This in itself does not prove that the country was not in a revolutionary situation in 1831–32. A statement such as Roebuck's only shows that in 1848 he recalled the effort to practice deception. But it does seem to raise the question of whether there was a discrepancy between the rhetoric and the reality when the claim was made that the country was threatened with revolution.

Public Opinion and the Reform Bill

Roebuck's claim, while it cast doubt on the belief that there was a revolutionary situation in 1832, did not question the existence of widespread support for the government and its Reform

---

10. *History of the Whig Ministry, 2,* 308–09. However, in the *History* there were fewer frank avowals of efforts to manipulate than in the anonymous article published in 1848. There were many descriptions of what public opinion was "believed" to have been. For example, he said, "The nation . . . had resolved . . . to have it by peaceful means, if possible, but if that were not possible, by FORCE. That such was the state of the public feeling was believed by a very large portion of the opponents of the measure": ibid., p. 259. For other examples, see pp. 218, 295, and 310–12; and *Bentley's Miscellany, 23,* 520–21.

11. *History of the Whig Ministry, 2,* 309.

Bill. This was evident in the elections in the spring of 1831, in the many petitions in support of the Bill that were presented, and in the numerous meetings organized at which resolutions in support of the Bill were passed.

Evidence of considerable popular support for the Reform Bill did not go unchallenged, however. The Opposition tended to argue that public opinion was by no means so unanimous nor so intensely interested in the Reform Bill as its supporters claimed. Already, in June 1831, Wellington writing from London reported that "the fever of Reform has passed away and has been succeeded by an apathy on the subject in this town which is quite remarkable."[1] This note was frequently sounded in Parliament throughout August and September when Tory speakers alluded to a "reaction" in public opinion, a claim in which they were supported by the evidence of success enjoyed by anti-Reformers in several by-elections. It was also noted that a City of London petition for reform had only 4,000 signatures whereas an earlier petition from the City had 9,000, from which it was "inferred . . . that there was a doubt in the public mind as to the character of the Bill."[2] Even after the riots in Nottingham and at Bristol this line was taken. In December, for example, it was rumored that London Reform leaders were disappointed with meetings organized in support of the Bill.[3] As noted previously, Henry Hunt, like the Tories (and much to their gratification), was opposed to the Bill and claimed that, since the people's interests were not served by it, they therefore were indifferent as to its

1. *Despatches, 7,* 465; also see pp. 493, 518–19, and 556–57; A. S. Turberville, *House of Lords in the Age of Reform* (Fairlawn, N.J., Essential Books, 1958), p. 270.

2. Halevy, *Triumph of Reform,* p. 39; Haddington, *Hansard, 7* (Oct. 5, 1831), 1320; also see Wharncliffe, col. 1309–11.

3. Caroline Grosvenor and Lord Stuart of Wortley, *The First Lady Wharncliffe and Her Family (1779–1856), 2* (London, Heinemann, 1927), 102; also see p. 145. Wharncliffe reported in October that "several persons . . . [present at Westminster and other Reform meetings] had represented them as absolutely ridiculous, and had stated, that the persons who acted the principal part on these occasions were positively ashamed of them": *Hansard, 7* (Oct. 5, 1831), 1314–15.

passage.[4] While many on the Opposition side denied the existence of a unanimous and intensely excited public opinion, there were exceptions. Some few, like Croker or Perceval, had genuine apprehensions of revolution and saw England as being in a situation comparable to France in 1788.[5] Yet even Croker, while believing that revolutionary excitement was real, thought that it was provoked by the Whigs for "factitious" reasons and could therefore be calmed.[6] The Waverers, who based their wish to compromise on a belief that public feeling did portend real danger, were in a minority. Most opponents of the Bill, while acknowledging that there was some demand for reform, thought it could be satisfied with a more moderate measure than the Whig Bill.[7]

One of the ways in which the Opposition attempted to prove its case was by casting doubts on the validity of the petitions presented in support of the Reform Bill. When the Duke of Devonshire presented a petition from Derby in support of the Bill, the Marquess of Londonderry offered "a counter-petition"

4. Ibid., *8*, 634–40. When on Oct. 10 Hunt was minimizing the extent of popular interest in the Bill there was "much noise and coughing," upon which Croker rose to order to state a hope that "the House would listen" to Hunt, "as he seldom troubled them at any great length": ibid., *8*, 463.

5. Croker: "When we look to the history of past ages, when we see what is passing around us, we draw . . . a conclusion . . . that the course which you are pursuing will lead to revolution": ibid., *11* (March 19, 1832), 465. Peel also "had attended to the progress of great revolutions in other countries, and was not insensible to their symptoms in our own. . . . Long before the bloody days of Marat and of Danton, there were pages in the history of that Revolution which were but too faithful types of the events of present times. Therein we might read of Ministers, once popular, unable to stem the tide on which they had floated to power": ibid., *9* (Dec. 6, 1831), 82.

6. Ibid., *3* (March 4, 1831), 106; also 87; and "State of the Government," *Quarterly Review, 46* (Nov. 1831), 297 n.

7. *Blackwood's Magazine* presented a variety of views which, together, indicate an image of public opinion divided between increasing indifference to the Bill among ordinary men and fanatical, unbending attachment to the Bill among reformers, with some of the populace occasionally being misled by the reformers. It was uncertain as to whether there would be violence, but it was generally thought to be unlikely. "The excitements of the press," it said, "are getting stale and vapid": *Blackwood's, 30* (1831), 313, 328, 337; *31* (1832), 1–9, 31, 142–43, 465.

from the town with a smaller number of signatures (100 as against 4,670) and at the same time reported that a Derby solicitor had sent him information "throwing light on the character of the petitions presented by so many of their Lordships in favor of the Reform Bill." The Derby meeting at which the reform petition was adopted, it was said, was not unanimous; three fourths of those signing it were said to have never heard it read; one person "boasted of his having signed it . . . ten or twelve times" and, it was said, a three-year-old child was helped to sign the petition.[8] On another occasion, after a petition from Nottingham with 13,000 signatures had been presented, the Duke of Newcastle presented an anti-Reform petition from the same town and stated that "a great proportion of the inhabitants of Nottingham was adverse to the measure." He also attempted to discredit a Reform petition from Worksop by claiming that it was signed "chiefly by Catholics and Protestant Dissenters."[9] But when Wharncliffe disputed the validity of petitions from the City of London, Grey, in reply, said, "Facts would speak for themselves,"[10] and the fact undoubtedly was that the number of signatures attached to Reform petitions by far outnumbered that on anti-Reform petitions. However, most Tories remained suspicious of Reform petitions and could not bring themselves to believe that the apparently large numbers of signatures represented what people really believed. The *Annual Register* referred to the "manufacturers of petitions" and called the large assemblies of the political unions "a new mode of petitioning" that used "alarm and intimidation" to gain apparent support from persons afraid to express the disapproval they actually felt; persons "who loved not the violent changes . . . were driven into acquiescence," and others, "who would actively have resisted the change, were overawed from any public expression of their sentiments."[11]

8. *Hansard, 7* (Oct. 4, 1831), 1123–24.
9. Ibid., col. 1129–30.
10. Ibid., *7* (Oct. 5, 1831), 1318.
11. *Annual Register for 1831,* pp. 78–80. "There would be a petition from a town—a petition from different bodies in that town—petitions from its political union—and all this was, to a great extent, nothing more than the voice of the same men thrice repeated. Neither the quality nor

The Opposition also sought to discredit the claim that public opinion was stirred and excited about reform by questioning the accuracy of press reports. It was widely believed that the press exaggerated, and Wellington thought many reports were "fabricated."[12] The public press, according to Wharncliffe, "had most grossly exaggerated the feeling which prevailed on the subject in London and its neighborhood."[13] Henry Hunt, representing the Radical Opposition, claimed that the "corrupt Press" misrepresented public feeling as being universally favorable to the Bill. When a meeting at Birmingham, "said to consist of a [sic] 150,000 persons," was favorable to the Bill, the Press "made the most of it"; but at a meeting at Manchester the Whigs, who organized it, were "completely beaten, and therefore the account of it was almost suppressed by the public papers."[14] When Opposition spokesmen were not prepared to challenge the claims that tens and even hundreds of thousands of persons attended public meetings, doubts about their significance were raised by suggestions that the crowds were filled with women and children or spectators attending only from curiosity.[15] However, sometimes the figures themselves were disputed. At an Edinburgh meeting, for

---

the quantity of names was ever examined": ibid., pp. 78–79. On the other hand, not only the reformers were suspected of practicing deception. It was reported, on the authority of a *Times* correspondent, that an anti-Reform petition from Norwich and presented by Eldon, which was represented as having 13,500 signatures (a figure later corrected to 3,500), really had only 1,300: *Manch. Guard.,* Oct. 22, 1831, p. 2.

12. *Despatches, 8,* 562.

13. *Hansard, 7* (Oct. 5, 1831), 1314–15. In the *Quarterly Review* it was said the Ministers "were deceived or alarmed by the idea that the people were unanimous and irresistible in their enthusiasm for the Bill": "State of the Government," *Quarterly Review, 46* (Nov. 1831), 302–03. Also see "Progress of Misgovernment": ibid. (Jan. 1832), 589.

14. *Hansard, 8* (Oct. 17, 1831), 858. The papers said the Manchester meeting "was in favour of the Reform Bill, but the truth was, that an amendment was carried, and the meeting had petitioned for Universal Suffrage, Annual Parliaments, and Vote by Ballot": ibid., col. 859. The working-class union's amendments did in fact prevail with large majorities: Foster to Melbourne, Oct. 12, 1831, H.O. 52/13.

15. *Hansard, 12* (May 11, 1832), 761, 874.

example, at which 60,000 persons were said to have attended, the actual attendance, according to the Opposition was only 8,000 persons.[16] A certain measure of skepticism about the claims made in support of the Reform Bill was appropriate, for there was a good deal of exaggeration by government supporters. By the same token, the Opposition was also tempted to exaggerate. Both sides claimed to see the facts in a way that lent support to its position.

Testimony that has greater value, however, comes from the reluctant admission of evidence that weakens one's own case, and the Opposition was obliged to do this more often than government supporters. For despite skepticism, it had difficulty sustaining its claim that there was apathy. Wharncliffe, even while suggesting that public enthusiasm was grossly exaggerated, "at the same time willingly added his belief, that a vast majority of the people were looking for Reform." The Earl of Haddington also thought the public, especially in London, had become doubtful about the Bill, but confessed that "he was not one of those who did not admit the existence of a strong feeling in the great body of the public in favour of the measure." And in May 1832 Baring "admitted that there was a portion of the people eager for Reform, and that so great was that portion . . . that it would neither be safe nor consistent with the peace and tranquillity of the country not to give every consideration to the substantive opinion of that portion of the people."[17] These admissions are in keeping with other evidence. Anti-Reform petitions, when they were presented, were signed by comparatively few persons, and in order to bolster

16. Ibid., col. 871–73; also see col. 1404, 1408, 1411. Actually one estimate of only 700 was made. For another example of a May 1832 meeting at Dublin, for which estimates ranged from 60,000 to 1,000, see ibid., *13*, 293–94. In still another case, in March 1831, when Morpeth presented a petition from "the freeholders and inhabitants of the county of York, assembled at a county meeting," he was challenged by three opposition speakers who claimed that the meeting was "a decided failure" and that "a thinner county meeting was never known to have occurred in the Castle-Yard of York within the memory of man": ibid., *3* (March 28, 1831), 1088–91.

17. Ibid., *7* (Oct. 5, 1831), 1315, 1320; *12* (May 10, 1832), 799; *13* (June 4, 1832), 369.

them it became necessary to argue that they represented the property of the district, thus implying that large numbers were not relevant.[18] Anti-Reform meetings were infrequent and also quite meager in attendance. The *Times,* calling such a meeting at Liverpool a "hole-and-corner" affair, reported that estimates of the attendance varied from 20 to "upwards of 50." However, a local source reported that 1,500 signatures were collected in support of its petition. Cockburn took note of an anti-Reform meeting at Edinburgh, attended by 800 persons, but "all the old remnants," with few of the middle ranks and almost none of the lower. In Parliament the taunt was made that "in no instance had those who were adverse to Reform convened any public meetings," and that they "did not deem it advisable to attend any public meetings at which the question came under discussion."[19] Even discounting for exaggeration and for inflated lists of signatures on petitions and fluctuating interest, it seems clear that public opinion was, on the whole, favorable to the Reform Bill. This is clearly indicated by the apparent ease with which leaders of the Reform agitation could collect signatures for petitions and organize (in many if not all cases) public meetings. Even if there is reasonable doubt about their size, reports of a very large number of such meetings appeared in the newspapers in October 1831 and the following May. This conclusion is also supported by considering the failure of the Tory opposition to organize any significant agitation against the Reform Bill.[20] (The working-class opposition to the Bill is another matter, for it represented a de-

18. Londonderry, ibid., 7 (Oct. 4, 1831), 1124; Eastnor, 9 (Dec. 16, 1831), 325–26.

19. *Times,* Nov. 24, 1831, p. 3. The Liverpool petition was not opposed to all reform but held the Bill to have gone too far: J. A. Picton, *Memorials of Liverpool, 1* (London, 1875), 440; Cockburn, *Memorials, 1,* 26; *Scotsman,* Nov. 30, 1831, pp. 2, 3; Vincent, *Hansard, 9* (Dec. 6, 1831), 43.

20. These were very rare occasions when a politically oriented mob acted on behalf of the Boroughmongers and in opposition to Reform. One such case occurred in early June 1831 at Whitehaven: *Birm. J.,* June 4, 1831, p. 2; *Exam.,* June 5, 1831, p. 360. Also at Girvan on April 25, 1831, when Orangemen attacked pro-Reform demonstrators: A. H. Baillie to Melbourne, July 13, 1831, H.O. 48/28, f. 75; see p. 144, n. 11 below.

mand for more extensive change than was offered, not resistance to reform as such.)

"Much was said that no one really believed"—Roebuck

Public opinion was favorable to the Reform Bill. About this there can be no doubt. It was at times even an excited public that made demands for reform. But was this revolutionary excitement? Is it appropriate to interpret the events of 1831–32 in the context of the French Revolution? Was it so difficult to maintain public order that one must assume the country to have been in a revolutionary situation? For that matter, short of revolutionary excitement, one may ask whether "the public fury" of which Halevy (among many others) spoke, was so pervasive and typical as has been represented.[1]

At least those who made greatest use of the rhetoric of revolution did not think that it corresponded to reality. Parkes and Place—certainly well-placed observers—reveal in private correspondence with friends that they did not believe all that they said in public about the threat of revolution. Writing to Grote on October 16, 1831, just a week after the Lords' rejection of the second Bill, Place expressed concern that public opinion had "reached its crisis . . . and has passed it without producing any good effect on the ministers." The danger was that public opinion, "rapidly declining . . . may settle down among the working classes and to a great extent among the middle classes into sulkiness," and that, "the common people shall become sullen as their immediate superiors indifferent, they will concur in nothing ministers will propose, by any demonstrations publicly made." It was for this reason that he feared, not an outbreak, but moderation, and thus he chastised Grote for what he thought an overcautious speech delivered to an assembly of merchants and bankers.[2] At this time he also told Burdett that there was a "falling off of the

1. Halevy, *Triumph of Reform*, p. 41; also 39, 40, 43, 45.
2. Place to Grote, Oct. 16, 1831. In his reply, Grote indicated that he shared Place's estimate of public feeling, and for this reason was unable to speak out any more. "I am quite satisfied that it would have been impossible to carry the meeting along with me, had I attempted to raise

excitement" and that "the people are settling down into sulki-ness."[3] James Mill seems to have shared this estimate; "I am terrified, mainly," he wrote to Fonblanque, "at any collapse in the public mind." Yet, despite his concern about sullenness among the people, this was the very time when Place spoke the "language of menace" and "wholesome terror" to the Ministry. Three days before writing confidentially to Grote he had led the deputation to Grey (described by Roebuck), to whom he expressed "appre-hension that [a prorogation till after Christmas] might lead to a violent revolution, the result of which no man could predict."[4] One of Place's colleagues, Bowyer, a Clerkenwell bookseller who was later to serve on the Council of the National Political Union, has also recorded that "much apprehension still existed [in early October] as to whether any popular movement would take place in the event of the Bill being rejected, sufficient to work upon the fears of the Court, and to retain the Ministry in office"; and he noted that after the rejection "no movement of the working people, of any important character, seemed likely to take place."[5] But such apprehension did not prevent Place from warning Hob-house (who had the ear of Cabinet Ministers) that impatience among the people was such that "[financial] Panic is now in an incipient state." Lord Grey, he warned, ought to make an un-equivocal declaration of his determination to have the "whole Bill." "The delay of such a declaration," Place wrote, "may put a stop in one hour to the circulation of Bank of England notes, shut up all the shops and factories and turn the whole of the working people into the streets." If this "incipient panic" were to

---

mistrust of Ministers." And Mrs. Grote: "But if those Bankers and traders were to be got together *at all,* you must adapt your style to their stomachs." Grote to Place, Oct. 19, 1831; Mrs. Grote to Place, Oct. 19, 1831: Add. MSS 35,149, ff. 98–100, 105–08.

3. Place to Burdett, Oct. 19, 1831: Add. MSS 35,149, f. 102. It will be very difficult, Place adds, "to induce [the people] again to shew so much zeal in so quiet a way."

4. James Mill to Fonblanque, Oct. 25, 1831, Mill-Taylor Collection, *49A,* 1; Place to Parkes, Oct. 13, 1831, Add. MSS 35,149, f. 90b.

5. "Mr. Bowyer's Narrative of the Procession [Oct. 12, 1831] to the King to present an Address": Add. MSS 35,149, f. 343–43b.

"be developed," then "the whole Government is destroyed at once, never again to be restored in its present form."[6]

The riots in Derby and Nottingham and Bristol did not change Place's evaluation of popular interest in the Reform Bill. In November Place had so little confidence in the willingness of any large number of people to stand up for reform that he confided to Colonel Thompson that "repealing the Habeas Corpus Act, and a few dragoons in the streets would quash Reform."[7] A couple of months later he again indicated "that when the Lords threw out the last Bill [October 8, 1831] there was so little real feeling or spirit in the people that it required all the efforts of a few individuals to found the National Political Union, and that the Birmingham Union was just kept alive by the subscription of three men who sent £50 apiece and saved it." Place also indicated "that even now [January 26, 1832] the National Political Union was mere moonshine, and the Birmingham the same."[8] Later, in the spring of 1832, according to Parkes, Place "thought further Public Meetings not successfully practicable," and while Place later denied this, he did admit that the people "had sunk into a state of repose" and that "it was with very great difficulty that I and my friends could devise means to keep the 'National Political Union' in existence." It is also worth noting that, apart from the initial meeting on October 31, 1831, his Union sponsored no open-air public meetings throughout the period of the Reform Bill agitation.[9]

6. Place to Hobhouse, Oct. 11, 1831: Add. MSS 35,149, f. 84b.

7. T. Perronet Thompson to John Bowring, Nov. 15, 1831: Johnson, *General T. Perronet Thompson*, p. 176.

8. Hobhouse, "Diary," Jan. 26, 1832, in Broughton, *Recollections, 4*, 164–65. Hobhouse also wrote, "I had no notion of the apathy or disgust of the people, but he [Place] assured me he was right." Yet it has been assumed that Place genuinely felt alarm whenever he uttered alarmist warnings; for example, see Wallas, *Place*, pp. 265, 306; J. R. M. Butler, *Passing of the Great Reform Bill*, p. 294; Woodward, *Age of Reform*, p. 83.

9. Parkes to Place, Jan. 8, 1837, and Place to Parkes, Jan. 27, 1837: Add. MSS 35,150, ff. 218b, 233. The following general meetings of members were held, all indoors: Nov. 10, postponed from Nov. 9 and Dec. 1, 1831 (at Crown and Anchor Tavern); Feb. 2, Feb. 6 and 7 (for election of Council), May 3, 9, 10, 12, 16, 1832 (at Saville House); May 21, 1832

The same discrepancy between accounts of public feeling that were sent to the press or to the Ministers directly and descriptions given to intimates can be found in some of Parkes' descriptions of extra-Parliamentary activities at Birmingham. While he did not go so far as Place, he clearly indicated how serious he believed the threat of revolution to be when in October he boasted that "six of us here could order the people, as a field officer at a review puts his regiment through their exercise."[10] Such docility among the people was hardly compatible with a genuine belief that revolution was imminent. Far from really thinking the people difficult to control, he said "it is just possible that we may be able to bring about a Revolution but it would be through the worst of the people." As for organizing resistance, Parkes confessed that "if a Tory juste milieu comes in we *shall* have a half measure," for "there is *not* sufficient virtue in even the best part of the people to resist, and to enforce their rights."[11] To Place he complained, "I do all I can . . . considering the *mixed* state of the Public."[12] And in April 1832, Parkes was said to have complained about "how difficult it is to keep the people together."[13] While portraying the Birmingham leaders to the government as militant and reckless, he privately complained that he did as much as he could. "I draw the resolutions," he said, "as

---

(at City of London Tavern). According to the *Times,* May 17, 1832, p. 5, a crowd of 8,000 outside on May 16 was addressed before the meeting took place within. "Minutes of the Council," in PCN, Set 63, *1,* ff. 41–42, 59b, 84–88, 126b, 128–32, 135b. On the May meetings see pp. 198–99 below, especially n. 13.

10. He also reported that the "Government is afraid of the people breaking loose; it is impossible, if they but stick to the helm": Parkes to Grote, Oct. 4, 1831, in Harriet Grote, *Life of George Grote,* pp. 68–69.

11. Parkes to Grote, Nov. 28, 1831: Add. MSS 34,149, ff. 128–29.

12. Parkes to Place, Oct. 24, 1831: Add. MSS 35,149, f. 115.

13. He was also reported as saying that " 'he knew how difficult it was; for that he had a great deal to do with them': and then he said that he came from Birmingham." The statement was made in conversation at a bookseller's and reported to Cobbett, who published it along with an account of the conversation in his *Political Register.* The unidentified person sending the letter reported that the bookseller identified the speaker as Joseph Parkes. Of course, Parkes denied having made the statements: "To

strong a dose as the patients would swallow, and their stomachs would retain."[14] Yet, despite these circumstances, he had warned Althorp, with whom he conducted a highly confidential correspondence and with whom he had a secret interview, that it is "no use now shying the word Revolution: they [the Cabinet] must make one or the People *will*."[15]

Place's confession that the National Political Union had been "moonshine" is confirmed by the facts of membership. The dues were one shilling quarterly, and since the accounts of the Union survive, the number of dues-paying members can be inferred from Table 1. Since it is conceivable that all the payments during the second quarter and 6,017 of the payments during the third quarter were made by the original subscribers, the membership

TABLE 1. Membership of the National Political Union

Quarter	Subscriptions	Number of persons (at 1 shilling each)
First Nov. 1, 1831, to Jan. 31, 1832	£300–17–1	6,017
Second Feb. 1, 1832, to April 30, 1832	80–18–0	1,618
Third May 1, 1832, to July 31, 1832	454– 4–0	9,084
	Total	16,719

the People of Birmingham, and to the Reformers in all the Great Towns," from William Cobbett, April 21, 1832, PCN, Set 17, *3*, f. 147a; *Birm. J.*, April 28, 1832, p. 2. The controversy provoked someone to write anonymously to the editor that the people had "settled into calmness and apathy." The editor observed that the writer "has not the faculty of seeing what is passing around him": ibid., May 5, 1832, p. 2.

14. Parkes to Grote, Oct. 26, 1831: Add. MSS 35,149, f. 117. For an indication of his role in preparing resolutions for a Birmingham meeting see his letter in *Birm. J.*, Oct. 29, 1831, p. 3. Such confessions to Grote did not prevent Parkes and Place from occasionally directing alarmist reports to him. Since he was known as a timid politician, they apparently thought he sometimes required such stimulation. For example, see Grote, *Posthumous Papers,* p. 41; Add. MSS 35,149, ff. 77, 99b, 106.

15. Parkes to Grote, n.d., but ca. Nov. 1831: Add. MSS 35,149, f. 81.

during this period could have been as little as 9,084. This, of course, is unlikely. On the other hand, it is unlikely that each payment during the three quarters was made by a different person. In a metropolis of 1,500,000[16] then, there were at least 9,084, and at the most 16,719, dues-paying members from the date the Union was organized (October 31, 1831) through May 1832, when the Reform Bill went through its last critical phase. About one third of this number (5,192) joined in November 1831, immediately after the formation of the Union. Thus, before the critical period in mid-December when, according to Perry, only one to three new members joined each day, there were fewer than 6,000 persons enrolled. This, of course, was a time when the Union was making extravagant claims on behalf of public opinion. However, there was a considerable accession later in May when 8,109 joined (5,662 before May 16).[17] This contrasts markedly with the 100,000 members Place hoped for and thought possible, but not with the actual attendance at the organizational meeting which was 3,000.[18]

Still more revealing are the results of the election to the Council, for they indicate the extent of participation in the Union's activities. The rules provided for an election at an annual general meeting in February, and in 1832 a Council was elected in accordance with Wakley's resolution that called for half the Council to consist of workingmen. The ballot included two lists of candidates, forty-eight on the working-class list and forty-seven on the

16. R. H. Mottram, "Town Life and London," *Early Victorian England,* ed. G. M. Young, *1* (London, Oxford, 1934), 169.

17. PCN, Set 63, *1,* ff. 2b, 24, 284b–87b. The figure for Nov. 1831 assumes that the entire £259–12–0 receipts until Nov. 29, 1831, was made up of subscriptions, although the entry indicates that it included donations as well. The one-shilling subscription is mentioned in "Declaration of Objects, Rules and Regulations" (a placard), 1831; also in Wallas, *Place,* p. 284. Perry, Add. MSS 27,822, f. 32b. The *Times,* May 14, 1832, p. 2, report that the Union had 15,000 members was an exaggeration by about one-third; and the claim that 2,000 had enrolled each day since May 8 more than doubled the actual enrollment.

18. Place to James Mill, Oct. 26, 1831: Add. MSS 35,149, f. 123b; Melbourne to Brougham, Oct. 31, 1831, Brougham Papers, 20,386. Wallas, *Place,* p. 282, said there were 20,000.

list "not of the working class." Each elector was called upon to strike out the names of candidates for whom they were not voting, and not more than thirty-six names were to remain on each of the two lists. The Minutes of the Council include information as to the number of votes received by each of the candidates. There were at least 624 participants, for the most popular candidate (Rev. W. J. Fox) received this many votes. But even if it is assumed that the supporters of the known Rotunda candidates never voted for any of the others (which meant casting only 19 votes instead of the 72 allowed), and that Place's supporters cast all the votes allowed so as to exclude Rotundaites (which in fact happened), then the number of participants is raised to 843, and this figure probably includes most of the 95 candidates.[19] These meager showings are in keeping with Place's acknowledgment (made in 1837) that "considerable bodies of the working classes" were "prevented . . . from joining the Political Unions in London, Manchester, Bristol, and other places, and . . . use[d] no efforts to promote the passing of the bill."[20]

19. NPU, "Minutes of the Council"; Balloting Lists: PCN, Set 63, *2*, f. 23; *1*, ff. 87b–88. There were 18,807 votes cast on the working-class list, 2,507 of them for the 11 known Rotunda candidates; and 20,495 on the nonworking-class list, 1,990 of them for the 8 known Rotundaites. It is assumed that there were as many supporters of Rotunda candidates as there were votes for the most successful Rotundaite (329), excluding Wakley (476) and Leonard (435), who both obviously received support from Place's followers. In Wakley's case it is explicable: see p. 85, n. 26 above. If instead the average vote received by Rotunda candidates is taken as an indication of their strength, the estimate of participants falls from 843 to 763.

20. Wallas, *Place*, p. 290, n. 2. The passage is from Add. MSS 27,792, f. 15, which was written in about 1837 when Place was writing a history of the agitation. Place then attributed the working-class apathy, among other things, to the expectation of and desire for revolution. The Union implicitly acknowledged its failure to gain middle-class as well as working-class adherents. For example—"The Union in spite of opposition and apathy has at length been definitely established," "While the members of the middle classes have exhibited *their* distrust by silence and apathy," and "In time the dread of taking part in new modes of proceeding will disappear from among the great body of the middle classes": No. 8. NPU, *Report of the Council, Feb. 2, 1832*, pp. 4–5 (signed by Rowland Detroisier, secretary, but not necessarily written by him). Place later said that as a

In evaluating the state of public feeling it is necessary to take into account the reports that as many as 150,000 and even upwards of 200,000 persons attended the meetings of the Union at Birmingham.[21] Meetings of this size would hardly have taken place if the Union there was also "moonshine." Yet it should be remembered that Parkes, with whom most if not all of these reports originated, had good reason to exaggerate, and the editors (of the *Morning Chronicle,* the *Examiner,* and the *Times*) who printed the figures were enthusiastic supporters of the Reform Bill and in some cases personal friends as well.

One way of evaluating Parkes' claims would be to establish how many persons could have stood on the meeting ground at New Hall Hill. This at least allows a check on overestimates. Parkes described New Hall Hill, where the meetings took place, as a "natural amphitheater" formed on twelve acres of "rising land." Another estimate, however, coming from a Union source and therefore not disposed to underestimate, described it as consisting of about six acres.[22] On contemporary maps it has a roughly triangular shape with a few buildings at the apex and a canal

---

result of Wakley's resolution providing for working class representation on the Council, "a comparative few who were not working-men joined us, and some of those who were not working-men left us": Wallas, *Place,* p. 284.

21. Referring to the meeting of May 7, 1832, the *Times* reported that "there must have been upwards of 200,000 persons present" just past noon, and that the number increased later: May 9, 1832, p. 1. Attwood, asking Brougham to present the petition agreed to at the meeting to the House of Lords, said he was "sure that *there were more than Two Hundred Thousand persons present in the course of the day."* Brougham repeated this figure in the Lords: Attwood to Brougham, May 7, 1832, Brougham Papers; *Hansard, 12,* 760. This meeting even had its attendance elevated to 250,000 in one report: Junius Redivivus, *Two Letters on the Character of the Duke of Wellington, and on Defence in the Streets* (London, 1832), pp. 9–10 (letter dated May 9, 1832). Most of the Birmingham meetings were held on Mondays, as it generally was an idle day with the manufacturers: A. Briggs, "Thomas Attwood and the Economic Background of the Birmingham Political Union," *Cambridge Historical Journal, 9* (1948), 201.

22. *Times,* Oct. 5, 1831; *Report of the Great Meeting held at Birmingham, May 7, 1832,* p. 3.

running through the area. A reproduction of a map on a placard announcing sale of the land by auction (in 1834) allows for a rough calculation of the available space. The area consisted of about 22,600 square yards—about four and a half acres and not the twelve acres claimed by Parkes.[23] If, on the average, there were four persons to the square yard (to adopt one formula used at the time), it would seem that there was sufficient space for about 90,000 persons, but this estimate does not take into account the canal running through the property, the effect of the natural slope on the possibility that four persons could stand on a square yard of ground, or the unequal density of most crowds. However, if the different rule-of-thumb method used by Foster, the experienced chief magistrate in Manchester, is adopted here, the estimated capacity would be greatly reduced. Foster assumed that about 6,000 or perhaps 7,000 persons would occupy an acre. According to this formula, New Hall Hill would hold perhaps 30,000 persons.[24]

Testimony of witnesses (and others) who were skeptical about the size of the Birmingham meetings can be found, but mainly from persons who opposed the Reform Bill. It is unlikely that

23. New Hall Hill appears to have been bounded by George, Graham, and Frederick Streets; the meeting area was separated from Mount Street by a few buildings. The area between Frederick and Camden Streets does not appear to have been included in what was known as New Hall Hill. This is evident from the John Kempson maps of Birmingham (1808; also 1810 but published April 1811), one of which is reproduced in Conrad Gill, *History of Birmingham, 1* (London, Oxford, 1952), in the pocket at the end of vol. 1. The Kempson map was used to identify the area included in New Hall Hill. The size of the area was calculated from the map appearing on the placard announcing the sale of this and adjacent properties: "New Hall Estate, Conditions of Sale, Nov. 17, 1834," Birmingham Collection, 256,362 (in Birmingham Reference Library).

24. The formula, four persons per square yard, was used in the Lords' dispute on the size of meetings: *Hansard, 12,* 1404. Foster to Melbourne, Oct. 13, 1831, H.O. 52/13. There are various sketches and paintings of the Birmingham Political Union meetings that give the impression of immense crowds. There is one in C. Gill, *History of Birmingham, 1,* Plate 21, opposite p. 210, reproduced from a lithograph which was based on "sketches taken during the three successive meetings in May 1832" by Henry Harris, a Birmingham artist. (I am grateful to Professor Gill for supplying this

a supporter of the Bill, if he was skeptical, would reveal his estimate. Place, in saying that the Birmingham Union was also "moonshine," was addressing Hobhouse, an old associate and perhaps a confidant. Some of the skepticism came from parties who had not witnessed the meetings. For example, referring to the meeting on October 3, 1831, which appears to have been the first convened at New Hall Hill by the Union, the *Annual Register* said that the 150,000 figure was "a gross exaggeration which nobody believed"; and the *Poor Man's Guardian,* which spoke for the working-class opposition, said in reference to the *Times* report that "the *Times*-server knows how to tell a story—and invent one, too, occasionally—when it suits its own purpose."[25] The *Times,* printing what most probably was Parkes' report, had described this meeting as having been attended by more than 100,000, and Ministers had the impression that 150,000 were present.[26] There were other skeptical estimates, and while they also came from interested parties, they were from eyewitnesses. One of these, sent anonymously to the Duke of Wellington, differs from the one appearing in the *Times* by an amount far exceeding the margin of error inherent in such estimates:

> I estimated the crowd at about eight or ten thousand, but, as I was unused to such calculations, I did not place much confidence in my own estimate. A relation of mine, a military man, thought that there were about 15,000, and that estimate has been further confirmed by the coinciding opinion of another military gentleman, stated without knowledge

---

information.) There is another illustration (artist unknown) in R. K. Dent, *Old and New Birmingham,* p. 407; and still another, only slightly different, in R. K. Dent, *The Making of Birmingham,* p. 360. Haydon did a sketch and a painting (incomplete) of one of the May 1832 meetings but, of course, he did not witness any of the meetings. He was "rendering . . . an event which he knew after all only by hearsay": P. J. Barlow, "Benjamin Robert Haydon and the Radicals," *Burlington Magazine, 99* (1957), 311–12.

25. *Annual Register for 1831,* Chr., p. 281; *Poor Man's Guardian,* Oct. 8, 1831, p. 111.

26. *Times,* Oct. 5, 1831, p. 4; Wakefield, *Attwood,* p. 179.

of the calculations of my relative. I am confident that there were not more than 15,000 or 20,000 on the ground at any one time. . . .

No one in the town, not even the magnifiers of such things, dreams that the numbers exceeded 30,000 or 40,000.

The writer also observed that "when the petition was read over to the meeting, as the petition of 100,000 people, *there was a laugh throughout the crowd at the deception.*"[27] This was the meeting about which a Walsall man wrote to E. J. Littleton, M.P. for Staffordshire and a supporter of the Bill, saying that "a favorite, and . . . a successful tactic, with the leaders of the Union has been to propagate most exaggerated notions of the importance and powers of the body; and no man better than Mr. Attwood knows how to array weakness in the garb of strength. It was thus a few weeks since he contrived to magnify a meeting of ten or twenty thousand idlers, mostly women and children into an assembly of one hundred and fifty thousand 'of the people.' "[28] It should be noted that the next meeting after the outdoors meeting of October 3 took place in Beardsworth's Repository, which held fewer than 20,000 persons.[29] Yet this was the time when popular

27. Anonymous (signed "H") to Wellington, Oct. 9, 1831, in Wellington, *Despatches, 7,* 559. Roebuck wrote of this meeting, "consisting, it was said, of 150,000 persons": *History, 2,* 218. Another example of skepticism from a Tory source concerns the meeting of May 7, 1832, which, according to Brougham and the *Times,* 200,000 persons attended. According to another of Wellington's correspondents, "the boasted meeting . . . which has been cried up as consisting of 200,000 persons, never amounted to more than a *quarter* of that number; indeed I was assured by a gentleman who was present with a military officer, that he computed the whole assembly as never exceeding 30,000": Rev. R. L. Freer to Wellington, May 14, 1832, in Wellington, *Despatches, 8,* 318–19.

28. Charles Porter to E. J. Littleton, M.P., Nov. 24 [perhaps 26th?], 1831: H.O. 40/29.

29. A report of a meeting of Jan. 25, 1830, indicated that the building was packed full, and it was said 12–15,000 were present. A report of a meeting on May 17, 1830, said there were 18–20,000 in the building. *Report of the Proceedings at the Meeting of the Inhabitants of Birmingham . . . 25th of January 1830,* p. 3; *Report of the Proceedings of the First Meeting of the Birmingham Political Union . . . May 17, 1830,* p. 3. One re-

resentment at the Lords' rejection of the Bill was said to have been most intense. Was the decision to hold this meeting indoors influenced by doubt as to the possibility of assembling a large number of persons?

It is hardly possible to evaluate these differing estimates with confidence. But it seems very unlikely that the Birmingham meetings attained the size attributed to them by the Union spokesmen and by the press at the time. The size of New Hall Hill made it unlikely, indeed, impossible. Consideration of the population of Birmingham and "environs" in 1831 (147,000) also made it unlikely, and even though the Union spokesmen claimed that those attending their meetings came from towns up to twenty miles from Birmingham, an examination of the number of persons associated with the unions of those towns, to say nothing of their populations, makes it difficult to believe that very large numbers came to Birmingham from them.[30] Table 2 gives the population of the towns from which, according to the Union, large numbers marched to Birmingham for the meeting of 200,000 on May 7,

---

port (which was sympathetic) said 9,000 or 10,000 were present: *Scotsman,* Oct. 26, 1831, p. 3. The *Times,* Oct. 22, 1831, p. 1, reported the meeting as having been held at Dees' Royal Hotel; but a local source reported it as beginning there and then adjourning to Beardsworth's Repository. The meeting was not called by the Union, but it was addressed by several Union notables, including Parkes: *Birm. J.,* Oct. 15, 1831, p. 2; Oct. 22, 1831, p. 2.

30. The population of Birmingham according to the Census of 1831 was 110,914, but this figure does not include neighboring areas that already were part of the "environs." Therefore, the 147,000 mentioned by Briggs is more realistic: *Press and Public,* p. 4. Since the following figures come from a Union source they may be assumed to represent the maximum size of the unions in neighboring towns. The Union claimed only that there were "upwards of a thousand enrolled members" at West Bromwich; a "little more than one hundred" at Oldbury; 400 at Hales Owen; "nearly five hundred" at Tipton; and "upwards of 600" at Walsall: *Political Union Register, 1* (March, 1832), 35–37, 39. A meeting of the Dudley Political Union on April 4, 1832, was attended by 50 persons: J. Smitheman to Magistrates at Dudley, April 10, 1832: H.O. 52/19. On the other hand, the Council of the Birmingham Political Union claimed to have received a petition of support signed by 25,000 townsmen: *Birm. J.,* Feb. 25, 1832, p. 3.

TABLE 2. Population of towns from which people marched to the Birmingham meeting of May 7, 1832

	Attendance claimed	Population in 1831
Grand Northern Division		
Wolverhampton		24,372
Bilston		14,492
Sedgeley		20,577
Willenhall	100,000	7,713
Wednesbury		8,437
Walsall		11,977
Darlaston		6,751
West Bromwich		15,327
Grand Western Division		
Stourbridge		13,874
Dudley		23,043
Harborne		4,227[a]
Cradley	25,000	2,022[b]
Lye Waste		No inf.
Oldbury		6,475
Rowley [Regis]		7,438
Hales Owen		5,954
Eastern Division		
Coventry		27,298[c]
Warwick		9,109
Bedworth		3,980[d]
Kenilworth	5,000	5,657
Leamington		6,746
Stratford-on-Avon		5,751
Southern Division		
Bromsgrove		9,712
Redditch		No inf.[e]
Studley		3,757
Worcester	10,000	27,362
Droitwich		5,571
Alcester		4,859

a. As a hamlet, 1,551.
b. As a township; 1,509 as a parish.
c. As a district or union.
d. As a parish.
e. But as a township combined with two others, 3,627.

1832.[31] The towns in the Northern Division, which were in most cases nearer to Birmingham than the others mentioned, had a total population that barely exceeded the number claimed to have marched to the Union meeting.

On the other hand, those who expressed skepticism about the reports were not without bias either. Yet the Lord Chancellor, while he was willing to use such reports, admitted that "there might be exaggeration . . . in describing the numbers assembled at them."[32] Some years later Parkes referred to these meetings when he spoke of himself as having been "the second or third idol of tens of thousands,"—hardly the language of one who believed the number to have been "upwards of 200,000."[33] It should also be noted that the Rev. Hugh Hutton, who addressed some of the meetings and had a quasi-official status in the Union, said that New Hall Hill was "capable of holding 80,000 persons." (He did not say how many it actually held.)[34]

However, regardless of the number it is clear that there was no real threat of a popular outbreak in Birmingham. The Union

31. The Union claims appear in Wakefield, *Attwood,* pp. 198–99 and in Gill, *History of Birmingham, 1,* 204. Gill warns (p. 209, n. 2) that the figures should be "read with caution, for the observers would be strongly tempted to exaggerate." The population figures are for "sub-districts" unless otherwise indicated; and they are from the 1831 census: *Census of Great Britain, 1851. Population Tables. I. Numbers of the Inhabitants, in the Years 1801, 1811, 1821, 1831, 1841, and 1851* (London, 1852).

32. *Hansard, 12* (May 11, 1832), 874–75; also see ibid., col. 760. Lord John Russell said of the meeting in Oct. 1831, which 150,000 were said to have attended, "He could not say that the meeting was so large as Mr. Attwood had represented it, but still it was a large meeting": ibid., *8* (Oct. 12, 1831), 598.

33. Parkes to Place, Jan. 8, 1837: Add. MSS 35,150, f. 219. Similar usage appears in the words of T. Aurelius Attwood, addressing a meeting allegedly of 200,000. "The thousands, and I may say tens of thousand . . . who are now present": *Report of the Great Meeting held at Birmingham, May 7, 1832,* p. 9.

34. Hugh Hutton to B. R. Haydon, May 26, 1832. Hutton was describing the scene to Haydon who had inquired about the prospect for painting one of the recent meetings. (Professor W. B. Pope of the University of Vermont kindly loaned me a microfilm copy of this and other unpublished letters in his possession. He also offered many helpful observations on Haydon in relation to the Birmingham politicians.)

leadership boasted about the peaceful disposition of the crowds and the quickness with which they disbanded at the end of the meetings. Therefore, while the considerable numbers attending such meetings provide evidence of public interest in reform, their peaceful disposition is hardly in keeping with the contention that there was the kind of feverish excitement that suggests the threat of revolution.

The Illumination in London; Election Riots in Scotland

There were many other places, however, where there were disturbances of the peace. There were demonstrations in London, in April and in October 1831, that were accompanied by some rioting. There were riots in Scotland during the election in 1831. And there were serious riots at Nottingham and Derby and at Bristol in October 1831. In addition, the rural incendiarism and machine breaking that had caused alarm during the winter of 1830–31 broke out again late in 1831. Some violence also accompanied the strikes that took place at this time—mainly among colliers and pitmen—in Durham and Northumberland, in Staffordshire, and in Wales. The violence that characterized industrial conflicts, while not an expression of political discontent, added to the nervousness about the stability of society that was experienced at this time.

The riots that occurred in London during the spring of 1831 hardly provide evidence of revolutionary excitement. The most serious were those accompanying the Illumination on the evening of April 27. The Illumination was called in order to celebrate the promise held out for the Reform Bill as a result of the decision to dissolve Parliament in the face of a one-vote majority by which the Bill was carried on its second reading. The Illumination took place just prior to the elections that began on April 29. The demonstration of illuminated shops and dwellings and the crowded streets indicate extensive support for the cause of Reform. The *Morning Chronicle* reported that it was "very general," and this was not contradicted by the Tory *Annual Register,* although it called it "pretty general." The *Chronicle* filled more than four columns with its list of commercial establishments in various parts of the metropolis that were illuminated for the occasion.[1] There was evidence of widespread approval. But what indication was there of revolutionary excitement? The only rioting was caused by "several thousand men" proceeding through parts of the city and the West End where they "smashed the windows of those persons who did not illuminate."[2] There were a great many broken windows; the following morning a police superintendent said it was "too numerous to detail at this early period." The town houses of prominent opponents of the Bill were stoned—among them the houses of the Duke of Wellington, the Marquess of Cleveland, and the Bishop of London. Various Tory club-houses were also stoned.[3] There is no indication of damage other than smashed windows, and this seems to have been taken in stride by those who recalled how, in accordance with "immemorial usage," this had frequently occurred during previous Illuminations.[4] According to the *Chronicle*, "This license has usually been taken by the mob, when parties have chosen to disregard the general feeling."[5] When Lord Lansdowne lightly treated

---

1. *Morn. Chr.*, April 28, 1831, p. 2; *Annual Register for 1831*, Chr., pp. 68–69. The Illumination was announced for April 25 but was postponed; this led the Opposition to call it a failure: ibid., p. 69; *Hansard, 4*, 128, 129, 154. The motives for participating in the Illumination must have been quite varied, inasmuch as the participants included the Bank of England and the India House. A firm at King's Street, Covent Garden, Hamburger and Co., also participated, as did Benbow's Coffee House on Fleet Street: *Morn. Chr.*, April 28, 1831, pp. 2–3.

2. Ibid., p. 3. Lady Wharncliffe, living on Curzon Street, reported "that we escaped without broken windows last night—tho' we were stout and would not light *one* candle. . . . We (in Curzon St.) were only treated with hisses and groans, and a lamp at the gate broken. . . . Boys are as much concern'd than men": Grosvenor and Stuart, *First Lady Wharncliffe, 2*, 75–76.

3. Report of Superintendent Thomas Baker, quoted in Reith, *British Police and the Democratic Ideal*, p. 95; *Morn. Chr.*, April 28, 1831, p. 3.

4. Torrens, *Melbourne, 1*, 367.

5. *Morn. Chr.*, April 28, 1831, p. 2. Brougham responded to complaints by peers who suffered broken windows by saying he "had lived through many illuminations, and he well remembered that on such occasions the people dealt out impartial justice, or, if they thought proper

what he called the "ludicrous outcry" against the mob and claimed that "the whole amount of damages done in the city [not including the West End] did not amount to 100.1.," the Marquess of Londonderry protested that his property had been "exposed to the outrages of the mob" and the damage amounted to more than £100. In reply, the Home Secretary said he "had never seen any illumination without the same destruction of property which had taken place at the last," and he added that Londonderry had not displayed "this morbid sensibility" when "the windows of Mr. Cobbett's house were smashed to pieces by the mob, because he refused to illuminate after the peace of Amiens."[6] Lansdowne and Melbourne certainly do not appear to have been overly apprehensive about the threat of revolution. Furthermore, the crowds in the streets do not seem to have been violently disposed. The *Morning Chronicle's* report suggests a festive atmosphere; "among the spectators were many persons of highly respectable appearance"; Lady Wharncliffe, after dining out, "went in the Coach and drove all about the most frequented streets, thro' *mob and all*."[7] Finally, it should be noted that the police, although inadequate in number and still inexperienced in dealing with unruly crowds, effectively handled the situation. When they did experience difficulty it appears to have been due to their instructions to show great restraint, "to avoid everything like violent measures, and upon no account to use their staffs unless as a matter of the greatest necessity"; for it was expected that the streets would be " greatly thronged by persons of all ages and classes, and that upon such an occasion the majority of such persons would be doubtless respectable." Thus a police superintendent, in reference to a disorderly missile-throwing crowd of two or three thousand, thought he "certainly could with a hundred men have completely swept the crowd away, but certainly

---

so to call it, injustice; for they could smite the Whig as well as the Tory." He referred to an occasion when, "by accident he did not illuminate . . . and he was hooted, and his house was pelted, and his windows broken": *Hansard, 4,* 155.

6. Ibid., col. 135, 140.

7. *Morn. Chr.,* April 28, 1831, p. 2; Grosvenor and Stuart, *First Lady Wharncliffe, 2,* 75–76.

not without the liability of doing much mischief . . . [to the] very considerable portion of respectable females and children from two years old upwards." When police arrived at Northumberland House, where windows were being broken, they assembled and "after much resistance . . . succeeded in forming a line in the street extending the length of the house, and eventually cleared the mob away." Still another superintendent, whose division was responsible for the area where the window smashing was most serious, reported "the crowds everywhere giving way on the appearance of the police force, and assembling afterwards at other points." The fact that after dispersal the crowd would reassemble indicates that police control was not complete. However, since in a metropolis of 1,500,000 a force of 1,116 was able to disperse disorderly crowds, and without using all the methods of crowd control available to them, it seems likely that either the violently inclined portion of the crowds was quite small or that their disposition was not so violent.[8]

Scotland was also disturbed in the spring, first on the occasion of celebrations of the initial success of the Reform Bill, and then during the elections. When applications were addressed to the magistrates requesting that an illumination be authorized, the authorities were reluctant, on the ground that the police force, consisting of 230 men, was not sufficient to control such activity, and that it would be better, therefore, to avoid provoking the populace. Official authorization came tardily, however, on the day of the proposed illumination (March 28). Many persons remained in the dark and consequently became the victims of the "political glass-breakers." There were eleven parties of rioters, each consisting of about 200 persons, that roamed over the fashionable streets, and there was one crowd (not riotous) of more than 2,000 persons. One of the crowd, Alexander Somerville, whose reflections on mob violence later played so prominent a part in his own life and in the passing of the Reform Bill, left

8. Reports of Superintendents J. A. Thomas and John May, quoted in Reith, *British Police and the Democratic Ideal,* pp. 91–95. Superintendent Thomas also reported that his men "were received by the populace with the greatest good feeling whenever they were called upon to act, and in many instances heartily cheered with cries of 'Bravo, Police!' ": ibid., p. 93.

an account of the riot as experienced by a member of the mob (a kind of document that is quite unusual).

> The sound of crashing glass and the facility of getting missiles to throw whetted the appetite of the ten thousand headed mob—a little taste of window breaking to it, being not unlike a little taste of worrying to the wild beast—and so to the work of destruction the mob rolled like a sea, and roared like storms meeting upon rocks and seas. It proclaimed itself the enemy of anti-reformers and of glass . . . this human sea, storm risen . . . bore upon its surf the seaweed that knew not whither it was carried. I was a piece of its sea-weed. I was now for the first time tossed upon the waves of a popular commotion. At the beginning there was a pleasing sensation of newness. Even the first sound of breaking glass was not unmusical. Combativeness and destructiveness were charmed. . . . as dash went the stones, smash fell the glass, and crash came the window frames— dash, smash, crash, from nine o'clock to near midnight.[9]

The damage appears to have been confined to window panes. Even Somerville, who tended to see the portents of revolution in almost any disturbance, was less than usually alarmist in his description of this event. Although the head of the police defensively claimed that it would have required 1,200 special constables to control the crowds, it is worth noting that the mayor thought that "twenty resolute men would have dispersed any of the assemblages that committed all the mischief." (The plausibility of this assertion depends on the size of the parties of rioters. Were they in groups of 200 or 10,000?)[10]

9. Alexander Somerville, *Autobiography of a Working Man,* ed., Carswell (London, Turnstile, 1951), pp. 92–94; G. Clerk and W. Dundas to Melbourne, April 13, 1831, H.O. 48/28, ff. 22–23; *Hansard, 3,* 1243. For a description of the window breaking on this occasion by a victim, see *Quarterly Review, 106* (July, 1859), 131.

10. J. Mitchell to Melbourne, Nov. 5, 1831; H.O. 102/41, f. 178b. There also was a riot at Dundee on March 30, 1831, when the authorities interfered with a political celebration, a move which, in the opinion of the Lord Lieutenant, was "not very prudent": Airlie to Melbourne, March 31, 1831; H.O. 48/28, ff. 18–19.

There were also scattered instances of rioting in Scotland during the elections in May, 1831. The rioting was done in the name of reform, and generally anti-Reform candidates or their supporters were the victims—for example, at Lanark the carriage of such a group, leaving an inn, was pelted with stones but not stopped. Those remaining within the inn were besieged by a crowd of 300 to 400, half of them boys, until the sheriff, who had allowed his force of 300 special constables to disband, called for military aid. The dragoons galloped through the streets and of course it was cleared. No one was injured. To take another example, at Haddington some persons had carried away anti-Reformers to prevent their voting. "The people do not look upon this as a moral offence; they know that there are enough of precedents for such proceedings." Therefore, while the sheriff was undertaking his inquiries a rescue of his prisoners was effected.[11]

The victims of the reform mobs described these disorders in the fiercest terms. Even Francis Jeffrey, the Lord Advocate, thought the elections were marked by "an unprecedented and somewhat alarming degree of excitement." But at the same time he was highly critical of most local officials whose conduct, he thought, unnecessarily led to the exacerbations of excitement and the exaggerated appearance of serious riot. They were too "warlike." "The worst thing," he said, "is a disposition in the local authorities, who are most of them very hostile to the popular feeling, to recur to the use of *military force*—to call in troops for their protection against every great assemblage of people." With

11. Jeffrey to Grey, May 18, 1831: Grey Papers, Durham. Sir J. Abercrombie to (Brougham?), May 29, 1831: H.O. 48/28, ff. 51–52. Dumbarton, Stirling, Maybole, and Ayr are also mentioned as scenes of election riots. However, not all the rioting was directed against anti-Reformers. Girvan, another Ayrshire town, provides an exception. It was a stronghold of Orangism, and the Reformers' alliance with O'Connell provoked Orange opposition to reform. Orangemen attacked a pro-Reform procession on April 25. In July there was resistance to an Orange procession, with several casualties, including one constable killed and four wounded by gunfire. Orange-and-Green disturbances were commonplace in Ayrshire, and ethnic-religious cleavages more than politics brought on the rioting. J. E. Handley, *The Irish in Scotland 1798–1845* (Cork Univ. Press, 1945), pp. 306–09; H.O. 48/28, ff. 73–90.

regard to Lanark, for example, where anti-Reform voters were besieged at an inn, he thought the small crowd would have dispersed on its own initiative if the sheriff had waited a few hours longer; and, in any case, he asked if "a moderate party of constables might not have kept . . . order, without having recourse to the dangerous expedient of calling in the military." He therefore warned Lord Grey against the exaggerated accounts that would be circulated regarding this "slight provincial tumult."[12]

There was one place, however, where the riots were much more formidable, leading Jeffrey to observe that bringing in soldiers "was rather more justifiable." After it became clear that Col. Blair, an anti-Reformer, had achieved a victory, neither he nor his supporters were safe. Those persons known to have voted for him were often threatened with injury, and in some cases their houses were attacked. A few of his more prominent supporters even felt obliged to flee. At nearby Maybole one house was attacked, and a crowd struggled with the police over the effigy of a Blair voter. The successful candidate and his entourage were chased onto a London-bound steamboat at Ardrossan, where they incurred serious injuries. Apparently the considerable number of Irish living in this county prompted one observer to warn that it would soon "be little better than the most disturbed county of Ireland."[13]

The seriousness of these disturbances led Jeffrey to initiate an investigation. In contrast to the indignant and alarmist reports filed by Blair's supporters, Jeffrey insisted that "the disorders in the County of Ayr were at no time by any means so formidable as might be inferred" from some of the reports that had been circulated. He acknowledged that disgraceful rioting had taken place, and that several persons, including the newly elected Member, had been seriously hurt. But, on the basis of three days' examination by his deputy, he discounted several alarmist accounts, one of them on the ground that its author was "misled

12. Jeffrey to Grey, May 18, May 27, 1831: Grey Papers.
13. Jeffrey to Grey, May 20, 1831: Grey Papers. D. Boyle to Earl of Glasgow, May 20, 1831; A. W. Hamilton to Glasgow, May 21, 1831; W. G. Bailie and others to M. P. Brown (Jeffrey's Deputy), May 24, 1831; all in H.O. 48/28, ff. 42–44, 49–50, 57–58.

by inaccurate information and exaggerated reports, too readily accredited by the apprehensions and desires of his informers." About another report, concerning disorder at Maybole, in which it was claimed that a house had been destroyed, inquiries by Jeffrey's deputy revealed that the house in question had in fact suffered damage to only fourteen panes of glass. Jeffrey thought this "a specimen of the way in which, in a moment of alarm, very insignificant occurrences are exaggerated." Taking still another example, he commented on the report written by A. W. Hamilton:

> The fact, I understand, is not only that no attack was ever made on his house, but that no tumult or assemblage of persons ever appeared near it. He also appeared before my Deputy at Ayr, and admitted these facts, and that there was no movement or proceeding as to his residence. . . . I should be inclined to suppose this gentleman rather of an apprehensive disposition.

On the basis of such inquiries he recommended that the government avoid establishing military stations at Ayr, even though the men who voted for Blair might still be in danger of suffering insult and perhaps even personal attack. Having admitted this, Jeffrey continued:

> But I would be wanting in the duty I owe to the Country or to the Govt., if I did not distinctly say, that to represent the Condition either of this or of any other County in Scotland as at all parallel to that of the most disturbed districts in Ireland, does appear to me a very great and unaccountable exaggeration.[14]

Increasing and reorganizing the constabulary forces was in his view quite sufficient. Disagreements about the seriousness of the rioting in Scotland and on the necessity of calling for military aid also took place in Parliament. However, the testimony of Alexander Cockburn, who tended to be alarmist, is worth noting: "Our Scotch elections are now all over . . . There has been more rioting at the elections than could have been wished, but still

14. Jeffrey to Phillipps, May 31, 1831: H.O. 48/28, ff. 53–56.

there has been less over the whole country than what commonly takes place at any one contested election in England."[15]

The Lords Reject the Reform Bill: Rioting in London

There were also disturbances in London during the days immediately after the Lords' rejection of the Bill. They mainly occurred in connection with a procession that was organized, with Place's help, by two London Radicals, Bowyer and Powell. Organized by parishes, people were to march to the palace and present an address in support of the Bill to the King. When it took place on October 12, 300,000 persons were said to have taken part.[1] The Home Secretary informed the deputations that the King could not receive their petitions, but they could present them through County Members. Hume received some of them in St. James Square and later left them at the palace. The procession then marched past the palace as a demonstration of its size and resolution. It consisted of "shopkeepers and superior artisans"; nevertheless, during the day there were attacks on some Tory peers as well as the usual broken windows.[2]

The procession stimulated some fear of revolution, at least among those already disposed to feel anxiety on this subject. One observer, who witnessed an attack on Apsley House that day, acknowledged that the "mere breaking of a pane or two of glass, under ordinary circumstances, was of no importance"; but on this occasion it appeared "to be a regular and organized out-

15. *Hansard, 4,* 362–67, 460–65; *Journal of Henry Cockburn, 1* (Edinburgh, 1874), 16–17.

1. *Morn. Chr.,* Oct. 13, 1831, p. 3; *Exam.,* Oct. 16, 1831, p. 667. The *Times,* Oct. 13, 1831, p. 3, said "at least 60,000 persons" marched. Carpenter's *Political Magazine* (Nov. 1831), p. 111, said the procession, six across, extended 2 miles and consisted of about 15,000. A foreign visitor, referring to a London procession during the Reform Bill crisis, possibly this one, said it consisted of 6,000 persons, not "the somewhat exaggerated computations of certain journals": Baron d'Haussez, *Great Britain in 1833, 1* (London, 1833), 183. Bowyer, a bookseller, and Powell, a clerk, both became members of the Council of the National Political Union.

2. Wallas, *Place,* pp. 275–76; Butler, *Reform Bill,* p. 293; Torrens, *Melbourne, 1,* 385–86; *Hansard, 8* (Oct. 12, 1831), 643–45.

rage." Many shops were closed, and some boarded up; while Hume interpreted their closing as an indication that respectable shopkeepers intended to take part in the procession, a member of the Opposition took their "barricading" as an indication that they shared his own fears. News of riots at Derby and Nottingham had arrived and must have colored the interpretation of the procession. One member, referring to them, thought London, "from one end to the other, had been all day occupied by a lawless and bloody-minded mob, ready to attack all those who would not administer to their evil passions."[3] These disturbances in London have been taken as evidence of "public fury" and as indicating that it was difficult to maintain order.[4]

The reports of the superintendents in charge of each of the seventeen divisions of the Metropolitan Police indicate the seriousness of these disturbances. Most of the superintendents reported that there were no unusual occurrences; thus, from G (Clerkenwell) division, "Nothing unusual occurred within this Division yesterday [Oct. 12], nor was any damage done to persons or property"; or, from H (Whitechapel), "Not a single occurrence worth noticing took place during the day"; or, from E (Holborn) division, "The whole of this Division was perfectly tranquil yesterday."[5] In some of the other divisions that were nearer the points on which the processions converged (St. James Square, Piccadilly, Pall Mall),[6] even though the police were required to

3. Ibid., col. 626 (Hume and Trevor) and 643 (Trench). Trevor's patron was Lord Londonderry, who was the target of personal attack this day.

4. Halevy, *Triumph of Reform*, p. 41.

5. "Reports of Police Superintendents on Processions of Oct. 12, 1831," H.O. 61/5. The superintendent of E division adds, "I was in attendance at the D station with a strong body of men to act in case of need, but their assistance was not required"; M (Southwark), S (Hampstead), T (Kensington), and V (Wandsworth) division superintendents all reported everything quiet. From N division (Islington) it was reported that a prisoner was rescued by the mob and a police constable was severely injured; and from P (Camberwell) division, that fifty constables drove a mob from the park where they were pulling up young trees.

6. Reconstructing the path of at least some of the processions from the police reports, it appears that they left Portman Place and marched down Regent Street, then up either the Mall or St. James Street to the

deal with marchers, they did so without difficulty. Thus, from
F (Covent Garden) division came the report that everything
"passed off yesterday perfectly quiet and tranquil. Strong parties
were occasionally sent out to protect the property of the inhabitants, but their services were not required." Several processions
marched through D (Marylebone) division, arriving in Portland
Place before proceeding down Regent Street, accompanied by
"strong parties" of police; but "they passed down very quietly"
and the superintendent reported that the day ended quietly.
Similarly, in L (Lambeth) division the police were called upon
to deal with persons who, while marching, wished to carry flags
ordinarily kept at the Rotunda; when they were refused, windows
were broken; "A Party of Police was sent . . . and the mob soon
dispersed very quietly."[7]

The only reports for this day that provide evidence of genuine
disturbance came from A (Whitehall) and C (St. James) divisions;
the scenes of greatest disturbance were St. James Square and at
Apsley House.[8] The attack on the Duke of Wellington's house
was made by "a great number of men and boys" who had followed one of the processions as it returned through the park from
the palace. Many windows were broken before two divisions
(from Greenwich and Kensington) arrived and, with two sections
of St. James division, "succeeded in dispersing the mob."[9] The

---

palace; then through St. James Square to Piccadilly, or from the Square
to the park and in the direction of Apsley House. Of course, not all the
marchers came from the north and west, nor did they all follow the
same path after passing the palace.

7. "Police Superintendents' Reports": H.O. 61/5.

8. N (Islington) and B (Westminster) divisions were used to reinforce
A (Whitehall) division. R (Greenwich) and T (Kensington) divisions reinforced C (St. James) division.

9. The commissioners explained the damage at Apsley House as in
part "owing to a misapprehension of the instructions of the Commissioners,
by the Superintendent of one [St. James] division, in not having distributed his men to the points to be particularly guarded, sufficiently early
after the Procession began to leave the Palace. In consequence of this,
the rabble, which accompanied one of the Processions on its return, had
an opportunity of breaking the windows of Apsley House": C. Rowan to
Lord Melbourne, Oct. 13, 1831, H.O. 61/5.

other scene of disorder was St. James Square, which was "in a constant state of confusion, from the different Parishes and mobs passing through it." Also, speeches were given there, by Hume among others. There were two serious incidents. During the afternoon stones were thrown at the Marquess of Bristol's windows; twenty-seven squares of glass were broken before "the Parishioners themselves rushed upon the mob and prevented further destruction." The other incident occurred early in the evening; it provides the only case during the day when a crowd of persons engaged the police in pitched battle (in contrast to scuffles). As a "large mob" was approaching St. James Square, a detachment of police attacked them; "after a short but severe struggle (a number of the mob being armed with bludgeons) the resolution of the Police prevailed and the mob took flight in every direction. The constables had to use their Truncheons freely on this occasion." However, "during the remainder of the night nothing serious occurred in this quarter (though the mobs passed frequently through)."

Apart from these two incidents the police maintained order without difficulty. It was necessary to attack a mob that had broken one pane of glass at Lord Dudley Stuart's house; but it was easily driven away. During the evening a disturbance in front of Lord Melbourne's house in Whitehall "was immediately put a stop to." There were cases of stones being thrown at the police, this leading to arrests. At St. James Palace there was "a little confusion" from the pressure of the crowd; as the inspector was reluctant to use violence, he called for reinforcements which "enabled us to clear the street."[10] The commissioners justifiably noted that "rioters were immediately dispersed by the Police whenever they could come up with them," and he implied that the riotous proceedings that did take place occurred only because

10. "Police Superintendents' Reports": H.O. 61/5. There were a few other encounters. Stones were thrown at the police, both near the palace gardens, where an inspector was injured, and near the entrance to the park at Carlton Terrace, where some men were taken into custody. A constable was "ill-used" and a prisoner rescued from him. Since the police were subjected to attack for nonpolitical reasons, not all of these attacks need have been connected with the Reform Bill.

the police were deliberately kept in "strong bodies" so long as crowds remained near the palace, thus leaving other parts of the town unpatrolled.[11]

Apart from the effectiveness and in most cases the ease with which the police put an end to disorderly proceedings, it should be noted that the superintendents who faced the greatest difficulties (St. James division) testified that "the conduct of the Parties who formed the Processions from the different Parishes was perfectly peaceable"; these persons were clearly distinguished from "the very lowest rabble who followed them" and by whom "the outrages were committed." There is a tendency to make "the mob" a scapegoat for any popular disturbance; but the phenomenon of a *lumpen proletariat* is not pure myth. The superintendent's distinction was also used by a Member of Parliament who witnessed the attack on Apsley House where the window smashing was begun by a mob that followed "respectable looking persons . . . very well dressed, walking four and four, and with ribands tied around their arms" that took no part in the attack.[12] The inspectors' observations about the main body of the persons marching are supported by reports from "several men in plain clothes" who were employed "in watching the movements, dispositions, etc. of the multitudes, . . . all their reports concurring in representing the disposition of the People as being perfectly peaceable."[13]

11. Rowan to Melbourne, Oct. 13, 1831: H.O. 61/5.
12. "Police Superintendents' Reports": H.O. 61/5; *Hansard, 8,* 642–43. However, Col. Trench, making these observations, thought the respectable marchers had signaled the mob following them to attack. On *lumpen proletariat,* cf. E. J. Hobsbawm, *Primitive Rebels. Studies in Archaic Forms of Social Movement in the 19th and 20th Centuries* (Manchester Univ. Press, 1959), p. 112.
13. "Police Superintendents' Reports": H.O. 61/5. In Parliament, Hume claimed that "no individual suffered the slightest molestation from those who took part in the procession." When he was interrupted by cries of "the Marquis of Londonderry," "the Duke of Wellington," and "Lord Bristol," Hume denied that marchers in the procession had committed the acts alluded to: *Hansard, 8* (Oct. 12, 1831), 627. Mr. Rutheven thought the people conducted themselves in a "peaceable manner . . . in a procession which, though its numbers rendered it formidable, was deprived

Sometimes the infrequency of disturbances is acknowledged, yet the belief that the country was in a revolutionary situation is nevertheless retained; this view usually rests on the assumption that intense popular emotion really existed but was concealed, and that it was on the brink of boiling over. Thus Harriet Martineau thought there would have been "immediate popular convulsion" if the Ministers had for even a moment vacillated.[14] However, there was another possibility—that quiescence reflected the absence of an intense wish for the Reform Bill among large sections of the London populace. According to Bowyer, the Clerkenwell reformer who had a leading part in organizing the procession of October 12, this possibility was considered by "many well informed Reformers." There was, he said, "much apprehension . . . as to whether any popular movement would take place in the event of the Bill being rejected, sufficient to work upon the fears of the Court, and to retain the Ministry in office." He reports that after the Lords' rejection, even though meetings were announced, "no movement of the Working people, of any important character, seemed likely to take place." In these circumstances the procession was announced. Its purpose was "committing this class of persons, and showing their continued disposition to uphold the Reform-Ministry, and to create, if possible, an impression that popular violence would be provoked if the Reform Bill were any longer obstructed." Although he had gloomy expectations before the procession, it should be said that Bowyer, proud of his achievement as one of the leading organizers, felt soon afterwards that "the public mind is in a positive *fever* of excitement." Yet even he could find little evidence of feverish excitement in disturbances to the peace. He thought the orderliness especially admirable. Leading with a friend one division of 5,000, "during the whole of our way, scarcely a single cheer, or,

---

of all terror by its quiet, and tranquil, and regular demeanour." In reply, Sir Henry Hardinge expressed astonishment that there could be "talk of the peaceable conduct of the mob" when a peer (Londonderry) had been attacked, struck off his horse, and wounded; yet he did "not mean to deny that many respectable persons, feeling strongly in favour of this measure of Reform, may have accompanied the procession": ibid., *8, 595.*
    14. Martineau, *Thirty Years' Peace, 2,* 427.

when we felt it necessary, a groan, was given, except by word of command!" (How this lack of spontaneous feeling fits with the feverish excitement is not explained.) Bowyer did not even claim that the "few disturbances" that did occur were an expression of widely held feelings; on the contrary, he seems to have welcomed them. "Little things of this sort," he said, "keep the public mind up to concert pitch. They give a kind of relief to our other measures."[15] Public feeling was such that some portion of the public met and marched on a wet day and with very little previous organization: but it was not the kind of feeling that showed any affinity with violence. These circumstances perhaps explain why, while there were so many meetings in and around London during mid-October, all calling for passage of the Reform Bill, there was so little disorder accompanying them.[16] They also make it less surprising that the crowd, which had assembled outside the Houses of Parliament on the night of October 7, when the fate of the Reform Bill depended on the vote in the Lords, was not to be found when, after the defeat of the Bill, the Lords emerged during the early hours of October 8.[17]

The disturbances that took place in London, at least, were quite petty. Cobbett, along with others, saw them in this light; having described "a trifling smashing of windows and a hustling and kicking and beating of Lord Londonderry," which he deplored, he suggested that acts of violence were inevitable among excited crowds, but that they need not reflect "any violent disposition"; and he concluded that "it must be a subject of admiration . . . that so little violence should have been committed . . . amongst such swarms of people all assembled upon the same

15. Bowyer to Place, Oct. 14, 1831, and "Mr. Bowyer's Narrative of the Procession to the King to present an Address": Add. MSS 35,149, ff. 92–94, 343–45. Hume described the situation, however, by saying that "never, in such a state of excitement, had there been so much discretion manifested": *Hansard, 8* (Oct. 12, 1831), 627.

16. The *Times*, during the week from Oct. 10 to Oct. 18, 1831, reports on many meetings in and about London but had little occasion to report disturbances accompanying them. There were a few isolated incidents.

17. Wellington, *Despatches, 7,* 561; H. Twiss, *The Public and Private Life of Lord Chancellor Eldon, 3* (London, 1844), 152; Grosvenor and Stuart, *First Lady Wharncliffe, 2,* 89.

spot." There were other incidents, in addition to the attack on Londonderry. The Duke of Cumberland was dragged from his horse and had to be rescued by the police; on October 10 windows were broken at the Duke of Newcastle's house; a mob of 6,000 at Palace Yard was dispersed by the police; and a crowd of 1,000 accompanying Hunt from the Rotunda to the House of Commons was turned back at Westminster Bridge. But reports from Police Superintendents and magistrates between October 5th and 12th, which had been especially requested by Melbourne, are almost uniform in describing tranquillity throughout London.[18] The kind of mild disorder that did occur, while it enhanced the nervousness of those who feared revolution, cannot sustain the historical interpretation that sees revolution beneath the surface of events in 1831.

Riots at Nottingham and Derby

Outside London there were some disturbances. At Nottingham one of the more serious riots took place. On October 9, a Sunday, there had been window smashing, and the mayor, while seeking

18. Cobbett, *Political Register, 74* (Oct. 15, 1831), 178–89. Cobbett knew of the riots in Derby and Nottingham when this was written. On the previous day, Oct. 11, the Duke of Newcastle, returning from the House of Lords, found his house "surrounded by a numerous and violent mob." The Marquess of Londonderry also was attacked on Oct. 11 (as on Oct. 12). In Parliament Street the mob "seized his cabriolet, endeavoured to drag him out of it, and one big strong fellow hit him a violent blow with a stick on his arm. . . . fortunately for him, the individual who was with him in the cabriolet drove the horse forward, and he thus escaped from the mob. . . . he, for one, was determined to carry arms about with him for his protection." However, Wharncliffe said he "did not think that the inhabitants of the metropolis had done any thing to disgrace themselves. He was happy to see such prudence exhibited by them. . . . they had not committed any thing in the way of disturbance of public order, beyond what he had reason to expect, or even so much." Windows were also broken at the north end of Bond St. *Times,* Oct. 13, 1831, p. 4; *Hansard, 8* (Oct. 11, 1831), 480–86, 495–97; Reports from Police Offices and reports of Police Superintendents, Oct. 8, 9, 10, 11, in H.O. 52/14 (Middlesex bundle); H.O. to magistrates, Oct. 5–12, in Mepol 1/50; magistrates' reports to H.O., Oct. 5–12, in Mepol 1/49.

to persuade a group of persons to disperse and return to their homes, was struck by a stone and trampled upon. The serious rioting took place the next day (October 10). A public meeting had been called to petition the King to stand by his Ministers. Troops were held in readiness, but the meeting went off peacefully, and most of the persons attending it went home afterward. Later that day, however, the military was again called out and the Riot Act read, for mobs were moving through the streets, "doing much injury to private property." They were "frequently dispersed" but, according to the officer commanding the troops, it was "totally impossible to prevent their reassembling, as the whole force under my command consisted of only about 75 men and horses—many of the former recruits." In these circumstances the commanding officer was unwilling to detach part of his force, so that when he was in the lower part of the town dispersing a mob attacking the House of Correction, he was unable to do anything about another mob that attacked Colwick Hall, outside Nottingham, where they destroyed furniture, stole jewelry, and unsuccessfully attempted to fire the house. Apparently the same body of persons then proceeded to the unoccupied and undefended Nottingham Castle which, in the face of no resistance, was burned. The next day (October 11) a mob of about 200 burned a factory outside Nottingham (Mr. Lowe's at Beeston), again without encountering resistance until the destruction was completed. There also were reports of attacks on houses, at the very least involving window breaking, in nearby places—Loughborough, Chaddesden, and Mansfield. Altogether there was a good deal of petty violence, in addition to the destruction of the castle, the factory, and the partial destruction of property at Colwick.[1] No lives were lost; two persons were wounded by pistol.

1. Letters to the Duke of Newcastle, in Newcastle Papers (hereafter NeC), 5,001, 5,010 (Univ. of Nottingham); Lt. Col. Joseph Thackwell to Duke of Newcastle, ca. Nov. 1, 1831; H. C. Wylly, *The Military Memoirs of Lieut.-General Sir Joseph Thackwell* (London, 1908), pp. 96–100; *Annual Register for 1831*, Chr., p. 161; Thackwell to Melbourne, Oct. 14, 1831; Portland to Melbourne, Oct. 16, 1831, in H.O. 52/15. Col. Thackwell also alluded to difficulties at Sharp's Mill, the racecourse, and other places; the mob also broke into Wollaton Park (outside Nottingham) but apparently did no damage. The Borough records show expenditures of £10–16–3

Seventeen prisoners were taken, all but two by the military.[2] The violent feelings of the crowd were directed against the property of "obnoxious individuals" who had signed an anti-Reform petition and whose names appeared in a local paper.[3] The Duke of Newcastle, whose castle was burned, attracted hostility for having evicted pro-Reform tenants and then defending his action by asking, "May I not do what I will with my own?"[4] Feelings were such that, after the riot, he was reluctant to enter Nottingham for fear of provoking another. He was also urged to

---

for materials and labor used in repairing Sharp's Mill; and the expenditure of £29–7–11 for sacks of meal or flour and wheat either destroyed or carried away by rioters. Also, one George Stretton, a printer, applied for £5–12–0 compensation for damage done to his shop and dwelling by the stone-throwing mob. The mob that set fire to the factory at Beeston also entered a public house and "helped themselves. They took cheese, bread, and pork, and had beer and spirits." The publican reported hearing one of them say, "We have done the job completely": *Annual Register for 1832*, Chr., p. 12. *Records of the Borough of Nottingham, 8* (Nottingham, 1952), 403–05. The *Times* reported that the mobs consisted of 3–4,000 persons, mainly "young men and boys from the country": Oct. 13, 1831, p. 4.

2. Additional prisoners apparently were taken later, for 25 persons were either held for trial or in custody for examination, 20 of them to be charged with incendiarism. Two bodies were found among the ruins of the castle. The mistress of Colwick Hall (Mrs. Musters) "tho' killed by the newspapers" was in fact safe: NeC 5,004, 5,010, 5,013, 5,052. T. C. Hine, *Nottingham, Its Castle* (Nottingham, 1876), p. 40, n. (quoting an account of 1834 by John Hicklin).

3. Wylly, *Thackwell*, p. 96; Hine, *Nottingham, Its Castle*, p. 39, n. One of the victims described the harassment by a mob—a brickbat was thrown, his windows broken, some of the window frames, the stonework and interior of the house injured—the result, he said, of a paragraph in *Sutton's Review* commenting on his signing the petition "against what is commonly called 'The Reform Bill.' " A. Manson to Duke of Newcastle, Oct. 9, 1831: NeC, not numbered. A prospective victim, hearing that the mob was to pay him a visit, distributed a handbill asserting that he had not signed the anti-Reform petition: H.O. 40/28, ff. 822, 823.

4. Butler, *Reform Bill*, p. 298. Newcastle had planned to double the rents of reformers, and perhaps did. Denman, a candidate at Nottingham, gave great publicity to Newcastle's resentful observation: John Martineau, *The Life of Henry Pelham, Fifth Duke of Newcastle* (London, 1908), p. 28.

stay away by the Home Secretary as well as by his agent. At his house at Clumber, near Nottingham, an attack was expected and elaborate defenses were set up, but it never took place.[5] However, those persons attending the public meeting on October 10 had returned to their homes peacefully and the rioting, which came later that day, was carried on in a town with no professional police force and where the military consisted of but 75 men (41 had been sent to Derby on October 9). The yeomanry were called out, but they were not on duty until October 11, after the most destructive rioting had taken place the day earlier. Special constables were sworn, but accounts of the rioting give few details as to the role they played.[6] While those taking part in the riots were clearly moved by intense feelings, their persistence and success were also due to the evident weakness of the forces of order. On the first day the military "succeeded in dispersing the crowds in various parts of the town," but found that "small knots of the lowest rabble, however, still continued to glide through dark alleys and passages, and frequently succeeded in breaking windows before they could be interrupted." The castle was burned only because there was a shortage of troops. It was initially attacked by fewer than 50 men, and there were only 150 present when the fire broke out. At the time, the force of 75 soldiers in Nottingham was protecting the House of Correction, and all observers agreed that the castle could have been saved by a small force. When such a force finally was brought into play, 18 constables and 5 dragoons were sufficient to disperse the crowd.[7] The commanding officer thought it "worthy of remark, that whenever the military came in contact with the populace, the latter in being dispersed did not offer the slightest resistance

5. Wylly, *Thackwell*, p. 95; Melbourne to Newcastle, Oct. 31, 1831, H.O. 41/10; Letters to Duke of Newcastle, NeC 5,002, 5,007, 5,010, 5,011, 5,025.

6. *Annual Register for 1831*, Chr., pp. 161–62; *Annual Register for 1832*, Chr., pp. 9–13; Wylly, *Thackwell*, pp. 95–105.

7. NeC 5,000, 5,004, 5,015, 5,026, 5,030; Hine, *Nottingham, Its Castle*, pp. 39–40, n. The castle was used only by a few lodgers, but no employees of the owner were in the building: Martineau, *Newcastle*, p. 31. Town Clerk to Melbourne, Oct. 14, 1831, H.O. 52/15.

by throwing stones or otherwise."[8] It was only on October 11 with the arrival of five troops of yeomanry (almost 300 men and horses) that the available troops could be divided into separate parties, thus giving protection to several places at the same time. By October 12 order was restored and on the 13th the yeomanry dispensed with. By October 15 the Home Office was sufficiently confident about the state of the town (and Derby as well) that the 15th Hussars were considered to be available for service elsewhere if needed.[9]

Meanwhile rioting had taken place at Derby. Property damage was much less severe than at Nottingham, but at least three persons lost their lives. On Saturday evening, October 8, when news of the Lords' rejection arrived, there was "dejection" but no disturbances until a group of anti-Reformers loudly cheered. In retaliation a crowd formed and proceeded to break the windows at a shop where signatures had been collected for an anti-Reform petition. The crowd broke windows at the houses of six other anti-Reformers, and they also uprooted shrubbery and pulled up palisades. Three prisoners were taken.

The next morning (Sunday, October 9) the mayor called a

8. Wylly, *Thackwell*, pp. 96, 98. Col. Thackwell later mentioned exceptions to this statement. On Oct. 11 stones were thrown at the yeomanry and at the regulars, but the mob "were quickly chased away and a prisoner taken." That evening when prisoners were taken from the barracks to the county jail, stones were thrown which struck some of the escort. "A pistol shot was then fired which wounded two people, and this at once stopped the hostile proceedings of the mob, and from that moment they melted away, nor did they ever again make head in any part of the town": ibid., p. 100. The *Times* reported several skirmishes between populace and soldiers but that "the mob have never come into direct collision with the military, and have continued to disperse on their approach." The paper incorrectly stated that there was a regiment of hussars at Nottingham: Oct. 12, 1831, p. 5; Oct. 13, 1831, p. 4.

9. Wylly, pp. 100–01; Oskar Teichman, "The Yeomanry as an Aid to Civil Power, 1795–1867," part 2, 1831–1867, *Journal of the Society for Army Research, 19* (1940), 128; S. M. Phillipps to Gen. Bouverie, Oct. 13, 1831, H.O. 41/10, f. 228; Bouverie to Phillipps, Oct. 15, 1831, H.O. 40/29. The Home Office was informed on Oct. 13 that "all appearance of Riot has entirely ceased": mayor and magistrates to Melbourne, Oct. 13, 1831, H.O. 52/15.

meeting to consider measures to be taken in the event of additional disturbances, and this was the occasion of the first of the two serious episodes in the rioting at Derby. Among the mayor's audience was a group that called for the release of the prisoners who had been arrested the evening before. When this was not even considered, they proceeded to the borough jail to attempt a rescue. Shots were fired from the jail, and one bystander was killed; but the gate was smashed and 23 prisoners were released. An attempt was next made on the county jail. It was repulsed, but the four shots fired in its defense wounded three persons and killed a fourth (again apparently an innocent person) before the crowd dispersed. The nearest troops were at Nottingham, and the military aid from that place (a cavalry troop consisting of 41 soldiers and 3 officers) arrived at Derby some time during the early afternoon of October 9.[10] The attacks on both the jails as well as the window breaking of the day before had taken place before the soldiers arrived.

On the afternoon of October 9 some of the mob left Derby for Little Chester where they were not resisted as they attacked a house, breaking windows, pulling up ironwork, and setting furniture afire. Returning to Derby in the darkness they broke windows of both Reformers and anti-Reformers indiscriminately. When they threw stones at the windows of the Post Office "the military began to act, and with so much success, that before nine o'clock, the town was pretty well cleared."[11]

The second and final episode took place the following day (October 10). The mayor refused a request for a public meeting to protest the Lords' rejection of the Bill, but as an alternative he proposed setting up stalls where petitions to the government could be signed. When these were put up during the afternoon, they were immediately destroyed by a mob. The Riot Act was

10. Wylly, *Thackwell*, p. 95; Major Buckley to Melbourne, Oct. 10, 1831; under-sheriff at Derby to Melbourne, Oct. 11, 1831; C. H. Colville, Sheriff, to Melbourne, Oct. 14, 1831; "Statement of the Circumstances and Time of the Attack on the County Gaol," enclosed with J. Barber to Melbourne, Oct. 25, 1831; statement of J. Roberts, Keeper of Borough Gaol, Oct. 26, 1831, H.O. 52/12.

11. *Times*, Oct. 15, 1831, p. 5.

read, the soldiers were called, shots were fired, one man was wounded, and another innocent man standing at the door of a public house was accidentally killed.[12]

By the evening of the 10th the disturbances were ended. Special constables paraded the streets;[13] rain fell; and the yeomanry had arrived.[14] Altogether there were at least three deaths and "several" wounded.[15] The rioters were effectively dispersed whenever the soldiers made contact with them, but the soldiers adopted the unusual procedure of using firearms, apparently because occasional shots were directed at them from the crowd. Most of the damage was done in the absence of the soldiers. While the mayor

12. Ibid., Oct. 11, 1831, p. 4; Oct. 13, 1831, p. 4; Oct. 12, 1831, p. 5; Oct. 15, 1831, p. 5; *Derby Riots, The Trial of the Eleven Persons Charged with Breaking Open the Gaol of the Borough of Derby* (Derby, 1832), pp. iii–iv. It is difficult to know the composition of the crowds. It was claimed that there were few Derby adults among the rioters and that they mainly were youths and females: *Times,* Oct. 15, 1831, p. 5. A witness at the trial said that the 20 or 30 persons he spoke with appeared to be country people, and another observer thought many of the rioters, especially on Oct. 10, came from nearby villages: *Derby Riots. The Trial,* p. 21, and W. Lockett to Duke of Devonshire, Oct. 10, 1831, H.O. 52/12.

13. There is conflicting evidence with regard to the special constables. They were said to have paraded the streets, checking public houses on Oct. 10: *Times,* Oct. 15, 1831, p. 5. But another source reported that the "respectable inhabitants refuse to be made special constables." *Morn. Chr.,* Oct. 12, 1831, p. 2. Some months later when 11 men were tried for breaking into the jail, the judge noted that, "while the transaction . . . took place in broad day-light, and in the presence of many respectable persons, . . . no one of that character [came] forward on the prosecution," and he said that it appeared such persons either had a "criminal sympathy" with the rioters or "were afraid to appear against them." The prosecution relied on a witness who clearly had received a considerable sum of money for testifying and who had testified at the trial of a Nottingham rioter who was executed: *Derby Riots. The Trial,* pp. 10–11, 23.

14. Most of the rioting had ended when the yeomanry arrived—the Burton troop at 8 P.M. on Oct. 10; the Radborne troop during the night of the 10th; and at 11 P.M. two troops of Leicestershire yeomanry: *Times,* Oct. 15, 1831, p. 5.

15. There is conflicting evidence about the number of casualties. Cf. *Times,* Oct. 11, 1831, p. 4; Oct. 15, 1831, p. 5; and Town Clerk to Melbourne, Oct. 19, 1831, H.O. 52/12.

could not have prevented much of the rioting, the two most serious riots occurred after he had given the populace an occasion for coming together, first by calling the meeting on October 9, and then on the 10th by arranging for petitions to be signed.

The Bristol Riots

The riots at Bristol on October 29–31 were the occasion of violence unmatched by any other disturbance during the Reform Bill years. They began when Sir Charles Wetherell, Recorder of Bristol, arrived for the gaol delivery, an occasion that called for a public procession that he was unwilling to forego despite the anticipation of difficulty by the municipal authorities.[1] Wetherell prominently opposed the Bill in Parliament and, perhaps more important, he sat for Boroughbridge, a pocket borough that made him the nominee of the Duke of Newcastle, who thus figures, at least indirectly, as a target of riots in Bristol as well as in Nottingham. The crowds that assembled threw stones at the Guildhall and later the Mansion House, and at any building in which he was thought to be present; the crowd was so aggressive that it was necessary for the recorder to flee from the town in disguise during the night. The Riot Act was read and military aid called upon, but nevertheless the mob on this first day (October 29) "was only the same kind of mob that they have on elections—it was merely such a mob as they very often have."[2] The next day, however, the mob became much more destructive and late on Sunday, October 30, several public buildings were demolished and burned—the Bridewell, the gaol, the toll house, the dock gates, the bishop's palace, the Mansion House, the custom house, the excise house, and several private houses in Queen

1. George Lamb to B. N. Claxton, Oct. 17, 1831, H.O. 41/10, ff. 246–47; *Hansard*, 9 (Dec. 6, 1831), 59–61; *Trial of Charles Pinney, Esq. on an Information Charging him with Neglect of Duty in his office as Mayor of Bristol, during the Riots* (Bristol, 1833), pp. 252–53, 393.

2. Ibid., p. 404. Also, *Question:* "It appears that Bristol is always a very riotous place at elections?" *Mr. Hare, under-sheriff:* "At elections it is"; *Question:* "And there are bludgeon men hired to keep the peace?" *Mr. Hare:* "There are persons hired so called," in ibid., p. 266.

Square.[3] It is uncertain how many casualties there were. The highest (but widely challenged) contemporary estimate was 500, which mainly consisted of wounded. There were also uncounted persons believed to have died in burning buildings. The official estimate was 12 killed, 94 wounded.[4] Of the 102 prisoners taken, 81 were convicted, 31 of capital crimes. The sentence was carried out in four cases.[5]

3. Ibid., p. 407; John Eagles, *The Bristol Riots, their Causes, Progress, and Consequences* (Bristol, 1832), pp. 293–96. Apart from Corporation or Crown property, the damage was done at 35 addresses on or in the vicinity of Queen Square; this does not include 5 warehouses in the same area. This damage amounted to almost £56,000, not including legal and other costs. Of course, much more was claimed than this, which represents the amount given in damages (in all cases but one by agreement between the claimant and the Commission): *Report of the Commissioners Appointed under the Bristol Damages Compensation Act* (Bristol, 1835), pp. 7–9, 12, 14, and tables following p. 15.

4. Halevy, *Triumph of Reform,* p. 43; "The Riots at Bristol," *United Service Journal, 3* (1831), part 3, 441. Major Mackworth gave high estimates (at least 250), but combined killed and wounded in one figure: "Personal Narrative of Major Digby Mackworth," ibid., pp. 445–46. He was challenged by a Bristol editor who said there were 12 killed (from shots, 2; sword cuts, 2; burning, 6; excessive drinking, 2; and he indicates to which hospitals they were taken); and 96 wounded (from shots, 10; sword cuts and "contusions from the horses," 49; drinking, 2; other causes, unconnected with the military, 35; and again indicates hospitals where treatment was given). He adds that "besides the above, very many suffered in various ways. Some died before they could be conveyed to the Infirmary, and others were fearful of applying for assistance, dreading detection": W. H. Somerton, *A Narrative of the Bristol Riots* (Bristol, n.d. but 1832), pp. 29, 37. The discrepancy between these estimates may not be so great as appears, for Mackworth was inferring the number wounded according to "the usual proportion of wounded" to killed, a formula his colleague, Major Beckwith, gave as 100 to 1. The latter, however, confessed that he had no idea as to the number, as on the 31st "everything was done at a gallop": Mackworth to Somerset, Oct. 31, 1831, and Nov. 4, 1831; report of Major Beckwith, Nov. 2, 1831 (copies), in H.O. 40/28, ff. 27, 128, 192.

5. Eagles, *The Bristol Riots,* pp. 258–60. One man was sentenced to 14 years' transportation; 6 for 7 years' transportation; 11 to 2 years' imprisonment with hard labor; 32 to similar terms ranging from 1 month to 1 year; 20 were tried and acquitted; 8 were brought to trial but no evidence was offered against them.

The riots at Bristol have been interpreted in two different ways. They are usually taken as a clear indication of revolutionary fervor. Cole and Postgate, for example, saw them as an occasion for "the workers" to take "command of the city for several days" and as one of the chief events that justify the conclusion that "never since 1688 had Great Britain been so near actual revolution as in 1831." On the other hand, it can be argued that the riots could have been prevented and that they were not a portent of revolution; this judgment gets at least partial support from Halevy who notes the comparative ease with which order was finally restored at Bristol as compared with the 40,000 soldiers required to suppress the riots at Lyons in 1832.[6]

What evidence supports this argument? First of all, considerable force was available to those responsible for maintaining public order but was not used in accordance with orthodox military procedure. Three troops of cavalry had been sent to Bristol at the magistrates' request and were in the city on October 29. In addition, there were about 300 pensioners (retired soldiers) in the neighborhood and available for service in these situations, but they were not called. Yeomanry could also have been called, but it was not available until the last day when two troops aided the Dragoons in putting an end to the riots.[7]

The military units were commanded by Colonel Brereton, who faced a court-martial for his conduct at Bristol. On some occasions he refused to obey the mayor's request that the troops take any action necessary to disperse the mob. On other occasions he acted against the mob, but with tactics not adequate to the task. His reluctance to act could not have been motivated by concern about his legal responsibility for loss of life, for it continued to be evident after the mayor gave him broad discretion. He was

6. Cole and Postgate, *The Common People*, p. 248; Woodward, *Age of Reform*, p. 80; Halevy, *Triumph of Reform*, p. 51.

7. Two troops of 14th Light Dragoons were ordered to Clifton and one troop of 3rd Dragoon Guards to Bath as early as Oct. 22. The troops entered Bristol on the morning of Oct. 29: Somerset to Melbourne, Dec. 6, 1831, H.O. 40/28, ff. 271–72; *The Courts-Martial upon imputed neglect of duty during the Bristol Riots* (Bristol, Philip Rose, 1832), p. 79; *Trial of Pinney*, pp. 300, 308, 411.

deeply concerned about the possibility of civilian lives being lost in any conflict. When he wished to remove some of the troops from the town he explained that "they had the misfortune to kill a man on the preceding evening [October 29], and had again fired on the people that morning." When a subordinate officer acted independently and charged the crowds, Colonel Brereton "sat upon his horse, and said nothing; he gave no orders," and "remonstrated" with him. When the subordinate reported his own determination to disperse the mob the Colonel said, "If you do so, it is on your own responsibility."[8] The Colonel's humane sympathies made him reluctant to carry out the obligations required by his professional situation. As a result, when he did not withdraw into complete passiveness, he gave equivocal orders that left the troops uncertain as to what they were meant to do and what was forbidden. Thus, on one occasion he ordered the troops "to use the flat of the swords as *much as possible,* and not to proceed to extremities till absolutely necessary," and this order shortly after it was given was rescinded. This concern about the result of actual conflict led him to adopt a tactical position that had the effect of avoiding immediate conflict without intimidating the crowds. Having allowed attacks on the crowds, but having prevented the troops from attacking with the vigor or frequency that would have suppressed the rioting, he was faced with a mob that was provoked but not intimidated by fear of military retaliation. On one occasion he did not allow the troops to return the fire that was directed at them from the mob. And on still another he sent a troop to a gaol that was under attack with no orders except that they were "on no account to use any violence."[9]

There are several considerations that help to explain the hesitation and occasional passivity that prevented Colonel Brereton from ordering those severe measures which, in retrospect, and in the view of his superior officers, should have been undertaken. In addition to his humane feelings, and related to them, was the fact that he had lived in Bristol as head of the recruiting depart-

8. Ibid., pp. 420, 263, 187. However, Col. Brereton said the magistrates would not authorize him to use force: ibid., p. 186. But the court held that he had been authorized.

9. Eagles, *Bristol Riots,* pp. 288, 327; also see pp. 300, 309.

ment there for the previous three years, and knew many of the inhabitants.[10] This was contrary to orthodox principles of crowd control, and unusual in British practice as well, for ordinarily the officer commanding cavalry troops used for suppressing riots was moved to the town on very short notice and had little opportunity to develop any attachments to the populace. Indeed, this consideration also influenced the army's desire that such troops be provided barracks rather than billets, and it also was an objection to the use of yeomanry against rioting. Another explanation of Brereton's indecisiveness can be traced to confusion about the laws defining the responsibilities of military officers on such duty. Military regulations, sanctioned by the civil courts, held that a soldier was obliged to act against rioters even if the action was not authorized by a magistrate and regardless of whether the magistrate accompanied the soldiers. Personal responsibility was reduced by having civil authority to act, but even without such authority there was an obligation to act.[11] Yet there was a good deal of uncertainty about this anything but clearly defined obligation. Another officer serving at Bristol (Captain Warrington, 3rd Dragoons) faced a court-martial, and his defense in large part rested upon the claim that it was "the invariable custom for every detachment of military employed on that service, to be accompanied by one or more Magistrates," a claim he supported with a printed order issued during his service with the cavalry used against the rural incendiaries and machine breakers in 1830.[12] Thus Colonel Brereton was not alone in believing that he required the authority of magistrates, and his belief in part explains why,

10. Bryan Little, *The City and Council of Bristol* (London, Werner Laurie, 1954), p. 241; Wellington, *Despatches, 8,* 27; another reporter said he had been in Bristol eight years: *Courts-Martial,* p. 39.

11. *State Trials,* ed. Macdonell, n.s., *3* (Eyre and Spottiswoode, London, 1891) 1315.

12. "Instructions to Officers in Command of Detachments," issued at H.Q., Southwest District, Nov. 24, 1830, stated that an officer "is invariably to require a Magistrate to accompany him." Proceedings of Court Martial of Capt. Warrington: W.O. 71/280. *Courts-Martial,* pp. 78, 90. Warrington's main offense was that he absented himself from his quarters in order to consult the retired Gen. Pearson about his responsibility (p. 84); also see pp. 104–06.

for example, when he sent a detachment to the New Gaol (on October 30) which was under attack he said, according to the officer in charge of that detachment, "he could give me no orders to act, for he could find no magistrate to give him any orders."[13] It also affected his failure to arrange to keep in Bristol a troop of yeomanry (55 men) that arrived during the night of the 30th when some of the most destructive rioting was taking place, and left again because its commanding officer, having found Colonel Brereton, was unable to find a magistrate.[14] The continuing influence of Peterloo can be seen in this confusion over the legal obligation of the military officers who in a difficult situation had to choose between moderation and boldness and therefore the possibility, as one of them complained, of being accused of either rashness or indecision.[15]

Although Brereton's indecisiveness can be partially explained by his misunderstanding of his duty under military law and his humane reluctance to shed blood, his conduct also should be seen as a product of serious misjudgment of the situation. There is a pattern in his judgments of overestimating the difficulties of the situations and the power of his adversary and of underestimating the strength of his own forces. Thus on the 29th he tried to appease the crowd; on the 30th, seeing that this did not work, he thought only a strong military force could subdue what he later called "an overpowering, infuriated mob." On the other hand, he saw the military force as impotent; opposition to the mob on the 30th would have been "putting too much to hazard, supposing we had shot many of them, and dispersed them for the instant, they would have reassembled with considerably augmented numbers." On the afternoon of the 31st, after the rioting had stopped and despite the arrival of reserves, he still was pes-

13. Ibid., p. 35; also see p. 83.
14. This was the Doddington troop of Gloucestershire Yeomanry. Regulations prevented its commanding officer from acting on his own outside his own county: ibid., pp. 56, 60.
15. J. M. to Editor, in *United Service Journal, 3* (1831), part 3, 540–41. For evidence that Peterloo remained a landmark in contemporaries' memories, see *Peeps into the Past, being Passages from the Diary of Thomas Asline Ward,* ed. A. B. Bell (London, 1909), p. 301; T. Parkin to Melbourne, Oct. 20, 1832, H.O. 52/20.

simistic and expected "some desperate resistance, as the Colliers are coming in."[16]

This kind of judgment is best exemplified by his decision on October 30 to order the two troops of the 14th Dragoons, representing two thirds of his command, out of Bristol. Already on October 29 these troops had skirmished with the mob. Stones were thrown at the soldiers, injuring three of them; provoked by this, a shot was fired by a soldier, killing one of the rioters. Anger was now directed at the 14th who were restrained from responding to it as forcefully as they were able to do. There was additional skirmishing the next day, when another civilian was killed and three or four wounded by the 14th.[17] Colonel Brereton's response was to strike a bargain with the mob: if they would act peacefully and go to their homes, he would remove the 14th Dragoons from the city. He accordingly sent them to a town five miles away in order to avoid additional provocation to the mob. To its commanding officer he said, "It appears that the whole of the disturbance at this period is caused by the presence of the 14th Dragoons—you will be pleased, Sir, to take your troops home again immediately." Believing as he did that the disposition of the crowd was not excessively violent—on the first day he thought it would be sufficient to "ride through" and "walk away" the crowds—he decided that their anger was directed at the troops and that "the only chance of preserving the peace of the city was their removal."[18] Apparently he expected, or at least hoped, that by removing the soldiers there would be an abatement if not an end to all violence.

Several reasons were given in justification of this decision, and they all stem from his estimate of the relative strength of his forces and his adversary. The mob, he explained, "promised so

16. Brereton to Somerset, Oct. 30, 1831; Oct. 31, 1831 (copy); and Nov. 3, 1831 (copy); all in H.O. 40/28, ff. 21–22, 69–71, 149–54. The colliers did not arrive. He also thought emissaries from Birmingham had helped organize the mob. Col. Brereton and some of the riot scenes appear in Stanley J. Weyman's novel, *Chippinge* (London, 1906).

17. Brereton to Somerset, Oct. 30, 1831, H.O. 40/28 ff. 21–22; *Courts-Martial*, pp. 31–32.

18. Eagles, *Bristol Riots*, pp. 263, 287, 290; also see pp. 324–25. *Trial of Pinney*, p. 261; also see *Courts-Martial*, pp. 31–32.

earnestly to disperse to their homes, if the 14th should be withdrawn" and, with a "very revengeful disposition" toward those particular soldiers, they were "determined to massacre" them if they remained. Believing both these statements, Brereton justified his decision as a way of providing safety to the troops as well as the safety of the city. Expecting that reinforcements would be sent, he thought "it would be judicious to use every means that might abate their fury until the further aid was obtained." He also claimed that the soldiers were too exhausted to be effectively used.[19]

Colonel Brereton's decision was a matter of controversy, some of it connected with Corporation politics in Bristol. But the weight of professional opinion was against him. He did have the concurrence of a retired general living near Bristol who agreed that the troops ought to be removed.[20] Major Mackworth, an aide to Lord Hill, who was present throughout the three days, confirmed that on the 30th the populace was hostile to the soldiers and that the troops were very fatigued. But he did not concur in the decision to remove the troops, although he did recommend that the cavalry refresh at night, but without unsaddling. However, Captain Gage, commanding the two troops of the 14th Dragoons at Bristol, testified that Brereton did not address any inquiry to him about the condition and efficiency of his troops and that "the squadron was capable of performing any duty which cavalry could be called upon to perform." In addition, Major Beckwith, also of the 14th, thought that "there was from the beginning plenty of troops here to have prevented what has happened had they been properly employed," and in support of this he pointed out that on the morning of the 31st "the same squadron that had been ordered out of Bristol as being unable to pro-

19. Brereton to Somerset, Oct. 30, 1831; Nov. 3, 1831 (copy); and "Memorandum of occurrences at Bristol," Nov. 1, 1831, by Major Beckwith (copy); all in H.O. 40/28, ff. 22, 120, 152–53. Eagles, *Bristol Riots,* p. 326; Wellington, *Despatches, 8,* 27; *Trial of Pinney,* pp. 41–42, 186.

20. Brereton to Somerset, Oct. 30, 1831, which also states that "some other officers" concurred: H.O. 40/28, f. 22. Eagles, *Bristol Riots,* pp. 292, 301; *Courts-Martial,* p. 32; Wellington, *Despatches, 8,* 27. Brereton said the magistrates agreed to the arrangement; they denied it.

tect itself from the mob, without any assistance whatever . . . in about an hour . . . completely dispersed and intimidated the mob." Melbourne's first reaction to Colonel Brereton's decision was most skeptical. "The prudence of such a step," he said, "is very doubtful or rather not doubtful at all."[21]

The withdrawal of most of the troops accentuated the difficulty caused by the inadequacy of the civil force. This had been assembled with difficulty to begin with. On the first day it was found that many persons were unwilling to serve as special constables, and it was therefore necessary to hire men in this capacity. Of the 300 available on the first day, 200 went home before the day ended. Only 60 or 70 of the remaining 100 appeared as required on the morning of the second day. And those who did appear were poorly organized and even in disagreement with one another as to what was the proper course of action. They also refused to act without the aid and support of the troops, although most of these had been withdrawn. The indisposition to act among the special constables was matched by the magistrates' refusal to accompany a military officer who undertook to go out among the mob.[22]

---

21. Mackworth to Somerset, Oct. 31, 1831 (copy); Gen. Fane to Lord Hill, Jan. 13, 1832 (copy); and Beckwith to Somerset, Nov. 2, 1831 (copy); all in H.O. 40/28, ff. 25–26, 393, 125–26. *Courts-Martial*, p. 32; Melbourne to Brougham, Oct. 31, 1831, in Brougham Papers, 20,386; Eagles, *Bristol Riots*, p. 301. Melbourne also thought the magistrate had not taken sufficient precautions, but added, "It is impossible not to tremble for the situation in which [Col. Brereton] has left himself, by consenting to send the squadron of the 14th out of the town": Melbourne to Grey, Oct. 31, 1831, Grey Papers.

22. *Trial of Pinney*, pp. 185, 305, 307–08, 393, 405, 409, 411–13, 428–29. A large civil force, claimed to consist of 2,819 men, appeared only on Monday, Oct. 31. The Political Union enlisted members of the defense force only on this, the last day, when about 300 of its members formed part of this body. Its members were paid 3s. 6d. per day: ibid., pp. 254, 258, 264, 266–67, 413. Manchee says the original group of 300 special constables could have been larger, but that there was an "indisposition" among many persons to help protect Wetherell, who had "insulted" and "misrepresented" them in Parliament: T. J. Manchee, *The Origin of the Riots of Bristol, and the Causes of the Subsequent Outrages* (Bristol, n.d. but 1832), p. 13.

With the civil force small and unwilling to act, and with most of the troops withdrawn from the town, the mobs attacked public buildings and private dwellings with almost complete impunity. Most of the destruction took place while the 14th Dragoons were out of the town (late Sunday and early Monday, October 30–31). The aggressiveness of the mobs was increased by the apparent permissiveness of the troops that were present but inactive. When a mob assembled before the New Gaol a detachment of the 3rd Dragoon Guards was ordered out (this being the unit not withdrawn from Bristol). But Colonel Brereton ordered that in defending the building no violence was to be used against the rioters. The detachment thus "looked patiently on, while the rioters were busily and deeply engaged in their work of demolition."[23] The detachment departed, and 150 prisoners were released before the building was fired (after 3 P.M.). This incident, according to one observer, proved to be a catalyst:

> How to account for the most diabolical disposition which afterwards pervaded the multitude, is somewhat difficult, unless we again refer to the impunity with which every fresh outrage had hitherto been committed. The presence of the military at the New Gaol, and their speedy retreat must, in reality, have produced the greatest confidence in the mob, because it was a confession either of weakness or approval, —at least, so the mob interpreted it.[24]

This was followed by attacks on the toll houses (5 P.M.), the Bridewell (6:30), and Gloucester County Prison (7 P.M.): "The rioters, meeting with no kind of opposition . . . were now flushed with confidence of succeeding at whatever point they chose to direct their operations."[25] Soon after 7 o'clock the Mansion House was in flames, "to none of which firings was the slightest interruption attempted." Toward 8 P.M. the mob approached the

23. Eagles, *Bristol Riots,* pp. 293–94.
24. [Anon.] *A Narrative of the Dreadful Riots and Burnings, Which occurred in Bristol, on the 29th, 30th, and 31st of October, 1831, and the Destruction of Property and Lives Consequent upon them* (Bristol, Philip Rose, 1832), p. 15.
25. Somerton, *Narrative of Bristol Riots,* p. 24.

Bishop's Palace; Colonel Brereton arrived with a detachment, but it was "restricted from affording the slightest assistance to the constables and others to repress the outrages of the rioters . . . or to secure the prisoners which had been taken in the very act of plunder, or of outrage, within the Palace." The troops were then withdrawn, after which the "mob returned with an accession of numbers, the constables fled, and in less than half an hour the Bishop's Palace was in flames."[26]

It seems clear, from accounts of their effectiveness when they were allowed to act against the mobs, that the military forces could easily have prevented most of the rioting. On one occasion when an officer commanding a troop of the 14th Dragoons was left to his own discretion, "the rioters were promptly and effectually dispersed." On several occasions the mob dispersed upon the appearance of the cavalry and on others a small number of soldiers, in one case as few as four, effectively drove away a group of rioters. When, on the morning of the 31st, the one troop remaining in Bristol (consisting of about 25 soldiers and without any other aid) faced the rioters, their swords were "let loose" for the first time, and "the mob was promptly and repeatedly charged and dispersed," and when it was found that "bands of rioters and plunderers continued . . . to lurk" about, they were charged again and dispersed "in the most prompt and decisive manner."[27] When the two troops of the 14th Dragoons were brought back on October 31, again the mobs whenever encountered were "speedily dispersed" and the security of the city was restored.[28]

26. Eagles, *Bristol Riots*, p. 294; *Trial of Pinney*, p. 418; *State Trials*, ed. *Macdonell*, n.s., *3*, 1316; *Trials of the Persons Concerned in the Late Riots* (Bristol, Philip Rose, 1832), p. 23; Rev. Robert Gray (nephew of Bishop of Bristol) to Melbourne (?), Oct. 31, 1831, H.O. 40/28, ff. 58–59.

27. Eagles, *Bristol Riots*, pp. 288, 296–97; also see pp. 309–11; *Trials of Persons Concerned*, pp. 3, 68, 129; *Narrative of Dreadful Riots*, p. 11; *Trial of Pinney*, pp. 124–25, 148.

28. Eagles, *Bristol Riots*, p. 201; *Trial of Pinney*, pp. 186, 304–05, 413. There was a controversy about this charge by the 14th Dragoons. Somerton claimed that it was unnecessary, as the streets were mainly filled with innocent, respectable people many of whom were wounded, some killed. He also says the civil force, including the Political Union, were then organizing. Major Beckwith, who led the charge, claimed that the mob

Unanimity is not to be found among the observers of the riots. In contrast to most of the military officers, including the court that tried Colonel Brereton, there were several opponents to the Corporation of Bristol who mainly blamed the magistrates and therefore de-emphasized Brereton's responsibility as a way of strengthening their case against the Corporation. But these critics arrived at the same conclusion as the military officers—that the riots could have been prevented. They disagreed about the identification of the culpable party. Opponents of the Corporation charged the magistrates with many failings: not clearly giving Colonel Brereton authority to act; failing to organize the special constables; lacking the confidence of the populace and thus the ability to enlist a sufficient number of citizens as special constables; being themselves apathetic and irresolute, and even of being absent from the central scenes at critical times. Similarly, the civil force for which the magistrates were responsible was accused of being too severe and thus provocative (on the 29th), apathetic and irresolute (on the 30th), and generally negligent. Manchee, for example, said of the New Gaol that "twelve men might preserve it against any mob," and that "a very few resolute men might have laughed to scorn all the efforts of a dozen such mobs."[29] Yet no effort was made to save it. Place also blamed the civil authorities:

> Nothing could be more absurd, had he [the mayor] only an
> hour earlier with two or three others mounted their horses

---

was still plundering in Queen Square and along the quays, that the soldiers were assailed with stones and bottles, and that there was a report that additional houses were to be fired. The Rev. Dr. Carpenter, like Somerton, an opponent of the Corporation, was an eyewitness. He said innocent persons were on the streets, but that the order was "in the circumstances, right for the commanding officer to issue." Somerton, *Narrative of Bristol Riots,* p. 33; Nov. 1, 1831, H.O. 40/28, f. 122; Dr. L. Carpenter, "On the Bristol Riots," *Monthly Repository,* 5 (1831), 850.

29. Manchee, *Origin of the Riots,* pp. 29–30. Manchee (p. 29) exonerates Col. Brereton. Other opponents of the Corporation are somewhat equivocal in their judgments of him: Somerton, *Narrative of Bristol Riots,* p. 19; Place, Add. MSS 27,790, f. 146; Carpenter, *Monthly Repository,* 5 (1831), 847.

and gone quietly among the people they would have dispersed them. I have seen so much of large mobs, have assisted to disperse so many, and seen and been concerned in getting up so many meetings of immense numbers of people, that I may venture to say, that a very little judicious conduct on the part of the magistrates, even after the constables had shamefully misconducted themselves, would have dispersed even the Bristol mob.[30]

Thus, regardless of political views or civil or military status, there was agreement that the riots could have been prevented, indeed, easily prevented.[31]

In fact, both the magistrates and Colonel Brereton were culpable, although neither were quite so guilty as suggested in the biased reports that were inspired by Bristol political controversies and the invidious efforts to shift the blame. Brereton misunderstood the way military regulations defined his responsibility. Given his assumption that civil authority was required for his use of military force, he failed to establish effective communications with the magistrates. And in retrospect he does appear to have seriously misjudged the morale as well as the physical force of both the troops and the street crowds. On the other hand, the magistrates were not blameless. They had not effectively organized the constabulary. Nor had they established any permanent headquarters where they could be reached, so that, for example, when the yeomanry arrived during the night of the 30th they were not to be found. They also seem to have exercised what later proved to be poor judgment when on the 29th they directed the constables to appease the hostile crowd. Furthermore, they failed to exercise leadership in a way that might have given organization and morale to the civil force. The mayor faced a trial for neglect of duty, and although he was acquitted, he was severely

30. Place, "Account of the Bristol Riots" (written ca. 1834–36): Add. MSS 27,790, f. 145.

31. Somerton thought that deep discontents in the feudal social structure of Bristol made it very likely that hostility to the oligarchy would bring rioting as well as an unwillingness among the citizens to help maintain peace. However, he thought the riots unnecessary, all the same: *Narrative of Bristol Riots*, pp. 3–7, 29–30.

judged by public opinion. While such criticism was greatly exacerbated by the animosities of Bristol politics, it is clear that the magistrates' performance, though far from being criminal, was not worthy of emulation.[32]

An examination of the changing character of the street crowds —their size, composition, their attitudes, the words they used— will give additional support to the judgment that the riots might have been suppressed by the forces at hand. On the first of the three days (October 29th, a Saturday) the crowd was large, said to be "a dense mass of the populace," and it consisted of a variety of types of person, including some "depraved" persons "ripe for mischief," but also including many respectable persons, some of whom were there as spectators and others to express their disapproval of Sir Charles Wetherell.[33] There was a good deal of vituperative comment directed to him and to the Corporation with which he was affiliated. There were cries of "The King and Reform" and "We'll give them reaction," as well as hootings and expressions of contempt for the magistrates. These shouts were not made by the majority, but from various persons dispersed throughout the crowd.[34] There also was some violence—stones were thrown at the recorder during his brief appearances and at

32. Actually the mayor, unlike most of his brother magistrates, was a Reformer: *Trial of Pinney*, p. 49. There was an ad hoc committee of citizens established to inquire into the cause of the riots. Some of the deficiencies of the magistrates are illustrated in Major Beckwith's report of the conversation when he asked for a magistrate to accompany him in suppressing the riot. "They all refused to do so; upon which I put the same question to them individually . . . one stated that it would make him unpopular— another, that it would cause his shipping to be destroyed—another, his property . . . they also informed me that none of them knew how to ride on horseback, except one gentleman, and they pointed to the tall Mr. Alderman Hillhouse . . . [who then] said that he had not been on horseback for 18 years, and . . . he would hold any body responsible who said a second time that he could ride": ibid., p. 185.

33. Somerton, *Narrative of the Bristol Riots,* p. 12; *Narrative of the Dreadful Riots,* pp. 6, 10.

34. *Trial of Pinney,* pp. 38, 39; Somerton, *Narrative of the Bristol Riots,* p. 16; also see pp. 11, 12.

the mayor when, later in the day, he read the Riot Act. Missiles were also directed against the Mansion House windows, and in the evening efforts were made to break into it. But the respectable persons, who were clearly distinguishable, made up the vast majority, whereas the violence, though petty, came from a small group of about 50 persons. The majority (at 4 P.M.) were "moving about, but quiet in respect of their conduct. They were not acting offensively; not attempting to defend the Mansion-house, or to injure it; taking no part."[35] And in the evening the crowd was described in the same way:

> [they were] all classes; it appeared to me the violent classes were of a very low description, but the crowd surrounding was of the same description that I had seen in the morning, —all sorts of persons, all classes, respectable, well dressed people round; the actual agents of the mischief were the lowest.[36]

There seems no doubt that many of the respectable persons, although innocent of violence, had vicarious gratification from seeing the mob at work. For this reason a military officer who witnessed the scene reported that "party politics too had no mean share *at first* in countenancing if not encouraging the violence of the mob."[37] The crowd on this day appeared to another witness as similar to those usually found during elections. It was by no means unusual, and the testimony of an outsider who happened to witness the rioting on the 29th and some of it on the 30th is noteworthy:

> The mob appeared to me neither formidable in numbers or organization and it appeared to every one with whom I conversed that had there been the least energy or concert in the Civil Power that the riot might have been easily sup-

35. *Trial of Pinney*, p. 29; also see p. 258. On the presence of many spectators, see *Narrative of the Dreadful Riots*, p. 10.
36. *Trial of Pinney*, p. 261.
37. Mackworth to Somerset, Nov. 3, 1831 (copy): H.O. 40/28, f. 171.

pressed. Fifty of our London Police could, I am confident, have dispersed any one of the assemblages I witnessed.[38]

Next day (Sunday) there was the usual attendance at church, but by afternoon, with two of the three troops of cavalry removed and the remaining one not often on the streets, there was a gradual shift both in the composition, size, and activities of the populace. The opportunity to plunder and express elemental aggression with impunity attracted the lumpen-proletariat of the city which, although a tiny proportion of the total population, was larger than normal in a seafaring town such as Bristol. The persons predominating in the riotous mobs after midday on October 30th are most often identified as "the dregs of the city," sometimes as the Irish; and occasionally peasants and unemployed sailors are mentioned. Several observers also emphasized the youthfulness of the rioters.[39] The mob that was seen by midafternoon, when the demolition of buildings was under way, was described as follows:

> They did not consist of working men, mechanics, or artisans, or even working porters, but that they appeared to be of the grade of the shovel and pickaxe, or men that work in canals and dig out the foundations of houses, and such kind of work.[40]

38. P. S. L. Grenfell to Melbourne, Oct. 31, 1831: H.O. 40/28, ff. 63–64. The text of the letter indicates that he was in Bristol at least until midafternoon on Oct. 30. He also said he "was out a great deal both Saturday night and yesterday." Also see Somerton, *Narrative of the Bristol Riots,* pp. 30, 40.

39. *Narrative of the Dreadful Riots,* pp. 2, 5, 17–19; Carpenter, *Monthly Repository, 5* (1831), 847. Also, Beckwith to Somerset, Nov. 2, 1831 (copy), and Gore to Melbourne, Nov. 3, 1831: H.O. 40/28, ff. 128, 176. However, sailors were also seen defending property against rioters. Little points out that Bristol's declining importance as a port was especially hard on unskilled manual workers, that the percentage increase in the cost of relieving Bristol's paupers during the 15 years preceding 1831 had been almost three times that for all the country, and that the economic threat to the plantation trade due to Emancipation was already "in the air": Little, *City and Council of Bristol,* pp. 238–39.

40. *Trial of Pinney,* p. 104.

And another witness:

> They were, in appearance, of the poorest class, and the most
> ill-conducted. . . . they appeared to me to be sailors, and
> such men as are employed in the port of Bristol.[41]

And another witness described them as from "the lower grades
of society, some dressed in smock frocks, fustian coats, and
ragged attire generally—mean attire."[42] Confirmation of these
identifications came from the recovery of a great deal of the stolen
property in parts of the town described as the "lowest and dirt-
iest," adjectives the imprecision of which can only be reduced
by concrete description:

> The state of extreme filth in which many parts of this City
> now are, particularly those spots inhabited by the lower
> orders of Irish labourers in Host Street and Marsh Street
> where the apparently accumulated dirt of many years can
> be seen many feet deep. This horrible nuisance consists of
> [one word illegible], dead cats dogs and rabbits. Pig dung
> cesspools of stagnant water, decayed putrid vegetables and
> other such like dangerous substances. During the last few
> days hundreds of persons engaged like myself in searching
> different parts of the City for the property stolen during the
> late commotion have witnessed and can prove the above
> statement.[43]

41. Ibid., p. 124.
42. Ibid., p. 71; also see p. 126. The persons brought to trial were not
necessarily representative of the entire body of rioters, but an examination of their occupations, where given (in 25 cases of 102 brought to trial),
roughly confirms these descriptions but also indicates that the rioters were
a somewhat more varied group than the descriptions suggest. Insofar as
the unclear accounts allow for identification of occupation, 18 cases are
in keeping with the general descriptions of witnesses, 7 are exceptions:
Trials of the Persons Concerned, pp. 5, 25, 27, 34, 49, 57, 82, 101, 102,
104, 106–11, 117, 123, 124, 127, 131, 133–36.
43. H. N. Tomlins to Melbourne, Nov. 6, 1831: H.O. 40/28, ff. 196–97;
Narrative of the Dreadful Riots, p. 22, where it is noted that recovery of
stolen property in such areas shows that large numbers of the lower class
of Irish were employed in plunder if not incendiarism. An Irish priest

During the Sunday afternoon, and increasingly as evening approached, respectable people did not appear on the streets. In contrast to those seen in the morning, "they appeared to be a different sort of people,—dirty looking fellows." There never was a complete absence of spectators, but later that night "it was unsafe for any respectable person to remain in the Square." (The risk being theft not personal injury.[44]) Therefore it is not surprising that the crowds were much smaller in size than they were the previous day when persons of all ranks were seen in the crowd following the path of Sir Charles Wetherell. Although a few witnesses claimed that some of the crowds on Sunday numbered in the thousands, most give much smaller estimates, typically about 500, and the overt acts of violence were confined to smaller groups.[45] During the afternoon the mob vented its anger on the largely unprotected public buildings—on the three prisons, the Mansion House, the Bishop's Palace, and later the customs house. Although large quantities of spirits were found in some of these buildings, the motive was simple destructiveness. Later that night private homes in Queen Square were plundered before being burned by the small bands that are uniformly described as having been intoxicated, presumably with pilfered liquor.[46]

Was there still a political cast to this rioting? Possibly, during the Sunday afternoon. The attacks on the prisons may have been motivated by a desire to rescue those persons taken into custody by the constables or soldiers. But the other buildings—several of them Corporation property—may have had symbolic significance that was political, although Bristol (including ecclesiastical) more

offered to raise 200 volunteers to put down the riots, which the magistrates refused, but his testimony also indicates that some of his congregation may have plundered houses: *Trial of Pinney,* pp. 127, 129.

44. Ibid., p. 57; also see p. 126; Somerton, *Narrative of the Bristol Riots,* p. 31. On the presence of some spectators on Oct. 30, see *Trial of Pinney,* pp. 60, 64, 93, 103, 106.

45. *Trials of the Persons Concerned,* pp. 2, 3, 24, 41, 55; *Courts-Martial,* pp. 65, 69; *Trial of Pinney,* pp. 57, 70, 72, 93; Carpenter, *Monthly Repository,* 5 (1831), 847.

46. *Trials of the Persons Concerned,* pp. 8, 9, 11, 16, 17, 117, 119, 120; *Trial of Pinney,* p. 66; *Narrative of Dreadful Riots,* pp. 17, 19.

than national politics was the dominant motif. This is evident in occasional shouts of "Reform" or "d——d the b——y parsons," as well as in the exuberant, suicidal conduct of one Christopher Davis who, although intoxicated, stood out among the rioters as a man obviously not one of the dregs of society—he was a well-off, retired tradesman—and for his efforts to lead and encourage the mob. Among a quiet group he shouted: "The b——g parsons, the b——d bishops, the r——y corporation." He also expressed the wish that every church in Bristol be burned down, and said, "This is the end of your d——d magistrates and bishops."[47] Furthermore, on the Sunday there were still among the spectators politically minded persons who were tolerant of the mob, although they formed a minority of the assembled crowds.[48] But whatever political sentiments can be traced to rioters on the Sunday they represent occasional expressions noteworthy because they did not become widely adopted. There was no simple slogan such as was used during the Gordon riots or the Birmingham riots of 1791. In addition, those persons who were attached to the Political Union, who were probably the most activist on the reform side and most sensitive to the exclusiveness of the church and Corporation establishment, were notably aloof from the rioting.[49]

As the day wore on, however, whatever political motive activated that portion of the rioters soon disappeared. The violence was directed to property, not persons. Whereas missiles were thrown at the recorder and the mayor the day before, in many instances persons, including magistrates, safely walked among

47. *Trials of the Persons Concerned,* pp. 10, 35, 46, 106–11, 131; Pinney to Melbourne, Nov. 12, 1831, H.O. 40/28, f. 530.

48. *Trial of Pinney,* pp. 75, 306.

49. The political unions claimed that they offered to help suppress and prevent rioting from an early stage; others insisted that they did not come forth until Oct. 31 after most of the rioting ended. There was one suggestion that the leader of the Union, Herpath, was directing the mob, but this is most unlikely: Somerton, *Narrative of the Bristol Riots,* p. 22; *Trial of Pinney,* 264, 266–67; *Narrative of the Dreadful Riots,* p. 28; Herpath's account, quoted by Place, Add. MSS 27,790, ff. 153–54; Little, *City and Council of Bristol,* pp. 242, 246.

the rioting mob.[50] Furthermore, the buildings attacked were those in the vicinity of Queen Square, closest to the public buildings (other than prisons) that had been destroyed earlier in the day. Since many of the dwellings fired and plundered in Queen Square were lodginghouses for persons of modest means, it does not appear that rank, wealth, or politics of the victims played any important part in the selection of the targets.[51] Some contemporaries believed that the rioters were acting in accordance with a preconcerted plan; but this is doubtful, especially as the weapons they used—iron railings, clubs, timber from the quays, bottles, stones, and only very rarely firearms—were things at hand and hardly suggest advance preparation. Indeed, far from there having been an organized conspiracy, it is unlikely, as the composition of the mob on Sunday night indicates, that after the first day there was a conscious political purpose.

Meanwhile, most of the populace of 100,000, including those who had been on the streets from curiosity or in order to hoot, and perhaps even to pelt, the recorder, went to their homes, and the Sunday night "was one of fear and watchfulness." Even for those who looked on permissively at the disorder of October 29th the later scenes inspired terror and, once the danger ended, indignation. When on the morning of October 31st the two troops, removed the day before, were returned to the city, they were brought through "one of the worst parts of the city, inhabited by the lower orders, and at the doors we were welcomed with exclamations of delight and joy." Later that day still more soldiers were brought in, "much to the joy and security of all."[52] Had there been the makings of revolution, the situation on Sunday evening—with the magistrates feeling helpless, most of the soldiers departed, and the remaining ones encouraging rioters by their hesitancy—would have invited it. What in fact followed was a widespread expression of horror by the respectable among all

50. *Trials of the Persons Concerned*, pp. 23–24, 147; Add. MSS 27,790, f. 144; *Trial of Pinney*, pp. 102, 104.

51. J. Gardiner (post master at Bristol) to Sir Francis Freeling, Nov. 2, 1831 (copy): H.O. 40/28, f. 145.

52. Carpenter, *Monthly Repository*, 5 (1831), 849, 851; *Trial of Pinney*, p. 307.

classes, including the artisans. Thousands of persons tardily enlisted as special constables or as part of the *posse comitas* during
the subsequent week.[53]

In contrast to Bristol and Derby and Nottingham, the reaction
to the Lords' rejection elsewhere in the country was quite tame.
Whether this was due to more effective control by the civil authorities and their military support or to more tepid feelings
among the people is difficult to judge. In Scotland, where there
had been election riots in the spring, at most there were only
petty disturbances. From Ayrshire, where there had been some
disturbance earlier in the year, the Lord Lieutenant reported that
the rejection had not produced the excitement that might have
been expected. Only at Girvan was there disturbance, though not
serious, and political causes had only a small part in bringing it
about. Cockburn reported that at Edinburgh interest in the Bill
was great, with large crowds, sometimes numbering 10,000 waiting for news. When it arrived, he said, "after the first shock they
separated in silence." And the *Scotsman* reported that the people
"dignified their cause by calmness," and that there was "not the
slightest outward expression of irritation," though in the evening
some mischievous boys annoyed passengers and broke street
lamps before the police dispersed them.[54] At Leeds, a plan to
bring operatives and farm laborers away from work to protest
the Lords' rejection met with failure.[55] There were no dis-

53. Ibid., p. 413; *Narrative of the Dreadful Riots*, pp. 20–21; Mackworth to Somerset, Nov. 3, 1831 (copy), H.O. 40/28, f. 172.

54. Glasgow to Melbourne, Oct. 17, 1831, H.O. 102/41, f. 164; Cockburn, *Memorials, 1,* 24 (entry of Oct. 14, 1831); *Scotsman,* Oct. 12, 1831,
p. 7. Mrs. Arbuthnot recorded in her diary that "Chas's regt was sent
off at an hour's warning from Winchester to Edinburgh. But it turns out
the people are perfectly tranquil and take the loss of the Bill with a calmness and resignation. . . . Chas writes us word the people of Edinburgh
only desire *to be let alone,* and all over the country they are evidently
tired of the Bill": (entry of Oct. 23, 1831) *The Journal of Mrs. Arbuthnot
1820–1832,* eds. Francis Bamford and the Duke of Wellington, 2 (London,
Macmillan, 1950), 432.

55. A. S. Turberville and F. Beckwith, "Leeds and Parliamentary
Reform, 1820–1832," *The Thoresby Miscellany, 41,* 39. A report from
Leeds said, "This place is quiet, that is, there is no mischief done, except

turbances at Birmingham; an American resident there, asked to report to the Embassy in London on "the state of the Public mind in this place in regard to the rejection of the Reform Bill," was able to state that "all here is tranquil"; and Lord Lyttleton, a supporter of the Bill, reported from Birmingham that, while the public supported the Ministry, the city was "particularly quiet and prosperous and well-disposed just now."[56] Nor were there riots or any disturbances at Leicester, Sheffield, Hull, Newcastle, Sunderland, Durham, or Liverpool, where a Reform meeting of about 10,000 "separated in the most quiet and orderly manner."[57] This does not mean that there were no petty disturbances. At Darlington on October 16, Lord Tankerville, an anti-Reformer, was the target of stones thrown at his coach as he departed from the town. The commander of the Northern District, General Bouverie, reported that "symptoms of Riot" had appeared at Carlisle and that threats were directed against the Bishop, for

---

hanging and burning in effigy Wellington, Wharncliffe, and another Lord": *Times,* Oct. 15, 1831, p. 6. Cf. Hobsbawm: Leeds "demonstrated and rioted as enthusiastically for the Reform Bill as any other place," in "Methodism and the Threat of Revolution in Britain," *History Today* (Feb. 1957), p. 120.

56. Lyttleton to Earl Spencer, Oct. 29, 1831, in *Correspondence of Lyttleton,* p. 266. Peter Irving to Van Buren, Oct. 12, 1831, among Despatches from U.S. Ministers to Great Britain, 1791–1906, 38 (National Archives, Washington, D.C.). The first name of the correspondent is not legible, but his identity is clear from Pierre M. Irving, *Life and Letters of Washington Irving,* 2 (New York, 1869), 201. The letter is dated 12 Sept. 1831, but this is clearly an error. Apart from the internal evidence, the letter is postmarked Oct. 13, 1831; furthermore, an October date can be inferred from the whereabouts of the recipient and Washington Irving, who asked his brother to write it.

57. Patterson, *Radical Leicester,* p. 187; H.O. 41/10, ff. 233, 235; Sidney Pollard, *A History of Labour in Sheffield* (Liverpool Univ. Press, 1959), p. 44; William Banning to Sir Francis Freeling, Oct. 12, 1831, H.O. 40/29; Burbridge at Leicester to Phillipps, Oct. 13 and Oct. 14, 1831, H.O. 52/14. The Liverpool meeting was on Oct. 12. There was some disorder later in the month on the occasion of an election. As the successful candidate, Lord Sandon, took the chair, missiles were thrown; he was hit with a dead cat, but the "noble member . . . bore it all with impervious good temper." This comparative mildness is especially noteworthy inas-

whom protection was provided.[58] At Manchester after several days of complete tranquillity, there were a few petty disturbances. At a meeting on October 12, members of the National Union of Working Classes seized the hustings from the leaders of the more moderate union that had organized the meeting. But passions were not so aroused as to cause a fight; the "respectable" persons left the meeting, however, leaving only country people, Irish weavers, and "no inconsiderable number of thieves and pickpockets." The *Manchester Guardian* claimed that the "Huntite" union had urged people to come armed, but that "the bulk of the labouring classes . . . positively refused to have anything to do with such desperate schemes."[59] However, "it was thought to be inconsistent with the safety of the town, to permit [meetings of the "low" political union] to go on," and the magistrates, with military support, decided to prevent such a meeting on October 14. Actually, the meeting, consisting of 500 to 1,000 persons, dispersed before the troops arrived, but a mob of two or three hundred was found attacking a private dwelling; but it "dispersed in all directions upon seeing the troops," having broken a few panes of glass. The chief magistrate regretted the measures taken only because "one cannot prevent the exaggerations with which they may be reported." A meeting was planned for October 17 by the National Union of Working Classes; the mills were to be stopped and the employees forced to attend. The meeting was

---

much as Sandon, a son of Lord Harrowby and an advocate of a much more moderate Bill, had defeated a pro-Reform Bill candidate (Thornly): Picton, *Memorials of Liverpool, 1,* 438. There were meetings at Newcastle on Oct. 17 and 25, at Durham on Oct. 31, at Sunderland on Oct. 27 and Nov. 10: John Sykes, *Local Records; Historical Register of Remarkable Events, which have occurred in Northumberland and Durham, Newcastle-upon-Tyne, and Berwick-upon-Tweed, 2* (new ed., Newcastle, 1866), 320–22, 333–34. Mayor of Liverpool to Melbourne, Nov. 2, 1831, H.O. 52/13; Town Clerk at Hull to Melbourne, Oct. 12, 1831, H.O. 52/15.

58. T. Bowes at Darlington to Melbourne, Oct. 22, 1831, H.O. 52/12; Bouverie to Phillipps, Oct. 17, 1831, H.O. 40/29.

59. *Manch. Guard.,* Oct. 15, 1831, p. 3, and Nov. 12, 1831, pp. 3–4. The chief magistrate also reported that the 8–10,000 persons dispersed "in the most peaceable manner." Foster to Melbourne, Oct. 10, 11, 12, 13, 1831: H.O. 52/13.

canceled, the town was perfectly tranquil, and General Bouverie was not apprehensive about the maintenance of public order.[60]

On the whole, the country reacted to the Lords' rejection without violence. In London and most major towns order was preserved without difficulty. Where it was interrupted, it was quickly restored and, with the exception of Bristol, with no great difficulty.

Industrial Conflict

As November began there was much apprehension of disturbance even though no serious outbreaks were to occur. The events at Bristol could well have caused the nervousness, for the vulnerability of towns without professional police forces and their dependence on military aid was made evident to all. Apprehension was increased by the knowledge that Henry Hunt was touring Midland and northern towns. A proclamation was issued (November 2) warning subjects against violations of the law and urging them to come to the aid of the magistrates should disturbances take place.[1] The Home Secretary also prohibited a meeting that had been announced by the National Union of the Working Classes in London.

The disturbances that did take place in November and December were concentrated in the vicinity of Birmingham—in mining towns in Staffordshire, Warwickshire, and Worcestershire—though not in Birmingham itself. In most of these cases the Reform Bill was not the occasion for the disturbances; rather, it was a strike for higher wages by colliers (or for maintaining the previous wage in the face of owners' determination to reduce it), and the violence frequently was caused by disputes between men willing to work at a wage determined by the owners and those attempt-

60. Shaw to Somerset, Oct. 17, 1831, and Foster to Melbourne, Oct. 14, 15, 19, 1831: H.O. 52/13. Bouverie to Phillipps, Oct. 17, 20, 1831: H.O. 40/29. Bouverie also reported: "No meeting was attempted and every thing remained quiet. Delegates have been sent from Manchester through the neighborhood and as far as Macclesfield to endeavour to get a large meeting together upon Kersall Moor, should it take place, it will be watched and no mischief need be apprehended."

1. *Annual Register for 1831,* Chr., p. 178.

ing to make the strike effective.[2] Dudley was the most troubled place. Miners from this neighborhood marched on Wolverhampton on November 30; on the same day prisoners were released from the Oldbury court house before yeomanry and regular troops suppressed the riot, taking 120 prisoners in the process.[3] At Bilston the magistrates reported "riotous proceedings" among the colliers. There was "a spirit of obstinacy" that was made evident, not in rioting, but in "petty acts of aggression and robbery." The yeomanry was called out, special constables enlisted, and the regular troops at Wolverhampton and Birmingham were increased. Order was maintained but, in the opinion of a magistrate at Bilston, "maintained solely by force." The *Birmingham Journal* shared this view: "it is solely by the display and active watching of large bodies of soldiery that . . . such of the colliers as have not yet returned to work, are prevented from committing acts . . . [of a] flagrant nature."[4] There were disturbances at Wellington as well; and bands of men from Staffordshire tried to prevent the men from working at some of the colleries and ironworks in Shropshire. However, the troops were effectively used to prevent the assemblage of colliers disposed to riot and to frustrate most of the attempted turnouts.[5] Throughout this area the magistrates were exceedingly nervous, making gloomy prophecies and de-

2. George Dalton (at Dudley) to Home Office, Dec. 8, 1831, H.O. 40/29; Phillipps to magistrates at Dudley, and Phillipps to William Leigh at Bilston, Dec. 2, 1831, H.O. 41/10, ff. 451–52; magistrates at Dudley to Melbourne, Dec. 5, 7, 1831; and magistrates for Worcestershire and Staffordshire to Melbourne, Dec. 3, 1831, H.O. 52/15.

3. Teichman, "Yeomanry as Aid to Civil Power," *Journal of the Society for Army Historical Research, 19,* 135. Clerk of Justices at Halesowen to Melbourne, Dec. 3, 1831: H.O. 52/15.

4. J. Case and W. Leigh (at Bilston) to Melbourne, Nov. 30, 1831, and Leigh to Melbourne, Dec. 4, 1831, H.O. 52/15; Phillipps to magistrates at Wolverhampton, and Phillipps to magistrates at Dudley, Dec. 2, 1831, H.O. 41/10, ff. 450–52; *Birm. J.,* Dec. 10, 1831, p. 3.

5. B. Smith to Sir F. Freeling, Dec. 7, 1831, H.O. 40/29; *Birm. J.,* Dec. 10, 1831, p. 3. This letter clearly refers to miners and colliers, but Teichman erroneously refers to these riots (and others in nearby places) as the "last riots due to the Reform Bill": "Yeomanry as Aid to Civil Power," p. 136.

manding troops from the Home Office.[6] However, the disturbances did not achieve the seriousness of those at Nottingham, to say nothing of Bristol. Toward mid-December the strike ended and conflict subsided. Although minor disturbances continued to take place, most of the violence ended with the return of the colliers to work. It was then reported at Wolverhampton, Bilston, West Bromwich, Walsall, Tipton, Dudley, and Stourbridge, where the previous week there had been symptoms of disorder, "in no instance has violence been resorted to," indeed, "quietness prevails."[7]

These riots were never uncontrollable and damage and injury appears not to have been serious. However, the persistence of petty violence was the source of apprehension, for it was evidence of what a Home Office official called "the spirit of insubordination among the colliers."[8] While threats to public peace mainly came from the mining district around Dudley at this time, there were enough reports of scattered disturbances to add to this apprehension. There had been disturbances in the southwest at the end of October and early in November—at Blanford in Dorset, at Yeovil, Tiverton, and Exeter.[9] At Worcester a county reform meeting was undisturbed, but rioting broke out late at night abetted, per-

6. E. Grove (Lichfield) to Melbourne, Dec. 10, 1831, and magistrates at Dudley to Melbourne, Nov. 8, 1831: H.O. 52/15.

7. Magistrates at Dudley to Melbourne, Dec. 15, 1831, H.O. 52/15; Phillipps to clerk of the magistrates at Dudley, Dec. 16, 1831, H.O. 41/10, ff. 496–97; *Birm. J.*, Dec. 17, 1831, p. 3, and March 10, 1832, p. 3.

8. Phillipps to T. Badger (at Dudley), Dec. 1, 1831: H.O. 41/10, f. 447.

9. H.O. 41/10, ff. 261–63, 288–89, 293; Teichman, "Yeomanry as Aid to Civil Power," p. 134. The Bishop of Exeter made light of the disturbances of Nov. 5. Although he anticipated "serious mischief" and perhaps even "insurrection," next day he reported that "the night has gone off with little more excitement than is, I understand, usual on the 5th of November. . . . Though there were no regular troops at hand, the magistrates were able to put down the attempts of the mob": Phillpotts to Wellington, Nov. 5–6, 1831, in Wellington, *Despatches, 8,* 35–36. The disturbances at Tiverton arose from a strike by 380 lace workers for higher wages, and clearly did not involve reform politics: Mayor of Tiverton to Melbourne, Oct. 8, 24, 1831; however, at Sherborne, near Yeovil, disturbances on Oct. 19–22 had a political flavor: J. Goodford to Melbourne, Oct. 27, 1831, H.O. 52/12.

haps, by Guy Fawkes celebrations. After a peaceful day, a crowd congregated, attracted by fire alarms. This was followed by some broken windows, skirmishes with special constables, the reading of the Riot Act, and a call upon the military, which cleared the streets, but only after inflicting saber cuts on two persons and taking 27 prisoners.[10] Two days later (November 7) there was a disturbance at Coventry, but it was entirely apolitical. Disgruntled weavers met to discuss their grievances—the masters had only recently introduced new power looms and reduced the prices paid for weaving. About 200 of them attacked a newly erected factory where they demolished the power looms, threw silk and ribbons from the windows, and violently attacked the owner. Soon afterward the building was fired, the Riot Act read, the troops called and, following a typical pattern, the streets were · cleared, a few prisoners taken, and public order was restored.[11]

Incendiarism, mainly in some six southern counties, which had been so frequent during the winter of 1830–31, continued at this time, although the rioting and the breaking of threshing machines that had accompanied it now ceased.[12] There was also unrest in

10. C. Ridert (Worcester) to Home Office, Nov. 6, 1831, H.O. 52/15; G. Lamb to Mayor of Worcester, Nov. 7, 10, 1831, H.O. 41/10, ff. 350, 372–73; *Birm. J.*, Nov. 12, 1831, p. 3; T. C. Turberville, *Worcestershire in the Nineteenth Century* (London, 1852), pp. 273–75.

11. J. Morris, Mayor of Coventry to Lord Warwick, Nov. 8, 1831, H.O. 52/15; G. Lamb to Mayor of Coventry, Nov. 10, 1831, H.O. 41/10, ff. 370–71. The day following the riot a report was sent to the Home Office stating that the town "is perfectly tranquil and [there is] no appearance of it being again disturbed": S. Vale to Home Office, Nov. 8, 1831, H.O. 40/29. *Birm. J.*, Nov. 12, 1831, p. 3, and March 31, 1832, p. 3.

12. An insurance office complained that the government's measures were inadequate and claimed that the fires were breaking out even more often than the previous winter. Incendiarism "continues to increase and . . . the burnings of the present season far outnumber those of last Winter. . . . in some districts [it] seems to have now grown into an habitual indulgence": B. Beaumont, County Fire Office, Regent Street, to Melbourne, Dec. 15, 1831, H.O. 40/29. Halevy notes that these riots "were of a very mild description." There was looting, but personal violence was infrequent, and they were "all confined to particular areas": Halevy, *Triumph of Reform*, p. 9. J. L. Hammond and Barbara Hammond, *The Village Labourer*, 2 (London, Guild Books, 1948), 111, n. 1 and passim.

the coal districts of Wales and around Newcastle; while these districts were now quiet, during the previous spring this unrest had led to violence and there was a possibility that it could do so again. At Preston on November 7 there was serious rioting when "Hunt's mob" went to a local factory where they "forced the work people from the factories and workshops, and put a stop to all business." Their purpose was to increase the attendance at a meeting scheduled for this day. In the process they damaged machinery (in order to prevent work from continuing) and broke windows wherever they were resisted; at one place they also destroyed books and papers as well as part of the counting house. The mob then went to the jail, released a few prisoners, and set fire to the books and papers. There were several injuries, and the military was called before order was restored.[13] Such incidents were isolated, however. In mid-November Cockburn said of Scotland, where there had been disturbances during the elections in the previous spring, that the country "is still in a most excited and uncomfortable state, but disgraced by no violence."[14] In Leeds, even though Hunt was to speak, "everything went off quietly." He did not go to Woodhouse Moor "in consequence of the very few people which assembled to meet him"; instead he spoke from a hotel window "to about 200 persons who dispersed immediately." [15] However, there was enough evidence of unrest and in some cases of actual disturbance for Melbourne to comment on a report of a fire set on a heath that "altho' the damage may not be material, [it] is evidence of the prevalence of a most mischievous spirit."[16] While there were comparatively few disturbances, there was no genuine tranquillity either.

13. R. Sanderson (?) at Preston, to Freeling, Nov. 7, 1831, H.O. 40/29; Phillipps to Mayor of Preston, Nov. 16 (?), 1831, H.O. 41/10, f. 403; J. Dixon, Mayor of Preston, to Melbourne, Nov. 7, 9, 1831, H.O. 52/13. "All accounts from S. Wales concur in there being no cause for alarm there; at least of disturbance of a serious nature": Sir R. Jackson to Fitzroy Somerset, Nov. 27, 1831 (copy), H.O. 40/28, f. 263; also see his letter of Dec. 25, 1831, at f. 304.
14. *Memorials, 1,* 25 (entry of Nov. 14, 1831).
15. Bouverie to Phillipps, Nov. 10, 1831: H.O. 40/29.
16. Melbourne to Newcastle, Nov. 16, 1831: H.O. 41/10, f. 408.

The prevalence of grievances and hostilities under such unstable conditions made the country vulnerable to the harnessing of industrial and agricultural discontents to a political movement. Yet this did not take place. The rural disorders in the southern counties were not directed to political objects. The grievances all concerned the immediate environment of bread and work and hope and fear for the future. The cause—if one can be isolated— was the threat held out by the introduction of threshing machines (and this was a threat not only to employment but to the substance of life as it was experienced by the farm laborer).[17] There is no evidence that the rioters were seeking change in any political institution or that they saw any connection between their actions and the urban Reform movement. The fears engendered by incendiarism were stimulated by efforts of urban reformers like Place and Wakefield to facilitate the progress of the Parliamentary Reform agitation, and they contributed to the general fear of social upheaval.[18] But there is no evidence that the rioting in the countryside was the result of a coordinated plan (though this was suspected at the time) or that urban reformers seeking political

17. The grievances were "against the poor law, the game laws, tithe, enclosures, wage rates, machinery; with a background of unemployment and dear bread, during the wet ungenial years 1828–9, against which had flared up the Paris Revolution of July. A promise of 2 s. a day certain, wet or dry, often sent them away content." The threshing machine, Clapham points out, was slow to be introduced in southern England and the hand flail was still more common there than elsewhere in the country. The risings "occurred just when the battle of machine *versus* arms was well joined": J. H. Clapham, *An Economic History of Modern Britain. The Early Railway Age 1820–1850* (Cambridge Univ. Press, 1950), pp. 139–40. David Williams, *The Rebecca Riots. A Study in Agrarian Discontent* (Cardiff, Univ. of Wales Press, 1955), pp. 74, 109.

18. Place, *An Essay on the State of the Country*, pp. 13–15; Wakefield, *Swing Unmasked*, pp. 5–6, 45–46; Roebuck, *History of the Whig Ministry, 1*, 334–38; Vizetelly, *Glances Back, 1*, 65. The rural disorders were one of the dominant themes in the prints of the time, at least until March 1831, when the Reform Bill was introduced: M. Dorothy George, *English Political Caricature 1793–1832. A Study of Opinion and Propaganda, 2* (Oxford, Clarendon, 1959), 241–42.

goals were connected with the organizing or instigation of such riots.[19]

Nor is there any indication that the Midland miners who took part in the rioting were closely connected with the political movement. Magistrates reporting to the Home Office were emphatic in asserting that the disturbances in the mining areas of Staffordshire were apolitical. From Bilston in November 1831 they wrote that the riotous proceedings "are not connected in the remotest degree with any political feeling whatever," and the same observation came from Dudley and Wolverhampton.[20] Of course, magis-

---

19. The government attempted to connect Carlile and Cobbett with the disorders and prosecuted them for seditious libel—Carlile successfully, Cobbett not. Carlile's conviction does not establish that he instigated the rioting, nor did the prosecution's case depend on establishing that his publication addressed to the agricultural laborers was sold in or brought to the disturbed district: *State Trials*, ed. J. Macdonell, n.s. 2, 609–10. These riots had a primitive, "pre-political," even traditionalistic character, resembling what Talmon calls an "elemental outburst," more like a jacquerie than revolution. See J. L. Talmon, *Political Messianism. The Romantic Phrase* (London, Secker and Warburg, 1960), p. 26; George Rudé, *The Crowd in the French Revolution* (Oxford, Clarendon, 1959), p. 236; E. J. Hobsbawm, *Primitive Rebels*, pp. 2, 67, 79–80, and passim. There were riots in another rural district in June 1831, when men wandered through the Forest of Dean tearing down the fence enclosing timberland, but the Home Secretary was certain "that neither reform or any other political feeling has any thing to do with them." Melbourne to Grey, June 11, 1831, and Beaufort to Melbourne, June 15, 1831: H.O. 52/12. There also were continuing disturbances at Otmoor, in Oxfordshire, over the use of common land. Magistrates to Melbourne, April 27, July 10, 28, 1831: H.O. 52/15; W. H. Ashurst to Melbourne, Jan. 23, 1832: H.O. 52/19.

20. Case and Leigh to Melbourne, Nov. 30, 1831: H.O. 52/15. From Dudley came the statement, "The disturbance does not appear to be at all connected with politics": George Dalton to Home Office, Dec. 8, 1831. From Wolverhampton came the statement that "the present Disturbed state of this part of the Country . . . does not arise from any political cause but from the Depreciated state of trade and the consequent low price of labour to the Work People": William Penn and St. John Square to Melbourne, Dec. 19, 1831, H.O. 40/29. Mackintosh complained that the Opposition "have thrown all the danger of the times upon . . . Reform. They load it with as much odium as if the age were otherwise altogether exempt from turbulence and agitation": *Hansard, 4* (July 4, 1831), 691.

trates might not have been the most sophisticated analysts of causes in these matters. But such observations do indicate that in stating their grievances the colliers did not make frequent reference to the slogans and arguments connected with the Reform Bill. Yet if industrial discontents were to be the cause of violent action that was directed at political objects and rationalized in terms of the struggle over the Reform Bill, this was most likely to occur in the area around Birmingham late in 1831. Efforts were made to organize political unions. Meetings were held at which aspirations could be stated and hostilities expressed. Yet this did not lead to violence. The rioting that did take place was unconnected with Reform Bill politics.

The same holds for the mining districts of Wales and the area around Newcastle where there also was unrest. Here too the miners' grievances were not harnessed to the Reform agitation. In Wales the unrest was caused by resentments against the truck system, wage reductions, and lockouts by employers resisting efforts to organize trade union clubs. There were strikes as well as lockouts.[21] Violence was frequent and occasionally serious. The most notable example occurred at Merthyr in June 1831, when as many as 25 persons may have been killed as rioting miners attacked soldiers. Although disturbance had first occurred during the election in the previous month (the homes of three electors were attacked), and although political discussion had encouraged the statement of grievances, the riot in June was occasioned by the strike brought on by a reduction in wages by the mine owners.[22] During the politically critical months of October

21. Ness Edwards, *The History of the South Wales Miners* (London, Labour Publishing Co., 1926), pp. 10–15, 25–31; David Williams, *A History of Modern Wales* (London, John Murray, 1950), pp. 229–36. A. H. Dodd, *The Industrial Revolution in North Wales,* 2d ed. (Cardiff, Univ. of Wales, 1951), pp. 403–07.

22. See pp. 208–09, n. 16, below for an account of this episode and pp. 230–31, n. 39, for the related encounter between a mob and the yeomanry near Brecon. Williams (p. 233) indicates that the riot may have had a political cast, for while "the immediate cause was a reduction in . . . wages," he also says the town was "in ferment because of the agitation for parliamentary reform." Correspondence from magistrates and other investigators emphasizes the role of the strike and other nonpolitical

and November there was much unrest caused by a lockout of men who sought to organize a union. The suffering was great; yet, despite "a heritage of lawlessness and a tendency to unrest and extreme actions,"[23] this situation was not turned to a political purpose. Indeed, the men submitted and the union was driven underground. The violence that ensued was postponed until the following year when it included terror by the union to obtain compliance from the membership. The unrest and violence had begun long before 1830 and continued long after the passing of the Reform Bill, with which it had little connection.[24]

---

grievances. The complaints most prominently made concerned reduction in wages, the Court of Requests (which had jurisdiction over small debt cases), price of food and of tools used at work (the truck system still operated), and the practices of hucksters. Although there were shouts of "Reform" when the troops arrived, there was little evidence of political concern at the time of the riot. But it was evident a month earlier at the time of the election (a branch political union had been formed and Cobbett's paper had a circulation of 100). But "from [May 9] forward we [two military officers] find political motives to have disappeared except in name; and the partial reduction of wages . . . and the supposed grievances of the Court of Requests . . . formed the chief objects of popular excitement." At most, politics operated to encourage the expression of grievances and the belief that they ought to be remedied. Thus Col. Brotherton said, "though political feeling is not perhaps the *substantial* cause of these riots, it is a pretext mixed up with others. The word Reform according to their crude notions means high wages and cheap provisions." But the most important cause was the impunity with which the rioters were allowed to act early in May, when, "most unaccountably, the civil authorities did not interfere. The dangerous latitude allowed to the mob and the perfect impunity with which their fury was permitted to exhaust itself and remain afterwards unnoticed, certainly rendered them more audacious on the next occasion" (Brotherton). Ibid., pp. 233–34; Melbourne to Grey, June 17, 1831, Grey Papers; from (name illegible) to Freeling, June 7, 1831, H.O. 40/29. Melbourne to Bute, June 6, 1831; Phillipps to W. Thompson, June 9, 1831; all in H.O. 41/10, ff. 92–93, 99, 116. Col. Brotherton and Maj. Mackworth to Somerset, June 20, 1831 (copy); A. Hill to Melbourne, June 3, 1831; Brotherton to Somerset, June 14, 1831 (copy); all in H.O. 52/16.

23. Williams, *History of Modern Wales,* p. 232.

24. Williams mentions but gives no details about rioting at Carmarthen in October in response to the rejection of the Reform Bill: ibid., p. 176. On the role of industrial conflict in the unrest of October and November,

In the mining area around Newcastle there was much petty violence during the spring of 1831. Mine officials were attacked and machinery destroyed. Violence was also directed against other miners, especially those imported from other areas, in all cases the purpose being to maintain solidarity and prevent strike breaking. The disturbances were sufficiently serious to occupy much of General Bouverie's attention and many of his troops; but even so Lord Londonderry said confidently in April 1831 that "we could walk over their columns immediately with a handful of Dragoons."[25] The strike was settled favorably to the miners at this time, but the contract was to run only for one year. During this period the men were "in a very unsettled state and quite insubordinate,"[26] but the violence was petty and not organized, so that in March 1832, a judge at the Durham spring assizes could congratulate the county "on its freedom from outrage such as was prevalent in the South."[27] With the one-year engagement terminating in April 1832, strikes were resumed, and the violence became more serious. Again it was directed to the imported lead miners and to local men who refused to join the strike, one of whom was murdered. When steps were taken to evict the strikers' families from houses owned by the employers, more rioting took

---

see ibid., p. 235; Edwards, *South Wales Miners,* pp. 25–31. On the union underground—the so-called "Scotch cattle"—see ibid., pp. 29–36; Williams, *History of Modern Wales,* p. 236. Williams (pp. 229, 232) notes that industrialization was more rapid in Wales than in England and its social consequences therefore were more intensively experienced; also, there were no resident magistrates and few police in the mining areas.

25. Londonderry to Durham, April 6, 1831, in Lambton Papers. Bouverie, surveying the district for which he was responsible, indicated that he saw strike situations in this area as the major source of disturbance: Bouverie to Somerset, April 7, 1831 (copy), H.O. 40/29. E. Welbourne, *The Miners' Unions of Northumberland and Durham* (Cambridge Univ. Press, 1923), pp. 31–40; Sykes, *Local Records, 2,* 297–98.

26. T. R. Crawford and A. J. Camp to Bouverie, June 8, 1831, H.O. 40/29; *Hansard, 13* (June 29, 1832), 1152–58.

27. Welbourne, *Miners' Unions,* p. 35. However, in Dec. 1831, 1,000 pitmen had rioted because the owners had employed imported lead miners and put them to work: Sykes, *Local Records, 2,* 336–37.

place. The evictions were made only after pitched battles between striking pitmen and special constables reinforced by soldiers. This occurred in April and early May 1832, yet without any symptom of political feeling becoming evident. The Union organized meetings in connection with the strike, one before (March 3) and one after (April 14) the strike began. But both meetings, attended by 7,000 to 9,000 men, were peaceful, and no political discussion is reported as having taken place.[28]

The main connection between the miners and the Reform Bill agitation seems to have been through the miners' leader, Hepburn. He was an advocate of the Reform Bill, and he attended meetings organized on its behalf.[29] But even though he had great influence over the miners, he does not seem to have bridged the gap between their grievances and the Reform agitation. In June 1831 the magistrates thought "there does not exist any political feeling whatever amongst them."[30] Later there were three Reform meetings at which large numbers of miners were present. The only one of these that was convened on the Union's initiative was the meeting in August 1831, and it was only nominally political. Although its object was "to get up an address to his majesty, thanking him for his beneficent attention to the wants of his people, for the reform bill, and for the support he had given to his ministers," the meeting all but completely neglected this purpose and all the speakers, including Hepburn, addressed the 10,000 or

28. Ibid., pp. 343–44, 352–56. Bouverie to Phillipps, May 2, 7, 10, April 2, 9, 20, and March 15, 1832: H.O. 40/30.

29. Sykes, *Local Records, 2,* 320–21; Sidney Webb, *The Story of the Durham Miners 1662–1921* (London, Fabian Society, 1921), p. 31. He addressed a meeting of the Northern Political Union at Newcastle (Oct. 17) and urged support for the Ministry and looked forward to free trade and, ultimately, to universal suffrage—"then poor Hepburn, that works till his hands are horned over, will give a vote": *Newcastle Courant,* Oct. 22, 1831, p. 2.

30. Crawford and Camp to Bouverie, June 8, 1831: H.O. 40/29. Hobsbawm observes that miners "were an isolated body of men, often geographically separated from the rest of the working people and concerned less with politics than with their specialized economic struggles": "Methodism and the Threat of Revolution in Britain," *History Today* (Feb., 1957), 121–22.

so men present on their religious duties, their recent victory over the employers, the problems of enforcing the Union's rules, and their prospects. "The topic least commented on was that which they had met chiefly to discuss." No resolutions had been prepared, and it was agreed that signatures would be collected all the same and would be attached to resolutions that were to be formulated by a committee.[31] This meeting, like all the others, was peaceful.[32] The violence that did occur was committed in the context of the strike situation, and arose out of resentments against owners or fellow workers. Political questions did not provoke it. Indeed, had there been "political feeling" among the miners that was at all intense it could have been easily mobilized, for in addition to Hepburn, to whom they were devoted, the leaders who spoke at meetings were "chiefly Ranter-Preachers, who have acquired a considerable fluency"; and "the great mass are . . . ready tools of these designing individuals."[33] It is also noteworthy that one of the leading owners and opponents of the miners was Lord Londonderry, who in Parliament was a prominent opponent to the Reform Bill.

Disturbances in May 1832

The year 1832, compared with 1831, was calm. Home Office correspondence concerned with disturbances is much heavier for 1831. Reith reports that in London it was "a period of compara-

---

31. Sykes, *Local Records, 2,* 308–09. The petition received 11,561 signatures from employees of 57 collieries.

32. The other two meetings were Oct. 17, 1831, and May 15, 1832. About the latter meeting it is reported that men came from some of the nearby collieries; about the former it can be inferred from the 50,000 said to be present that miners were in the audience; furthermore, this was the meeting about which Gen. Bouverie had heard that the leaders "have issued orders for the attendance of all the Pitmen on the Tyne and Wear." Hepburn, among others, addressed the meeting: ibid., pp. 320–21, 356–57; *Newcastle Courant,* Oct. 22, 1831, p. 2; and Bouverie to Phillipps, Oct. 17, 1831, H.O. 40/29.

33. Crawford and Camp to Bouverie, June 8, 1831: H.O. 40/29. On Hepburn's influence over the men, see Welbourne, *Miners' Unions,* p. 33.

tive quiet for the [Police] Commissioners."[1] There were disturbances in the country, none of them serious, and all, with one exception, occasioned by industrial rather than political problems. In February, weavers at Manchester "manifested a very turbulent spirit," parading through the town and violently removing work from houses where it was being done despite the lowered wages.[2] In March there was a disturbance in London in which the police clashed with a crowd that gathered in response to the call of the National Union of Working Classes. A Royal Proclamation called for a day of "fasting and humiliation" on account of the cholera epidemic that had been under way for some months. The Union countered this by calling on Londoners to assemble at Finsbury Square in order to distribute food to the poor. After the crowd grew to large proportions, reportedly 25,000, some of whom pelted and insulted the police who had assembled in force, the decision was made to clear the square. This required half an hour, and twenty policemen were injured, two of them very seriously.[3] At about this time the disturbances in the Tyne mining area resumed, and while they were serious they did not appear overwhelming to the military authorities. There was only one regiment available to aid the civil power in the clothing district of Yorkshire and the coal district on the Tyne and Wear, and only three

1. Reith, *British Police and the Democratic Idea,* p. 102. There were 44 convictions for "Riot and Felony" in 1832 and 105 in 1831, and many of the 44 probably were for crimes committed in 1831, for example, the Bristol riots: *PP,* 1833 (135) *XXIX,* 5–10.

2. Bouverie to Phillipps, Feb. 26, 1832, H.O. 40/30; Phillipps to Foster, Feb. 25, 28, 1832; Phillipps to Bouverie, Feb. 25, 1832; all in H.O. 41/11, ff. 92–94, 98–99.

3. *Annual Register for 1832,* Chr., pp. 40–41. In contrast, the Fast Day in Newcastle "was observed . . . with all the solemnity befitting the occasion. All the shops . . . (with few exceptions) were closed; the manufactories were off work. . . . The day was most religiously observed at Durham, Sunderland, South and North Shields, Alnwick, and all the neighboring town": Sykes, *Local Records, 2,* 347. Also in Birmingham it was observed "with every becoming solemnity": *Birm. J.,* March 24, 1832, p. 2. At Carlisle there was a disturbance when 500 persons assembled to hear drum and fife music and burn an effigy. Mayor to Melbourne, March 24, 1831: H.O. 52/17.

regiments in the entire Northern District, which also included Lancashire, Leicestershire, Derbyshire, and Nottinghamshire. Yet General Bouverie did not think a fourth regiment necessary.[4]

In May 1832, when rioting might have been expected, there were many demonstrations organized for political purposes, but very little violence. The one exception was near York, at Bishopsthorpe; a crowd approached the Bishop's Palace where they burned an effigy of the Bishop and did some small damage to property. When troops appeared the crowd dispersed without military action.[5] Elsewhere there were demonstrations. At Worcester, bands marched and an effigy of the Duke was burned, but civil officials did not interfere and did not even enlist special constables.[6] At Manchester a meeting attracted not more than 10,000 persons and "all went off quietly."[7] In Scotland there were large meetings at Edinburgh and Glasgow but no disorder, not "even any disrespect."[8] At Nottingham the mayor called for military aid as a precaution, but twice public meetings "dissolved in good order."[9] The mining areas of Newcastle and Durham were peaceful even though the miners were on strike and anything but well disposed. General Bouverie wrote to the Home Office that the disturbance at Bishopsthorpe was "the only instance of Riot which has taken place in this [Northern] district and that generally speaking the meetings which have taken place have been conducted in the most orderly manner."[10]

4. Bouverie to Phillipps, April 12, 1832: H.O. 40/30.

5. Bouverie to Phillipps, May 21, 1832, H.O. 40/30; Phillipps to Bouverie, May 22, 1832, H.O. 41/11, ff. 156–57; Archbishop of York to Lord Harewood, May 16, 1832, H.O. 52/20; *Hansard, 12* (May 18, 1832), 1045.

6. Tymbs to Melbourne, May 18, 1832: H.O. 52/20.

7. Watkin, *Extracts from his Journal,* pp. 160–61.

8. Cockburn, *Memorials, 1,* 30.

9. *Records of the Borough of Nottingham, 8,* 404; Sykes, *Local Records, 2,* 356–59.

10. Bouverie to Phillipps, May 21, 1832, H.O. 40/30; *Newcastle Courant,* May 19, 1832, p. 2. The Chronicle in the *Annual Register* reported only one disturbance for May 1832; this was at Newcastle (May 4) and an effort to evict pitmen from their houses was the occasion for it. The *Annual Register* by no means reported all disturbances, but it did

London at this time of Parliamentary crisis was not the scene of rioting. There had been a disturbance at St. Bride's Church on May 13 where the Bishop of Litchfield was to preach a charity sermon. It was said that the parishioners had no part in it, and that the "improper behavior" was caused by a crowd made up in large part of boys. One person was taken into custody.[11] Elsewhere the town was said to be *"perfectly* quiet, and the *City* also." There were crowds near the Houses of Parliament, something not unusual in view of the changes in the government; but "they did nothing more than *hiss and groan* a little at two or three most obnoxious persons, but *no* violence." There were not even any large public meetings or processions such as occurred during the previous October. A meeting in Regents Park, addressed by Hume and other "gentleman radicals" was called a "complete failure." There were perhaps 4,000 persons present (20,000 according to the *Times*), but there was a "want of excitement and eagerness amongst them . . . nothing could be more *flat*."[12] It is also interesting that Place resisted a suggestion that processions be organized and that a large open public meeting be held on the outskirts of London.[13] Ordinarily he would have welcomed such proposals.

---

mention the major ones: *Annual Register for 1832*, Chr., pp. 65–66. The Warwick bundle in H.O. 52/20 contains no evidence of disturbance in Birmingham in 1832, except for a report in August of "riotous assembliages" at funerals of persons who had died of cholera.

11. *Hansard, 12* (May 15, 1832), 984.

12. Grosvenor and Stuart, *First Lady Wharncliffe, 2,* 143, 145–46. Referring to May 28, Lady Wharncliffe wrote, "the illuminations were beautiful, and I am told the streets [sic] so *immensely* crowded that carriages could hardly get along; yet every thing was perfectly quiet and peaceable. I cannot but think this a good sign, and that we are still a good deal more *loyal* than we thought": ibid., p. 147. Lord Ellenborough wrote in his diary on May 12 that, "In London all is quiet. The meetings have been rather failures. In the country all is quiet": Aspinall, ed., *Three Diaries*, p. 250. There is no difficulty in finding expressions of nervousness in May, but evidence of actual disturbance is more difficult to find.

13. Wakley proposed the open meeting and processions at a special general meeting of members of the National Political Union on May 10. Since he had led the working-class opposition to Place, it is tempting to speculate that he made this proposal in the hope of embarrassing the supporters of the Reform Bill. However, he had expressed support of the

It has been suggested that his reluctance arose from fear of the turbulence of London crowds;[14] however, in view of the evidence of quiescence in London at this time, it is much more likely that Place was afraid that such a meeting would nourish skepticism about the claims that were being made as to the vigor and impatience of public feelings.[15]

The Tradition of Rioting

The significance of the rioting that did take place in 1831–32 can be exaggerated if it is not seen as the exercise of a "right to riot" which, as Halevy has pointed out, "was an integral part of the national traditions."[1] Far from being unusual, rioting was to be found in most areas of life. Of course, industrial conflict was frequently the occasion of disturbances. Machine breaking had taken place in some of the new factories as well as in the countryside where threshing machines were frequently destroyed.

Reform Bill at this time, so this may not have been his purpose. When Wakley's resolution was discussed in the Council of the Union, Place took the chair, although this was not always his practice. The first time the resolution was taken up (May 11), "after considerable discussion," it was deferred; when it was taken up again (May 14), the Council approved an alternative plan of holding separate district meetings in the metropolis, and Wakley's proposal of a general meeting of several metropolitan unions was rejected (22 votes to 6), "after a very lengthened discussion." It was then moved, and carried, that the secretary be directed to inform the next general meeting (Wakley's resolution had been carried at such a meeting on May 10) "that the Council have considered it not expedient to call an open General Meeting of the Union at the present moment": PCN, Set 63, 1, ff. 129–32; Times, May 11, 1832, p. 4.

14. Wallas, Place, p. 306. Place later said, "Had this meeting been called more than a half million of persons would have attended." Halevy, following Wallas, gave credit to Place's Union for preventing a popular outburst at this time: Triumph of Reform, p. 56.

15. "The great art in agitation," Parkes said, "is to maintain the standard—to make no new efforts which do not come up to the mark of former action on Public Opinion." Parkes to Cobden, Oct. 15, 1841: Cobden Papers.

1. Halevy, England in 1815, p. 148. Halevy also notes that "riot belonged to English political tradition."

Strikers often used violence against imported labor, and occasionally the new life in the factories seems to have been the object of severe hostility. Sometimes even religious issues led to violence, not only in the famous riots of 1780 in London and 1791 in Birmingham, but as late as 1835 in Lanarkshire when tension between Catholics and Protestants led to many skirmishes and, on one occasion, to the sacking and burning of a Catholic church.[2] Elections were regularly the occasion for rioting, so much that it was, according to Jennings, "a recognized election technique," as it kept some of the respectable electors away from the poll.[3] Bristol was thought to be "always a riotous place" at election times; indeed what were locally called "bludgeon men" (i.e. special constables) were part of the scene on such occasions. The under-sheriff said that at elections "the usual exhibitions have taken place there, amounting as much to riot, as the demolition of the Mansion-house on the Saturday night [October 29, 1831]; in fact," he said, "I believe there had never been a contested Election in my time, at Bristol, in which that ceremony has not formed a part."[4] Thus "civil commotions . . . erupted constantly throughout this period,"[5] and not only in such major events as the Gordon riots (1780), the Birmingham riots (1791), and Peterloo (1819). Nor was it confined to particular areas of discontent such as were expressed in the Corn Law riots (1812–15), the Reform agitation of 1816–20, the Luddism of 1812–15, the rural incendiarism of late 1830, the Poor Law riots of the mid and late 1830's, the Rebecca riots of 1839–43, the Plug Plot riots of 1842, or the other Chartist disturbances that broke out at various

2. Alison, *Life and Writings, 1,* 359–61.
3. Ivor Jennings, *Party Politics, I. Appeals to the People* (Cambridge Univ. Press, 1960), p. 117. In contrast to the situation in May 1832, there was widespread rioting during the elections in Dec. 1832, most notably at Huddersfield, Sheffield, Kendall, Wolverhampton, Nuneaton, Walsall, Halesowen, Frome, Norwich, Stamford, Bolton, Preston, Bury, and Carmarthen. Most of the rioting was petty, but at Sheffield it was serious. H.O. 52/18, 19, 20, 21, passim.
4. *Trial of Pinney,* pp. 253, 266.
5. Allen, *Queen's Peace,* p. 104.

times between 1839 and 1848. There were also many petty disturbances which only recently have begun to attract the attention of historians, yet which were a part of what has been aptly called "our former national pastime of rioting."[6]

In the larger perspective of this tradition of rioting, the riots of 1831–32 do not stand out as being more serious than many of the others. On the contrary, many of the others are more symptomatic of instability than the riots that accompanied the passing of the Reform Act. In some of the mining communities of Durham, Staffordshire, and Wales grievances combined with an absence of legal restraints so frequently led to disturbance of the peace that this seemed to have been an endemic condition. Technological unemployment combined with the breakdown of the traditional structure of family life produced similar results among the handloom weavers of Manchester.[7] And then there was Ireland—throughout this period the scene of intermittent disturbances that indicated an alienation much more serious than

6. Ibid., p. 114. "There was . . . much legislation under George IV and Victoria concerning malicious damage and the riotous and felonous destruction of houses. Our history," Allen writes, "contains only too many examples of the necessity for these restraints." And he also observes, "howevermuch it may shock my readers, that we are a lawless people and only for a short time have we been on good behavior": ibid., pp. 50, 126–27. It has also been noted that "There was, of course, nothing new in a riotous England. An earlier generation fifty years ago [i.e. in the eighteenth century] had accepted riots almost as a matter of course, and had endured them with a composure bordering upon indifference": E. C. P. Lascelles, "Charity," in Early Victorian England, 1830–1865, ed. G. M. Young, 2, 317. Rose observes that price-fixing riots "abound in English history from at least 1693 until 1847," and they were not confined to prices of grain. R. B. Rose, "Eighteenth Century Price Riots and Public Policy in England," International Review of Social History, 6 (1961), 279. Also see Watkin, Extracts from his Journal, pp. 108–09, 131; Gash, Peel, pp. 251, 312, 346, 358, 359, 361, 365–66, 601, 618.

7. Arthur Redford and I. S. Russell, The History of Local Government in Manchester, 1 (London, Longmans, 1939), 323; J. F. M. Ludlow and Lloyd Jones, Progress of the Working Class, pp. 22–23; Neil Smelser, Social Change in the Industrial Revolution (London, Routledge and Kegan Paul, 1959), pp. 245–50.

that found in England.[8] The same comparison can be made with the disturbances during the Chartist period, especially those known as the Plug Plot riots in 1842. They were more continuous and spread over a larger region than any of the Reform riots, and they revealed a rancor and vigor that is not easily found in accounts of rioting in 1831–32. The Home Secretary in 1842, Sir James Graham, unlike Melbourne ten years earlier, faced a danger that he recognized to be urgent; a disposition to insurrection was widespread, not confined, as Melbourne saw it in 1831–32, to a small minority of the radical leadership. The country did not face a very great risk of revolution at this time; but if the risk was ever very great, it was so in 1842 and not in 1831.[9]

8. For example, in June 1831, the month when 20 to 25 persons were killed in riots at Merthyr, Hunt in the House reported that "twenty or thirty of the populace in Ireland had been slain by the Yeomanry Cavalry in an affray about tithes": *Hansard, 4* (June 23, 1831), 269. Cf. Robert Curtis, *The History of the Royal Irish Constabulary* (Dublin, 1869), pp. 26–32. Police killed 13 and wounded many on May 23, 1831; the yeomanry shot (apparently mortally) 17 persons and wounded many more on June 18, 1831; and 16 police were killed as the result of a battle with the peasantry on Dec. 14, 1831.

9. Parker, *Life and Letters of Sir James Graham, 1,* 320–22, 329; F. C. Mather, *Public Order in the Age of the Chartists,* p. 228.

CHAPTER 5

The Conditions for Avoiding Revolution

The soil that nurtures revolution is not easily analyzed; widespread disorders and severe discontent need not produce violent upheavals, while rioting such as occurred in Britain in 1831, even though it was on the whole petty, could in some circumstances lead to revolution. For example, if the forces available for defending the established order are few in number or poor in quality, a revolutionary impulse that is initially weak and diffuse might be stimulated by the absence of resistance and grow until it overcomes the forces of the defense. The seriousness of a threat of revolution must therefore be judged by the adequacy of the defending forces as well as by the potency and organization of the revolutionary impulse.

The Police and the Army

The machinery for defense of the established order was grossly inadequate, especially on the civil side. The modern idea of a professional police force was still a novelty.[1] In London, where the Metropolitan Police had been established only in 1829, there was still much suspicion and some outright hostility directed to the police. Outside London the creation of modern police forces had to await the passing of the Municipal Corporations Act in

---

1. Before the nineteenth century, "there were no 'police' in our sense of the term, which is quite modern. To Blackstone, to Dr. Johnson, and even to Macaulay, 'police' meant only certain public services, very rudimentary at that, such as scavenging, 'street-keeping,' prevention of nuisances, some vague attempt at controlling traffic in cities, and the like": Allen, *Queen's Peace,* pp. 92–93.

1835 and the Rural Police Acts of 1839–40.[2] In the absence of a professional police force that aimed at the prevention of disorder, most communities had to rely on antiquated machinery that was put into operation only when disorder was imminent. Responsibility for maintaining order in 1831–32 rested with local officials. The only regular force consisted of the High Constable of the Hundred and the petty constables of the parishes and townships. When rioting threatened, this force was meant to be enlarged by the enlistment of special constables. This was to be done by the magistrates, who had over-all responsibility for maintaining the peace. If the additional force of special constables proved insufficient, the magistrates were authorized to call out the local yeomanry and to requisition regular military forces if they were available. They also had authority to prohibit public meetings that threatened the peace, to read the Riot Act, to issue warrants for the arrest of rioters, and to order both troops and special constables to fire on a rioting mob. When the local machinery of order was unable to cope with disturbances, the magistrates called on the Home Office for aid, and when the situation was sufficiently serious the Home Secretary could quarter troops in a disturbed area, call out certain classes of pensioners, divert the yeomanry from their own county, and have arms issued to the special constables. In these circumstances the Home Secretary determined the strategy for the defensive forces. But normally responsibility remained with local officials, and public order depended on local resources.[3]

Since in most communities the regular force of constables was usually too small to deal with a disturbance that had the makings of a riot,[4] the magistrates, short of calling on the yeomanry or

2. Mather, *Public Order in the Age of the Chartists,* pp. 112, 128. Of course the legislation itself did not immediately lead to the establishment of efficient or even adequate forces: ibid., pp. 112–20, 133. For examples of the "unpoliced" condition of many growing communities, see Gash, *Peel,* pp. 248–50, 342, 505–06.

3. Mather, pp. 36–38, 54, 75. The Sheriff and Lord Lieutenant, as officials of the county administration, nominally had important roles, but in fact the Sheriff's role was negligible and the Lord Lieutenant's became uncertain because of his frequent nonresidence: ibid., pp. 47, 49.

4. Ibid., p. 74.

regular troops, relied on special constables, and the difficulties attending this illustrate the inadequacy of the system. For one thing, it was often difficult to enlist citizens as special constables; many, either from timidity or apathy, avoided the duty. At Merthyr Tydvil, in June 1831, householders refused to take the oaths.[5] Even those sworn in were often found to be unreliable. At Bristol, only a small proportion of the special constables that had been sworn appeared on the second day of rioting.[6] An additional difficulty was the small number of persons eligible in the communities where rioting frequently occurred. In many of these areas there was a comparatively small middle class and much suspicion that the working class might sympathize with the rioters. Thus the town clerk at Kidderminster, urging the Home Secretary not to remove the troops stationed there, explained that in this town of 16,000 there were not enough dependable persons available as special constables to do any good in the event of disturbance. At Merthyr the magistrate complained that as the population consisted "of a very few masters and all the rest workmen, an efficient constabulary force cannot be organized, for want of the intermediate grade between these two

5. H.O. 41/10, f. 145; also at Chaddesden, near Derby; Wilmot to Melbourne, Nov. 23, 1831, H.O. 52/12. The difficulty was such that an act was passed (Oct. 15, 1831) that defined in greater detail than the law had previously done the circumstances in which those appointed as special constables were subject to penalty for refusing to take the oath, for failing to appear, and for disobeying commands. It held for England and Wales only: 1 & 2 Will. IV. c. 41, s. 7, 8. Cf. 1 Geo. IV. c. 37; also compare for penalties to which constables were subject. Copies were printed and widely distributed by the Home Office; for example, see H.O. 41/10, f. 268 (Oct. 21, 1831).

6. *Trial of Charles Pinney*, p. 262. Also see pp. 393, 405, 412. On the other hand, in Jan. 1832, when preparations were being made for the trials of the rioters, there was a great willingness to serve: *Trials of the Persons Concerned in the Late Riots*, pp. 2, 3, 7. The sheriff of Lanarkshire said the special constables in Glasgow were "from the higher class of shopkeepers" and they rarely would show up; and if they did, they were "exceedingly little to be relied upon; they will not fight, they all run": *PP*, 1838 (2), VIII, ques. 1959, 1961, 1963. He also told of an occasion when he swore in 100 special constables and only one appeared: Alison, *My Life and Writings, 1*, 376.

parties."[7] Even when these difficulties were overcome, the special constables usually were unarmed (except for a constable's staff or a baton)[8] and untrained, and of uncertain value in the event of serious rioting.

The inadequacy of the local civil forces made it more likely that a small disturbance would grow into a serious riot, and these were the circumstances in which the magistrates could call for military aid. Such assistance as was sent served as a substitute for the almost nonexistent local police force and not as an emergency supplement to it. Therefore, the government's use of troops was not so significant as it would be if troops had had to be called in only after a well-organized and adequately staffed police force found itself unable to cope with rioting crowds. Thus at Wigan (population 22,000), where there were two policemen and a poorly organized and small body of special constables, the authorities were helpless to prevent the rescue of a man arrested for theft during an election riot. And they were equally helpless when the mob paraded the streets in triumph, displaying the rescued man, after which they proceeded to re-enact the riots that had taken place on election day, attacking the same two houses they had previously assaulted. Military aid was requested from Ashton (five miles away), "but before their arrival the work of destruction had been consummated and the mob retired jeering and laughing at the Military for having come when all was over." Even though the constabulary force was reorganized with the assistance of police officers from Manchester and London, it was necessary to call for military protection when it removed prisoners to another town.[9] At Carmarthen in June 1831, because of the "unaccountable degree of apathy . . . amongst the principal inhabitants," it was impossible to improvise a police force by enlisting special

7. Town Clerk to Melbourne, Nov. 14, 1831, H.O. 52/15; Mather, *Public Order in the Age of the Chartists,* pp. 58, 83–85; A. Hill to Melbourne, June 3, 1831, H.O. 52/16.

8. Mather, p. 81.

9. Bridgeman to Melbourne, May 3, 1831; Mayor of Wigan to Melbourne, May 24, 1831; Roby to Melbourne, May 31, 1831; Shaw to Somerset, May 25, June 6, 1831; all in H.O. 52/13. Bouverie to Phillipps, June 4, 1831; H.O. 40/29.

constables, and thus it was necessary to call for military aid.[10] In the fall of 1831 the Board of Admiralty, when called on to supply a naval force when disorder threatened during a strike of seamen in the River Tyne, complained that the navy was being asked to supply police, which was not its proper function. It acknowledged "that throughout the River Tyne, where a legal check is much wanted, there is no Police whatever"; but it held that the Corporation at Newcastle and the Lord Lieutenant "have jointly ample means for providing a Police, which would secure good order in the River without resorting to the . . . employment of the King's Forces for this purpose."[11] Early in 1832 General Bouverie urged that "an efficient Police may be established at Manchester," and that "the Military Force, now so indispensable, might be much reduced as soon as the Police has become efficient."[12]

That the troops, usually cavalry, served as mounted police rather than fully armed soldiers is indicated by the small numbers in these military detachments as well as by the character of the action in which they engaged. Typically a troop, consisting by regulation of 40 to 100 men, would be sent to a scene of rioting. Actually, the size of a troop was nearer the smaller of these figures. When a troop was sent to Derby from Nottingham on October 10, 1831, it consisted of 3 officers and 41 men. Alexander Somerville reported that in his regiment a troop consisted of 55 men. At Bristol during the rioting the three troops together were made up of 93 men, and one of them (3rd Dragoons) of

10. Melbourne to Cawdor, June 11, 1831; H.O. 41/10, ff. 106–07.

11. Graham to Melbourne, Oct. 22, 1831: Graham Papers, Letters, M-S. Also, the "real fact is that the Corporations do not like to bear the necessary expense; and the Duke [of Northumberland, the Lord Lieutenant], who seeks their favor, connives at the above." Melbourne expressed his agreement with Graham.

12. Bouverie to Phillipps, Feb. 7, 1832: H.O. 40/30. In 1752 Henry Fielding said, "to these two [the Justice of the Peace and the soldier] it is entirely owing that they [the mob] have not long since rooted all the other orders out of the Commonwealth": quoted by Leon Radzinowicz, in *A History of English Criminal Law and Its Administration from 1750*, 3 (London, Stevens, 1956), 1.

but 25.[13] The police-like function performed by these troops is also indicated by the methods they used when facing rioters. They rarely acted like cavalry—charging rapidly and using sabers or firearms—but on the third day of rioting at Bristol they did. Usually the approach of a cavalry force was sufficient to intimidate a riotous crowd, as well it should, since the movement of a mounted force, whether of policemen or cavalry, can appear most formidable. Thus General Bouverie, describing the approach of cavalry toward a group of two or three hundred window breakers at Manchester, reported that "the mob dispersed in all directions upon seeing the troops."[14] It was generally the case that the troops easily dispersed riotous crowds even though paving stones, staves, and pikes (rarely firearms) were used against them. And they usually accomplished this without resorting to their lethal weapons. There are many reports from officers describing the speed and effectiveness with which the troops, especially the cavalry, restrained rioters without engaging them in pitched battle.[15]

There were occasions when it was necessary to use military rather than police methods in order to restrain rioters. In such cases the troops effectively suppressed the rioting (there is one exception[16]), which was to be expected in view of their superi-

13. Great Britain, War Office, *Regulations and Allowances applicable to Corps of Yeomanry Cavalry* (1831), p. 3; Somerville, *Autobiography of a Working Man,* p. 161. Somerville says the sergeants, farriers, troop sergeants-major, and bandsmen were included in the numerical strength of 55 to each troop: ibid., pp. 161–62. Wylly, *Thackwell,* p. 95.

14. Bouverie to Phillipps, Oct. 17, 1831: H.O. 40/29. In the same report there is another description of the cavalry "passing through a considerable number of groups of people, who opened out and dispersed quietly."

15. Bouverie to Phillipps, May 15, 1831, H.O. 40/29; Col. Shaw to Bouverie, Nov. 20, 1831 (copy), H.O. 40/29; Major H. Pratt to Col. Shaw, Feb. 25, 1831 (copy), H.O. 50/14.

16. At Merthyr Tydfil on June 3, 1831, there was a collision between striking workers and infantry soldiers (93d Highlanders). Rioting was effectively suppressed, but not without the use of firearms that caused many deaths (estimates range from 8 to 26). There was no effective civil force, and the striking workers had committed violence with impunity, both in early May and on June 2, the day before the 135 soldiers arrived. After delegates had negotiated, but without agreement, with the iron-

ority in weapons and training.[17] But where it became necessary to use these harsh methods, the rioting had become exacerbated by the absence of effective resistance by an adequate police force when the disturbance began. Had the riotous crowds been resisted initially (for example, at Bristol or Derby), it is unlikely that the more severe methods would have been required subsequently. This point is made by a Manchester municipal committee which reported that, "Instances of riot have often occurred and considerable damage has been sustained, when the aid of the military has been called in, but which easily might have been suppressed

masters, they found the newly arrived soldiers assembled before the Castle Inn. The delegates apparently agreed to have the men disperse within an hour. But voices came from the crowd: "The masters have brought the soldiers against us" (some of the magistrates were ironmasters); "the soldiers there were no more than a gooseberry in their hands to squeeze." A call was made to disarm the soldiers, and the riot began. The order to fire was given only after several soldiers were struck with sticks and 30 muskets taken, and after some of the crowd got between the soldiers and the Inn. This quickly cleared the streets. There is no evidence in H.O. records that the soldiers panicked (cf. Williams, pp. 233–34). Indeed, several witnesses emphasized the forbearance of the soldiers in the face of attack, and a magistrate commended "their cool, intrepid, and effective conduct." See p. 192, n. 22, above for sources; also depositions of W. Thomas, June 20, 1831, and T. Chinse, June 8, 1831; A. Hill to Phillipps, June 26, 1831; E. Thomas to Bute, June 16, 1831 (copy); all in H.O. 52/16. Edwards, *South Wales Miners*, p. 15; *Hansard, 4,* 204–06, 397; H.O. 41/10, ff. 99–116.

17. An obstacle, at Bristol and elsewhere, to the complete effectiveness of cavalry was the presence of narrow alleys through which the mounted soldiers could not pursue rioters. A War Office manual for yeomanry offered "precautions on the March in Disturbed Districts," and rather pointedly noted that, "Steadiness and order will . . . produce much more effect and intimidation than any misplaced impetuosity. . . . as long as cavalry maintain their ranks with steadiness and order, and do not expose themselves to fall into confusion by attempting too great rapidity of movement, they are irresistible by any description of force except a thoroughly-disciplined infantry formed in square to receive them": Great Britain, War Office, *An Abridgement of the Regulations, for the formation and movements of the Cavalry, adapted to the use of Yeomanry Corps* (1833), p. 149. Harriet Martineau describes an encounter (presumably fictional) between an angry mob and soldiers who disperse it: *The Rioters* (2d ed., London, 1842), pp. 46–48.

in its origin by the civil power had there been a sufficiently numerous and properly organized police force."[18] Most typically, however, the troops restrained and dispersed rioters by conducting themselves as policemen rather than as soldiers, and it therefore appears that adequate police forces, had they existed in 1831, would have made military assistance to the civil power all but unnecessary. The Home Secretary apparently held this view, for when requests came for military aid, in the great majority of such cases he responded, not with troops even when they were available, but with appeals that special constables be enlisted.[19] Furthermore, had adequate local police forces existed, the disturbances might have been prevented, and certainly they would not have assumed the proportions they did during the inevitable delay while the soldiers were being brought in. In view of the police-like function typically performed by the small detachments of soldiers and their effectiveness in this role, the use of the military cannot in itself be taken as an indication of the existence of revolutionary crisis.

This conclusion gains support from an examination of the situation in London. Here was the one place with a professional, although still inexperienced, police force; and even though its tactics were not yet fully developed nor the confidence of the populace fully achieved, the Metropolitan Police effectively prevented serious riots and never found it necessary to call for military aid. Although they frequently came into conflict with crowds, never were they doubtful as to the outcome. An officer who had

18. Redford, *History of Local Government in Manchester, 1*, 370. The committee wrote this in 1836, but their statement certainly reflects their experience in 1831–32. When Russell looked back on this period, he noted that magistrates "had not the means of putting down the infractions of the peace by the civil power without calling in aid of the military force. They had no means, nor funds at their disposal. . . . There were districts containing many thousand inhabitants, and having only one, two, or three constables at the disposal of the magistrates": *Hansard, 51* (Jan. 31, 1840), 1055.

19. For example, Melbourne to Westmorland, Oct. 31, 1831; Lamb to Mayor at Bridgewater, Nov. 8, 1831; Lamb to Clerk of Magistrates at Thornbury, Nov. 10, 1831; Lamb to R. Clerk at Bognor, Nov. 10, 1831; and Melbourne to Muneby (?) at Derby, Nov. 23, 1831; all in H.O. 41/10, ff. 300–01, 357, 370, 377, 430–33.

been present "at all the principal scenes of popular commotion" through two decades, including "The Reform riots," testified to this before a Parliamentary Committee:

> QUESTION: Do you think the police was sufficient to prevent the employment of the military on those occasions?
>
> REPLY: The military have never been called out since the establishment of the force; we have never felt the slightest doubt of being able to preserve the peace.[20]

The success of the police in London was in part due to their use of preventive tactics, which required that they intervene in crowd activities when it became evident that riotous conduct was about to take place. It seems likely that, had there been a professional police force in places such as Bristol, Nottingham, and Derby, the rioting in those towns would not have become so serious or have appeared symptomatic of revolutionary ferment.[21]

20. *PP,* 1852–53 (715), XXXVI (2d report), ques. 2831–32 (F. M. Mallalieu). Reith also asserts that the police had the situation under control, but in reference to the disturbances of 1830–32 he says the riots "ended well, but indecisively, for the police," and he notes that "skirmishing never ceased." While there was enough skirmishing, his estimate of at least one day of disturbance (in connection with the Procession of Oct. 12, 1831) exaggerates the difficulties experienced by the police: Reith, *British Police and the Democratic Ideal,* pp. 96–98. In June 1830 the police force consisted of 3,314 men, the population within the Metropolitan Police District was 1,212,491, thus there were 2.7 police per 1,000 population: John Wade, ed., *The Extraordinary Black Book* (London, 1831), p. 548.

21. Melbourne paid tribute to the police in 1835 and noted that "Since the . . . establishment of the London police, though we have passed through times likely enough to have produced disturbances of the public peace, yet we have not been obliged to call out a single soldier in quelling riot. This is a great recommendation, especially when [formerly] . . . on occasion of riots perfectly insignificant in their character, towns were thrown into great alarm, and the destruction of property was hazarded to a great degree by cavalry being stationed among the inhabitants for several days": *Hansard, 29* (Aug. 3, 1835), 1354. Chadwick, one of the originators of the preventive principle, expressed great confidence that a police force could prevent rioting: *PP, 1852–53* (715), XXXVI, ques. 3642.

While the military arm, unlike much of the civil machinery, performed its duties effectively in 1831–32, it was hampered in this by a serious deficiency that could have tipped the scales had there been a genuine revolutionary situation. While the number of soldiers available to be sent to a scene of rioting was usually adequate, there was an over-all shortage of troops, leading the government in 1831 to authorize the enlistment of an additional 7,261 into the army, though the real increase was much less.[22] Because of the shortage, soldiers could not be sent to every place from which requests were made for military aid. Such requests were supported by statements describing symptoms of unrest and anticipating an outbreak. In response, the Home Secretary usually urged the magistrates to swear in special constables. While in some cases he treated such requests as alarmist, in others he clearly wished to comply but regretted his inability to do so. When an increase in military strength was requested at Edinburgh after the civil force was proved inadequate during a riot on March 28, 1831, the Home Secretary observed that it would be "highly in-convenient" to comply and instead urged that 1,200 special con-stables be sworn. On another occasion magistrates were told that "it is not improbable that he [General Bouverie] may be un-able at present to detach so large a military force as that for which you apply in consequence of the numerous applications for military aid from various other parts of the Northern Dis-trict."[23] The shortage was exemplified by the situation faced in early November 1831, when disorders were expected in London.

22. *Hansard, 10* (Feb. 17, 1832), 482. The effective strength of the army in Great Britain (excluding Ireland) on Jan. 1, 1832, was 4,690 cavalry, 3,899 foot guards, and 16,494 infantry, making a total of 25,083, a figure that is raised to 28,772 if officers are included. This figure is in sharp contrast with Place's statement that there were only 11,000 soldiers, made when he was explaining how he would have organized a coup in May 1832 had Wellington formed a government: Wallas, *Place,* pp. 293–94. *PP,* 1831–32 (317), XXVII, 118–21. In addition, there were 19,047 in the yeomanry; but there were serious delays before a corps could be assembled and brought to the scene of disturbance as well as other objections to their use (see p. 232, n. 41, below). Ibid. (80), pp. 451–53.

23. Melbourne to Clerk and Dundas, April 16, 1831, and Phillipps to Tillet and Twinlove, May 24, 1831: H.O. 41/10, ff. 8–10, 63–64.

"You would scarcely believe it possible," an official at the Horse Guards wrote, "that after having scraped together every *disposable sword* and *Bayonet* within 50 miles of London, our utmost disposable force is 1347 mounted Swords [and] 2301 Bayonets and of the former I have included 94 Surrey Yeomanry, and of the latter 629 Marines . . . forms more than ¼ part of the whole disposable Inf[antry]," and he added, "We need not fear a Military Despotism at least."[24] Another example may be taken from the riots at Derby and Nottingham on October 10, 1831. Colonel Thackwell, in command at Nottingham, sent one troop to Derby and then discovered, when rioting occurred at Nottingham, that he could have used the departed detachment. At the same time General Bouverie from Manchester received calls for assistance from both Nottingham and Derby which he acknowledged to be "extremely urgent," but he reported: "I do not think that I can with safety detach any thing from this part of the district at present."[25] There were only three regiments in the Northern District during the early part of 1832, and this figure probably had not greatly changed during the preceding year.[26] The shortage had the effect of creating considerable strain on the defense of public order whenever riots occurred at several places simultaneously. The government was greatly de-

24. Sir Willoughby Gordon (the Quarter-Master General) to Graham, Nov. 9, 1831: Graham Papers, Letters, C-H.

25. Bouverie to Phillipps, Oct. 11, 1831: H.O. 40/29.

26. There is a discrepancy in the information given by Gen. Bouverie in 1832 and Gen. Jackson in 1839. Gen. Jackson presented figures to the Home Office indicating that in 1832 in the Northern District there were 4,716 infantry, 738 cavalry, and 287 artillery soldiers—altogether 5,741. Yet Gen. Bouverie, Commander in the North District, and presumably informed as to what forces were under his command, reported that there were three regiments in the district (April 1832). The size of a regiment could vary greatly. A cavalry regiment, for example, could consist of from 5 to 12 troops, and each troop could consist of from 40 to 100 men; thus a regiment could vary from 200 to 1,200. The only way this information could reconcile the figures from Jackson and Bouverie would be by assuming that Bouverie was referring only to cavalry regiments, but this seems unlikely. Bouverie to Phillipps, April 12, 1832: H.O. 40/30. Jackson's figures are cited in Mather, *Public Order in the Age of the Chartists,* p. 159.

pendent on the army's ability to shift troops quickly from one locality to another, wherever the need was most pressing, but the cholera epidemic sometimes caused troops to be quarantined, and this added to the difficulty.[27] In this event the shortage caused occasional strain but nothing worse. Its significance lies in the opportunity it created for organized insurrection which, of course, never broke out.[28]

The over-all shortage of troops, the small number of troops sent to a scene of rioting, the absence (outside London) of a professional police force, the inadequacy of the antiquated civil machinery for defending order—all these circumstances created an opportunity for revolution. Had there been a really serious threat of revolution arising from widespread and acute discontent, making the populace vulnerable to mobilization into revolutionary activities, this opportunity probably would have been exploited. But it was not exploited—perhaps because this particular ingredient of a revolutionary situation was not present.

Reliability of the Army: The Case of Alexander Somerville

No matter how adequate the size of the military force, if it is unreliable it will contribute little to the defense of public order. Since the soldiers originally shared the economic and social circumstances of many of the discontented persons who went into the riotous mobs, it was possible that they would feel sympathetic or even share political views that would impair their performance. If the populace came to believe that the soldiers felt a sympathy for their cause, or even a reluctance to use violence against them as fellow-subjects, the confidence and aggressiveness of the mob would likely have increased. It is difficult to believe that this did not happen at Bristol where the riots mounted in fury and destructiveness as it became evident that the soldiers were not

27. For example in June 1832, troops at York, Leeds, and Hull were in quarantine: Bouverie to Somerset, June 12, 1832 (copy), H.O. 50/14.

28. Thus the general in command at Birmingham in May 1832 said that if there was an insurrection he would be unable to deal with it, as he had only two troops of cavalry at Birmingham and a small infantry detachment at Dudley: Aspinall, ed., *Three Diaries*, p. 258.

exercising the force they clearly possessed. On the first day (October 29) the commanding officer even took off his hat and cheered the mob in response to their having uttered a cheer for the troops. Confident that the crowd could be managed and desperately anxious to avoid bloodshed, he also ordered the troops to "walk away" the crowd, and it was said that he gave an order that firearms were not to be used. What must have been decisive was his ordering two troops of cavalry (of the three present) away from the scene and later away from the town when he was convinced that their presence provoked the mob to violence. Colonel Brereton's court-martial held him personally responsible for the increased severity of the rioting; there is no evidence that the troops shared Brereton's reluctance and indecisiveness; on the contrary, they appear to have been bewildered if not contemptuous of his conduct, and the court-martial expressed its "highest admiration" for the other officers and men under his command.[1] While the conduct of the soldiers, therefore, does not reveal unreliability of the army, it does indicate how a riot can become increasingly destructive and approach insurrection as the forces defending public order appear weak and perhaps sympathetic to the populace. It is significant that the days following the riots at Bristol became one of the most riotous periods of the fifteen months' agitation for the Reform Bill. These uprisings were on the whole not serious and were easily suppressed. But the meetings, demonstrations, and strikes that took place perhaps might not have led to rioting had the events at Bristol been managed differently.

During the period of the Reform Bill agitation claims were occasionally made that the soldiers would not fire on the people and in a crisis would even mutiny. At Birmingham it was as-

1. *Reports of State Trials,* ed. John Macdonell, n.s., *3,* 1315–16. Actually, Col. Brereton was in command by virtue of being senior officer present: he was not the regularly assigned officer in command of the troops. Capt. Warrington, commanding the troop of 3d Dragoons at Bristol, also faced a court-martial, but the charges against him were much less severe than those against Col. Brereton; see p. 165, n. 12. The Court's judgment was not influenced by reports, of which it must have known, that some of the soldiers had accepted plundered liquors from some of the mob: *Trial of Pinney,* pp. 47, 77, 97.

serted that Wellington "has no sword,—or if he have, it is a useless . . . semblance of a weapon. . . . The soldiers will not murder the people. There is not one man out of one hundred of the whole British army, that is prepared to flesh his sword in the blood of his countrymen."[2] And a speaker, addressing the Working Class Union at Manchester, warned the government "that soldiers, though they did happen to have scarlet coats, had feelings in common with the people, and had fathers, and brothers, and friends" among those assembled.[3]

The only evidence in support of such claims comes from the incident in which Alexander Somerville played a leading part. Somerville, less than six months in the army, was stationed in Birmingham with the 2nd Dragoons (known as the Scots Greys) during the crisis of May 1832. He was sympathetic with the Reform cause and had observed how many Birmingham people wore an insigne indicating membership in the Political Union. However, he became alarmed when on May 13 (a time when the Duke of Wellington was still trying to form a government), the barracks gates were locked in order to keep visitors out (they were usually left open), and an order was issued that swords were to be rough-sharpened (to inflict a ragged wound), for he assumed

2. *Reports of the Principal Staffordshire Reform Meetings, Held on Monday, the 14th of May, 1832*, p. 2; also see *Birm. J.*, Oct. 8, 1831, p. 4, reporting meeting of Oct. 3. Place, writing later (probably in 1837), expressed doubt about the willingness of the soldiers to fight the people, but it is doubtful that he felt this in 1831–32: Wallas, *Place*, pp. 308, 316. There was a recent precedent for speculation about the unreliability of the soldiers. During the 1820's there had been considerable anxiety about the loyalty of the troops dealing with disturbances in Ireland. This could have carried over to 1831. During the twenties, however, there were large numbers of Irish Catholic soldiers serving in regiments that were used in Ireland: Reynolds, *Catholic Emancipation Crisis*, pp. 147–48.

3. *Manch. Guard.*, Dec. 3, 1831, p. 3, reporting the meeting of Nov. 28. Apparently this did not reassure the audience, for there were several panics when the crowd ran off as someone shouted that the soldiers were coming. There were occasional riots that were not caused by political or industrial issues, but which arose from private quarrels between soldiers and citizens. For example, at Bolton on Aug. 2, 1831 (a Fair Day), and Burnley, on Dec. 6, 1831. Trevor to Melbourne, Aug. 4, 1831, and Shaw to Bouverie, Dec. 11, 1831 (copy), H.O. 52/13.

that preparations were being made to attack the populace. "The danger now seemed imminent," he wrote. "Those of us who had held private and confidential conversations on the subject, had agreed that the best means of preventing a collision with the re- form movement and the national will, as expressed by the House of Commons, was to give circulation to the fact that we were not to be depended upon to put down meetings, or prevent the people of Birmingham from journeying to London, to present their peti- tions, and support the House of Commons by their presence, if they chose to undertake the journey." Somerville and his com- panions "caused letters to be written . . . to that effect." They were sent to Wellington, to Lord Hill at the War Office, to un- named individuals at Birmingham, and some were dropped in the streets. Apparently it was hoped that, as a result, rumors would be spread that the Scots Greys, and perhaps the soldiers generally, could not be relied upon.[4] There was such a rumor about, at least during the latter half of May; officers of Somer- ville's regiment admitted hearing a rumor that their soldiers had joined the union and "would not act against the mob," and this was reported in the press as well. Somerville thought this move was decisive, that the rumor "drew forth the letter . . . announcing that his majesty had succeeded, for the safety of the nation, in inducing as many anti-reform peers to withdraw their opposition, as would allow the bill to pass."[5] It has been widely held that the

4. Somerville, *Autobiography of a Working Man*, pp. 156–57.

5. "Report of Court of Inquiry on the Case of Alexander Somerville," *PP* 1831–32 (714) XXVII, 24; *Scotsman*, May 19, 1832, p. 2, where the rumor was reported and denied; *Autobiography*, p. 146. Somerville also wrote that "the rumour industriously spread and conveyed to the highest quarters, and founded on a well-determined resolution of certain soldiers, that the army was not to be relied upon, if the constitutional voice of the country was attempted to be suppressed by the unconstitutional use of military power": ibid., p. 158. With "the approach of revolution . . . at Birmingham in 1832," Somerville writes, he "arrested its progress and its peril. It was I . . . [who] sent letters to the King and to the commander of the forces in London, warning them that the garrison of Birmingham could not be relied on. The King's letters to the Anti-Reform Lords . . . was the direct result": *Conservative Science of Nations. Being the First Complete Narrative of Somerville's Diligent Life in the Service of Public Safety in Britain* (Montreal, 1860), p. 46.

government and the Duke of Wellington felt uncertain about the reliability of the army, and Somerville's account of this affair has provided the evidence for this belief.[6]

This incident could have influenced Wellington's decision to yield; it also could have influenced marginal supporters of the Bill in the House of Commons not to support a Tory government. But does it provide evidence of unreliability of the soldiers? The only evidence (apart from rumors) of unreliability in the Scots Greys consists of the fact that anonymous letters were sent; and from various accounts written by Somerville, in most cases long after the event.[7] In addition to his unrevealing testimony before the Court of Inquiry, the only near-contemporary statement of Somerville's that is available is the letter he sent to the editor of the *Weekly Dispatch*. Extracts of this letter (received May 24) appeared in the issue of May 27, 1832; it was written after the crisis was resolved, and gave the public its first information about the affair. In it Somerville insisted that rumors indicating that the Scots Greys were not to be fully relied upon were true; and he described the circumstances in which they would have disobeyed. This was the letter (not the anonymous letters written earlier) that led to the court-martial that brought him notoriety as well as one hundred lashes. Apparently suspected as the writer of the letter

6. Martineau, *Thirty Years' Peace*, 2, 472–75, where Somerville is quoted, and heavily relied upon. Evidence of the persistence of this belief is found in the words of an unnamed barrister reported in Henry Solly, *James Woodford, Carpenter and Chartist, 1* (London, 1881), 64–65. Knowledge of the letters was spread by certain papers which denied that Wellington had been influenced by such a consideration, by Somerville having sent a letter to the *Weekly Dispatch* stating the position of the soldiers, and by public discussion of the court-martial that followed.

7. Of course, since the anonymous letters of mid-May have not been found, it is conceivable that they were never written. A cursory search has not turned up any of them in the PRO or in the portion of the Grey Papers consisting of correspondence for 1832 between Grey and Lord Hill, Hobhouse, and Melbourne, nor are they among the anonymous letters sent to Grey in 1832. There were rumors that the Greys were not reliable, but these need not have originated in the anonymous letters, for they could have been inspired by claims that the soldiers had joined the union (see n. 28 below).

in the *Weekly Dispatch,* he was ordered to do exercises at the riding school that were difficult and perhaps impossible to perform. When in these circumstances he disobeyed an order he was brought before the commanding officer who, while holding a copy of the *Weekly Dispatch,* ordered a court-martial. It was soon suspected that the letter and not the disobedience was the occasion for the punishment, and a Court of Inquiry was established. As a result, a public subscription was raised to purchase Somerville's discharge. He subsequently pursued a career of "political authorship," during which he often referred to the events of 1832. It has been these accounts of what he and other soldiers might have done in May 1832, written long after the event, on which later historiography has mainly relied in order to substantiate the belief that the soldiers were unreliable.[8]

In all the accounts left by Somerville he insists that the disobedience planned by the soldiers would have taken place only if they had been ordered to attack people peacefully engaged in holding a public meeting or marching in a procession of petitioners. In most of his accounts he only states that in these circumstances they would have refused to obey. But in one of the several versions given by Somerville he claims that the soldiers planned to actively join the popular demonstration. This secret "project," which he had been invited to join by an "unrevealed association of the thinking men of the regiment," planned to "be ready, if marched against the people, to do so, with the understanding that when a certain soldier, well able from his natural abilities and long military experience, gave a signal agreed on— we were in an instant to gallop to the standard of the Unionists." This, he said, would have been followed by a "rapid march on London." This account appeared in a pamphlet of 1839, which

8. *Weekly Dispatch,* May 27, 1832, p. 172; Somerville, *Autobiography,* pp. 159, 162–76, 216–18, 222; Somerville, *Cobdenic Policy the Internal Enemy of England* (London, 1854), p. 17; *Hansard, 13* (June 19, 1832), 874, 883, 891–92; Broughton, *Recollections, 4,* 246–47, 250. The editor's comments suggest that he printed only extracts, yet when Somerville published the letter (with a few slight changes) he ran together the passages from the newspaper as if they were the entire letter. "Court of Inquiry," pp. 21–22, 64–70.

did not mention, however, the anonymous letters.[9] In contrast, later versions, like the letter sent to the *Weekly Dispatch,* state that the soldiers would have disobeyed (without giving a detailed description, such as the secret "project," of what the disobedience would have consisted); and they refer to and emphasize the anonymous letters. The different accounts are not inconsistent, but if none of them is incorrect, they are all incomplete. The evidence does not allow for a judgment of the accuracy of any of them.[10]

Somerville's statements hardly portray a mutinous army or even one with strong political sympathies. He denied that those who took part in the plotting were members of the Birmingham Political Union, and he insisted that only a few men from the regiment were involved with the Union.[11] Nor were the parties to it seeking to encourage rioting so as to foment a general insurrection; on the contrary, he said: "The Greys would do their duty if riots and outrages upon property were committed, [but] they would not draw their swords or triggers upon a deliberative public

9. Alexander Somerville, *Public and Personal Affairs. Being an Inquiry into the Physical Strength of the People, in which the Value of their Pikes and Rifles is Compared with that of the grape-shot, shells, and rockets, of the Woolwich artillery; also, an Exposure of Treacherous Patriots and Drunken Lawyers who have imposed upon the People, and are connected with Alderman Harmer, and the Weekly Dispatch, the whole comprising a Personal Narrative* (London [1839]), pp. 24–25.

10. Later versions include his *Autobiography* (originally published in 1848) pp. 157–60, and his *Diligent Life,* pp. 102–05. In each of these there is at most an allusion to the detailed project described in *Public and Personal Affairs.* When in 1853 he confesses to his "grave error," the "breach of military duty," and "treason," it seems to be the writing of "certain political letters" that he has in mind: *Cobdenic Policy,* pp. 17, 19, 20. Somerville's state of mind in later years—suspicious, resentful, obsessed with the fear of revolution, and sometimes influenced by excessive drinking—adds to the difficulty in evaluating his varied testimony.

11. *Autobiography,* p. 159. At one place he says only two of the soldiers had joined the union: *Public and Personal Affairs,* pp. 23–24. Later he referred to soldiers who "took the pay of the Birmingham Political Union"; and he said, "I knew the citizens of Birmingham who were subverting the dragoons, and know some of them still": *Diligent Life,* pp. 46, 105, 318.

meeting, or kill the people of Birmingham for attempting to leave their town with a petition to London." If "the unprincipled and lawless, who are everywhere more or less to be found," were "to commit outrages on property . . . *we* would have certainly considered ourselves, as soldiers, bound to put down such disorderly conduct. This, I say, we would have certainly felt to have been our duty; but, *against the liberties of our countrymen we would have never, never, never raised an arm!*"[12] He thus portrays the soldiers as calm, rational men, who foresaw imminent conflict between the army and a law-abiding populace. "The men of Birmingham and the midland counties," according to Somerville, "mustered strong and determinedly, and at the bidding of a leader, were ready to march [on London]." He also believed that the Duke of Wellington was about to order the army to oppose them. "Our regiment was booted and saddled, and primed and loaded with ball and cartridge, for days and nights together; and we knew that we would be the first called into conflict with the moving millions." He sees the soldiers as avoiding an evil still greater than one bloody encounter; for "the slightest show of retaliation on, or from, the military, would have let slip the contageous strife, to which the minds of the multitude were disposed." Somerville justifies the action contemplated by the soldiers as a way of avoiding a violent upheaval, and not as a means to promote revolution or even the passing of the Reform Bill. This is consistent with his statement that they were willing to suppress riots, and it explains the particular circumstances in which, according to Somerville, they would not have fought.[13]

While the Greys, as Somerville describes them, were not ripe for rebellion, the fact that they could visualize certain circumstances in which they would not obey orders indicates that there was some uncertainty about their performance. But how much? They never faced the circumstances in which, according to Somerville, they would have disobeyed. He was only stating an intention

---

12. *Autobiography,* pp. 157, 159; the second passage is from the letter published in the *Weekly Dispatch,* May 27, 1832, p. 172; the word "everywhere" appears in the slightly different version in the *Autobiography,* instead of the words, evidently misprinted, "ever either," in the newspaper.

13. *Public and Personal Affairs,* pp. 8, 14, 82.

agreed upon by some small proportion of the regiment.[14] But this intention, as he described it, was a response to a hypothetical situation that was not likely ever to exist. He (and his fellow soldiers) believed that the army would have been used to forcibly suppress peaceful activities of the Union.[15] But the army was never used for such a purpose in 1831–32. Even if the Duke of Wellington had formed a government, and even if resistance to it was organized, there is no evidence that he would have used troops to suppress legal and peaceful meetings. But the Duke did not form a government, and the Grey government had established a policy of not using the army unless there was a serious breach of the peace that local civil officials were unable to deal with. In fact, the Scots Greys were probably in Birmingham as much to aid the civil power in dealing with disturbances arising from intermittent conflict between colliers and mine owners in nearby towns (such as Walsall, Dudley, Bilston, and Wolverhampton) as for political disturbances. There had been much industrial conflict in the area, but no violence arising from political causes. Only the previous December, Melbourne had recommended the

14. There are two places where Somerville indicates that there may have been more than a few, but these statements are neither direct nor unambiguous, and they refer to the number that might have taken part in the "project," not to the number of persons who discussed it. He asked, "if fifty or twice as many dragoons, had galloped to the standard of the movement, what would have been their effect?" The other estimate is also embedded in a question: "Can any one say that the act of one half, or one third of a regiment of dragoons joining the people, would not have carried physical assistance and a great moral effect with it?" Elsewhere he describes how he was invited by a soldier "to meet him and a few others" to discuss the matter; and he refers to "the principal movers" and the "thinking men of the regiment," phrases that hardly suggest large numbers: ibid., pp. 24, 25, 82. He had never seen 4 of the 6 troops in his regiment: "Court of Inquiry," pp. 36, 61, 67.

15. Describing what he thought the "Soldiers *were threatened with,*" Somerville said Wellington, "as was expected, [was] about to put down the Political Unions by Proclamation, and force a refractory people to submit to military subjugation," and "The fractional minority [opposed to the Bill] resisted King and people, and threatened the country with military coercion": *Public and Personal Affairs,* pp. 9, 14. "History tell us, that all revolutions have had their immediate cause in some act of despotism": *Diligent Life,* p. 24.

establishment of a separate military district with headquarters at Dudley because of disturbances in the mining towns. And at that time the magistrates at Dudley were informed that additional cavalry was being sent to Birmingham in order to meet their needs.[16]

Furthermore, the soldiers' expectations about the conduct of the populace were equally unrealistic. Isolated by barracks life, they were dependent on newspapers and rumors for information and, to judge by Somerville, they seem to have believed all the exaggerated, threatening statements made at public meetings and in the press. He believed the statements in the press that the nation was unanimous, not only in its demand for Reform, but in its determination to have it by force if necessary. He noted that O'Connell made "strongly worded allusions to Charles the First" at "one of the great Westminster meetings," and he seems to have been greatly impressed by H. B. Churchill (secretary to the Council of the National Political Union) who urged the people to *"prepare their powder and melt their lead"* (italics given by Somerville). He also was struck by strongly worded speeches by Wakefield, Buller, and Major Revell (all associated with Place's Union), especially by the latter two for having alluded to the revolution of 1830 in Paris as a warning and example for England.[17] These

16. Phillipps to Magistrates at Dudley, Dec. 2, 1831 and Phillipps to Leigh, Bilston, Dec. 2, 1831: H.O. 41/10, ff. 451–52. Melbourne to Lord Hill, Dec. 19, 1831: H.O. 41/11, f. 2.

17. *Public and Personal Affairs,* pp. 8–10. Quoting a newspaper report on "another of the great metropolitan assemblages," Somerville attributes this statement to Buller: "We had got a Polignac Ministry (Tremendous groans.) . . . *There were but three days in Paris, and let them recollect the result (cheering and waving of hats.)*" He emphasized the apparent unanimity of the strong feelings. "The newspapers . . . contained reports from all quarters of the island." He quoted from papers published at Taunton, Plymouth, Exeter, Bolton, Liverpool, Boston, Sheffield, Manchester, Newcastle, and Dundee and reports from still other places appearing in London papers: ibid., pp. 10–13. Yet he also said that "most of the transactions beyond . . . Birmingham were unknown to us, though, from general rumour, we knew . . . that the country was alarmingly unanimous. When closed within the barracks . . . we had no communication with the townspeople night or day, and knew nothing of their movements": *Autobiography,* pp. 155–56.

speeches and many others prepared him to believe the rumor that the Birmingham Political Union would march to London, where it would be joined by other unions, till Attwood presided over 800,000 petitioners.[18] Accepting all this, he asked if "it can be supposed that soldiers were not to reflect on the possibilities that were before them, when in almost every speech at every meeting the sword and the musket were spoken of; when even the Leading Journal of Europe . . . spoke of our being compelled to lay down our arms, by the overwhelming force of 24,000,000." Somerville then added, "we did reflect, and spoke, and planned action too."[19] Somerville held to his belief that the march on London would have taken place and that the populace was disposed to use force and would have done so; yet he also seems to have wondered if his assessment of the situation was correct, for he asked, "[were] the whole host of liberal periodicals only shamming when they, from day to day, filled their papers with apprehensions of the dreaded revolution? Was there nothing meant but sound when O'Connell, Wakefield, Buller, and the others made speeches?"[20]

Since Somerville provides the only testimony in support of the contention that the Scots Greys would have disobeyed in certain hypothetical circumstances, his evaluation of the claim that the

18. *Public and Personal Affairs,* p. 14. "The men of Birmingham and the midland counties, mustered strong and determinedly, and at the bidding of a leader, were ready to march on the Metropolis, to public meetings, or to the battle-field": ibid., p. 82. The Union "was to march for London that night; and . . . we were to stop it on the road": *Autobiography,* pp. 155–56. Another soldier stationed at Weedon seems to have heard the same rumor: "great excitement prevailed. . . . However, all for this time passed quietly, although there was some talk of 80,000 or 90,000 men marching from Birmingham by this station on their way to London": *The Diary of Colour-Sergeant George Calladine 19th Foot 1793–1837,* ed. Michael L. Ferrar (London, 1922), pp. 169–70.

19. *Public and Personal Affairs,* p. 23. It was a time "when even the slightest shew of retaliation, on, or from, the military, would have let slip the contagious strife, to which the minds of the multitude were predisposed": ibid., p. 8; also see pp. 13, 25, 81, 82.

20. Ibid., p. 25. Also see his reference to the possibility that the press was "fooling the public" and that it was a "vile imposition": ibid., p. 82.

intention would have been carried out is worth considering. In 1839, in a pamphlet describing an imaginary insurrection at Birmingham and elsewhere, Somerville said there was a "hope that the military would not fight against the people, or that they would partially turn their services in favour of the insurrection, if not actually join the insurgents"; but he pointed out that "this hope was founded on delusive suppositions." Somerville then spoke in general terms that are applicable to the affair of 1832. "A soldier talking to a civilian, and telling what he will do in the case of a popular outbreak, is no authority on which you can found an opinion on the fidelity or infidelity of the army; he may be a thinking man, but whatever his individual opinions are, he is carried to the execution of his military duties, by the mindless mass of which he is himself a powerless atom." Then, in an allusion to his experience in 1832, he acknowledges that soldiers might conspire together, but he says "that no dependence ought to be placed by the people on such risks," and he specifically refers to the Dragoons at Birmingham in 1832 as "sufficient proof of this."[21] Since Somerville originally had claimed that some of the soldiers were unwilling to fight in certain hypothetical circumstances which, in any case, never arose, and since he himself later cast doubt on the claim, his evidence at most gives weak support to the belief that the soldiers in 1831–32 were unreliable, especially since there is no evidence that soldiers in his regiment or any other ever refused to obey orders during these months of continuous duty in varied circumstances.[22]

21. Alexander Somerville, *Warnings to the People on Street Warfare. A Series of Weekly Letters, in which all the Records of European Revolutions are quoted; and opinions on Field and Street Tactics Impartially Given for the Benefit of the Armed People*, Letter 2, p. 8 (n.d. but May 25, 1839). These letters are in large part a fictional account of insurrections, with horrific descriptions of the conflict between populace and army. They are set in Birmingham and Glasgow and are directed against physical-force Chartism. His purpose was to discourage them, not to suggest that an insurrection could even temporarily succeed: ibid., Letter 7, p. 5 and passim.

22. Somerville is in many ways a mystery. It is not clear what he really contemplated doing—or what he actually did—in May 1832 (to say nothing of his later career). The letters of mid-May, assuming that they

Apart from the ambiguous evidence provided by Alexander Somerville, there is no evidence of unreliability arising from political sympathies among the soldiers in 1831–32.[23] However, there were other rumors and allegations to this effect, and while they were never substantiated in the conduct of the soldiers, they, like Somerville's statements, might have been important had they

were actually written and sent, could have been written without believing that they provided a correct assessment of the soldiers' willingness to obey orders. He had an obsessive concern to prevent violent conflict between the army and the populace. This was made abundantly evident as the years passed. For example, in 1839 he privately published *Warnings to the People on Street Warfare,* in order to warn against the risks civilians faced when fighting disciplined troops. Again in 1848 when, as in 1839, there was a threat of disorder, he decided to publish his *Autobiography* instead of leaving it for posthumous publication. He explained that it "may be of more use at the present, than at a future time. If the [last chapters on a conspiracy in 1834] be of use to warn working men of the perils into which they are led by leaders whom they cannot control, he will gladly confess that good been done." In each of these cases (and there are others) he saw himself as interceding to save the country from unnecessary violence. In later years he saw this as his role in 1832. Carswell notes his "obsession of his own importance" and his belief that his "solitary martyrdom . . . saved a bloodbath in 1832," but assumes that his "repudiation of physical force" only came later. But there is a possibility that he already thought of himself as saving the country from revolution in 1832. The evidence is by no means unambiguous. But when he says that in 1832 he thought "that the best means of preventing a collision with the reform movement and the national will . . . was to give circulation to the fact that we [i.e. the Greys] were not to be depended upon," and when the over-riding character of his wish to prevent such a collision is considered, the possibility that the "fact" he circulated was not fact at all must not be ruled out, especially since this passage was altered in the 1860 version of his autobiography (which incorporated much of the earlier editions) so that what in the earlier edition was "the fact" later became "a report": John Carswell, "Introduction," in Somerville, *Autobiography,* pp. xiv–xv, xviii, xxiii, 160, n. 18; *Autobiography,* (2d ed., London, 1854), pp. 312–24, 349; *Diligent Life,* p. 103.

23. Referring to a later period, Mather says, "There is no evidence that the troops ever faltered in their duty when called upon to put down Chartist and other disturbances." "It seems likely then that the kind of political outlook which was liable to produce a refusal to obey orders was limited to a few exceptional soldiers": *Public Order in the Age of the Chartists,* pp. 179–80.

been believed. For even with little disaffection among the populace, if the government believes that the army cannot be relied upon, it will be reluctant to use it and thus greatly increase the opportunity for successful insurrection. "If revolutionary leaders can develop such a situation," says Chorley, "they will be in a position to launch an insurrection with fair hope of success. The effect is to produce a condition of nervousness on the part of the existing government so that its striking power will be in practice paralyzed or at least decisively weakened."[24] Perhaps sensing this, some of the less moderate radicals of the time claimed that the soldiers were on their side. Colonel Macerone's *Defensive Instructions for the People,* published in 1832, recommended that in civil conflict officers be the first targets, for "without their active superintendence and influence, the men, ashamed of and disgusted with their cause and occupation, would slacken their efforts, retire from the contest, or actually join *us.*"[25] Wakefield, in his 1831 pamphlet, *Householders in Danger,* also suggested that in conflict with the populace the soldiers would be reluctant to attack.[26] This belief was a persistent theme in radical literature.[27] Parkes claimed, in a letter to Grote—perhaps intending that Grote repeat the story—that "soldiers are enrolling themselves in our Union," but Somerville insisted that only a few had done so.[28] A speaker at Manchester on November 28, 1831, said "they had nothing to fear from the military, as he knew that

24. Katharine Chorley, *Armies and the Art of Revolution* (London, Faber, 1943), p. 87. Of course, in some circumstances the situation depends on the attitude of the officers rather than the rank and file: ibid., p. 92.

25. "Colonel Macerone's Defensive Instructions for the People," *United Service Journal, 4* (1832, part 2), 56.

26. But for a special reason; the 10,000 of "the lowest class of prostitutes" would mingle with the crowds and "be a shield" to them. The soldiers, in view of their "intimate connexion" with the 10,000, would be reluctant to fire at crowds of which they were a part!: *Householders in Danger* (1831), p. 8.

27. Dolby, *Cyclopaedia,* p. 17. The heading used by Dolby is, "Armies. Not to be Depended upon by those who most desire them."

28. Wallas, *Place,* p. 304; Somerville, *Autobiography,* p. 159. Grey had a report from Birmingham, dated May 13, that two soldiers had joined the union and had said their comrades were prepared to follow their

800 of the soldiers now in and about Manchester were for them."

Yet there is no indication that these claims raised serious doubts in the minds of military commanders or the government. When General Bouverie forwarded the report of the speech at Manchester to the War Office he noted: "The story of the troops I hold to be nonsense."[29] Despite the precedent and encouragement from Colonel Brereton at Bristol, the troops earned from the court that tried him "its highest admiration" for "the general good discipline maintained by the squadron of that regiment under the circumstances of *most peculiar* trial."[30] When the general in command at Birmingham wrote to the War Office to say that, because of the small size of his force (consisting of two troops of the Scots Greys and two companies of infantry at Dudley), he was incapable of resisting in case of insurrection, "Lord Hill, however, spoke very lightly to Lord Althorpe of the danger."[31]

---

example. He passed it on to Lord Hill, recommending that the troops be removed from Birmingham. His informant, whom he did not identify, but who evidently was a civilian (certainly not Somerville), did not say that the soldiers were unwilling to obey their officers: Grey to Hill, May 14, 1832, Grey Papers. On the other hand, since Somerville said he had "caused letters to be written," it is conceivable that this letter was inspired by him.

29. Shaw to Bouverie, Nov. 28, 1831 (copy); Bouverie to Somerset, Nov. 30, 1831 (copy): H.O. 40/29.

30. *State Trials,* Macdonell, ed., *3,* 1316. Also see Jackson to Somerset, Nov. 2, 1831 (copy), and Fane to Hill, Jan. 13, 1832 (copy): H.O. 40/28, ff. 141, 396.

31. Le Marchant's diary, May 15, 1832, in Aspinall, ed., *Three Diaries,* p. 258. The incapacity to resist of course refers to the smallness of the force and not to any suspected unreliability among the soldiers. The letter Somerville said he had written to Lord Hill could have arrived when Hill made this observation. Hill would have already received the letter mentioned in n. 28 above. The commanding officer at Birmingham is reported to have said, in response to a question about the reliability of the men, "They are firm as rocks": Somerville, *Diligent Life,* p. 20; "Court of Inquiry," p. 67. The Inspection Return of Aug. 9, 1832, for Somerville's regiment was almost enthusiastic in its report: W.O. 27/217. The Greys continued to serve in the area around Birmingham, particularly during the elections in Dec. 1832, when there were disturbances at Nuneaton, Walsall, and Wolverhampton. At the latter place they defended the supporters of the Tory candidate against the mob. H.O. 52/19, Staffordshire bundle, passim.

When anonymous letters inviting disloyalty were sent to the sergeants-major of Marine units, the Admiralty put commanding officers on their guard and ordered all such letters stopped by the post office. In reply the commanding officers reported "most favorably of the steady and loyal disposition of the men" and that the "men are true."[32] The army commanders' confidence in the troops was not based on a naïve unawareness of the problem, for they appear to have been sensitive to the sources of unreliability. Thus, for example, they often refused to station troops in towns until adequate barracks were provided, despite nervous demands from local officials, for they sought to avoid billeting the soldiers with the populace as this would scatter the force, making it vulnerable to attack, and allow the soldiers to develop attachments and sympathies with the populace.[33] Indeed, the army appears to have gone far toward that "political sterilization of the rank and file" which is necessary for the defense of the government when it is subject to insurrection.[34]

There was some disaffection—or, as Lord Melbourne called it, "party spirit"—among the yeomanry. In October 1831, after

32. Graham had only two such letters, both "in some feigned hand"; one had been turned in to the commanding officer (at Portsmouth) and the other had been stopped before being delivered (at Woolwich). None had been delivered at Chatham, and no report had yet arrived from Plymouth. It is assumed that the letters invited disloyalty, as Graham describes them as "most scandalously wicked and treasonable." The King thought it "serious and calling for attention and vigilance though not alarming": Graham to Taylor, Oct. 14, 1831, and Taylor to Graham, Oct. 14, 1831, in Graham Papers, the King and Sir H. Taylor. The warrant authorizing the post office to detain such letters was canceled after only 12 days: H.O. 79/4, f. 206b.

33. For example, when the Mayor of Liverpool requested troops as a precaution, he was told they could be sent when a building was available to house them, as scattered billets would not be used: Bouverie to Mayor of Liverpool, Nov. 4, 1831, H.O. 40/29; Chorley, *Armies and the Art of Revolution,* pp. 141–42, 158.

34. Ibid., p. 175. Chorley notes that this requires segregation from the civilian populace that is achieved by barracks life, the cultivation of an *esprit de corps,* and the dampening of initiative through paternalistic treatment. Long service for the ranks also contributes to its immunity from civilian political influences. She also notes that while these methods work for the rank and file, the officers are not subject to them: ibid.,

the Lords rejected the Bill, there were resignations in some of the troops commanded by Tories who had voted against it. Two entire troops resigned in Kent.[35] In the Yorkshire regiment commanded by Lord Wharncliffe a "mutinous Round Robin" was circulated demanding that he resign. This was by no means successful, however; a delegation informed him that while they did not share his opinions they had no wish to withdraw from the regiment. It was confined to one troop, from which twenty-two men resigned, and apparently there was no further difficulty.[36] The Home Secretary was also warned that the Dorsetshire yeomanry was unreliable.[37] In May 1832, the Hertfordshire yeomanry and thirty members of the Wolverhampton corps resigned after Grey's resignation was announced,[38] and Chorley asserts: "It is almost certain that the Duke of Wellington, had he formed an Anti-Reform Ministry, would have been unable to rely on them to help him hold down the country."[39] This evidence of

pp. 175–76, 180. Of course, when there is nervousness about the obedience of troops, they are not drawn from the region in which they are used nor from the social class against which they will be used (for example, recruitment is from rural areas if the troops are to be used against an urban proletariat).

35. Sanders, *Melbourne*, p. 134, n. 1.

36. Grosvenor and Stuart, *First Lady Wharncliffe*, 2, 91–92; "all the other troops of the Regt. . . . resisted the attempts of certain of the Doncaster troop to seduce them": Wharncliffe to Melbourne, Nov. 4, 1831, H.O. 52/15. There were also reports of party feeling and efforts to foment insubordination in a Lincolnshire militia regiment: Brownlow to Melbourne, Nov. 30, 1831, H.O. 52/14.

37. Sanders, *Melbourne*, pp. 134–35; also see Wellington, *Despatches, 8,* 29. But a different report on the Dorset yeomanry indicated that they were considered unsatisfactory because they were "dreadfully beaten" at Blandford and they were the object of strong hostility. Rev. J. Parsons to Melbourne, Oct. 22, 1831, H.O. 52/12.

38. Butler, *Reform Bill,* p. 422; *Scotsman,* May 19, 1832, p. 2. Mr. Robert Sidney, seconding a resolution put to a union meeting, announced his resignation from the yeomanry: *Reports of the Staffordshire Reform Meetings, May 14, 1832,* p. 5.

39. Chorley, *Armies and the Art of Revolution,* p. 167. However, of the 19,047 men in the yeomanry at this time, the troops said to be unreliable because of party feeling represent a tiny percentage. A small troop

strong party political feeling among the yeomanry does not affect the estimate formed of the army's reliability. First of all, the yeomanry, while it had a military appearance, was a civilian force under civilian control. The men were subject to military discipline only when on duty and in the unusual event of being placed under the command of regular military officers. Service was voluntary, and since the men had to supply their own horses and equipment, they were drawn from a propertied class. Also, in view of the purpose it served, an active identification with the established order was necessary in order to bring a man to volunteer, for service was inconvenient, often interfering with the harvest. The ranks were drawn mainly from tenant farmers or small landowners, and the officers from the squirearchy or aristocracy.[40] Thus they came from a segment of society that was entirely distinct from the classes to which the regular soldiers belonged, and the "party spirit" that in some cases influenced them was hardly the kind that typically causes disaffection among the ranks of the regular army. Furthermore, while some of the yeomanry resigned or objected to their commanding officers on political grounds, this was done while they were not on duty. When called upon to defend public order they served in most cases effectively, and when they failed to do so it was not because of unreliability arising from political views. The yeomanry holding Whig views had a common interest with their Tory officers in defending the social order against rioting mobs. Nonetheless, the Home Secretary,

---

called to Merthyr on June 3, 1831 (see p. 191, n. 22 above) was trapped by 1,200 men (some of them armed) as it approached the town, and it surrendered its arms without fighting. However, this was not done from political disaffection. The commander was stopped apart from his troop and was prevented from warning his men of the trap when a pistol was pointed at him. The small detachment thus rode into a defile where they were surprised and outnumbered. A professional officer was critical of their surrender, but the Lord Lieut. thought it not so bad as it appeared. But the troop was disbanded. Brotherton to Somerset, June 13, 1831 (copy) and Bute to Melbourne, June 9, 1831: H.O. 52/16; Teichman, "Yeomanry as Aid to Civil Power," p. 91.

40. Chorley, pp. 166–67; Mather, *Public Order in the Age of the Chartists,* pp. 142–43, 147.

aware of the difficulties attending use of the yeomanry, placed primary reliance on the army.[41]

Self-confidence of the Government

Even with an adequate and politically reliable military force a government may lack the "nerve" without which it cannot defend itself effectively. A demonstration can turn into an insurrection if the government gives the impression of being indecisive. The degree of confidence of the government is therefore relevant to an assessment of the imminence of revolution.

Among some local officials there was excessive nervousness bordering on panic. Letters from mayors and magistrates and anonymous persons flooded the Home Office with accounts showing that they felt threatened and vulnerable. After the riot in Worcester on November 5, the mayor wrote to Melbourne begging that the troops remain: "Although to all outward appearances the tranquility of the City is restored, yet . . . the removal of the military would be the first signal for acts of aggression on the part of the Mob." The riot and the expected removal of the troops created "a terror" in the minds of respectable inhabitants "which nothing but the actual presence of the Military *can allay*."[1] From Dudley came a request for troops to be stationed there: "not that we apprehend any immediate tumult," but, if a disturbance did take place, "we consider our situation almost

41. Referring to the yeomanry, Melbourne wrote, "We must not conceal from ourselves that the real weakness and inherent vice of all institutions of this nature, from a regiment of volunteers down to a *posse* of special constables, is that, being taken immediately from the body of the people, and not having habits of military obedience, they are at times of strong popular feeling either divided within themselves by discordant opinions, or so possessed and heated with the prevailing popular sentiment, that either they cannot be depended upon for acting at all, or are entirely incapable of conducting themselves with that steadiness, coolness, and impartiality which are so absolutely required in such circumstances": Melbourne to Sir Herbert Taylor, Oct. 25, 1831, in Sanders, *Melbourne*, pp. 134–35. Mather, *Public Order in the Age of the Chartists,* pp. 145–47.

1. Clifton to Melbourne, Nov. 9, 1831: H.O. 52/15.

defenceless."[2] In addition to such requests, there were also alarmist letters anonymously sent to the Home Office. One, signed
"Truth," came from Birmingham, announcing that the Council
of the Political Union had discussed a plan for arming its members; it was noted that since subscriptions were to be raised to
provide muskets for those unable to purchase their own, "it is
the *lower* and not the middling classes they intend to enrol."[3]
Credence may have been given to such claims by the appearance
of Colonel Macerone's *Defensive Instructions for the People,* in
which he offers instruction on tactics for street fighting as well as
for the home manufacture of weapons.[4]

2. Magistrates at Dudley to Melbourne, Nov. 8, 1831: H.O. 52/15.
For other examples see H.O. 52/15 and 52/20, the correspondence from
Yorkshire, Worcestershire, Staffordshire, Warwickshire, and Nottinghamshire in 1831 and 1832. In Jan. 1831 an unusual incident occurred at
Manchester. After a group of citizens wrote to the Home Office to inform
the authorities of "the disturbed state of the town," an antialarmist meeting was called and passed resolutions challenging the alarmists' observations. It was said that the town was "libellously declared to be disturbed,"
and that there was "indignation that in the midst of profound peace
that any one should . . . attempt to persuade Government that there was
ever the shadow of tumult amongst us. . . . [if] you receive any information to the contrary tendency there is every reason to believe that the
municipal authorities have been deceived by spies and informers." There
were strikes and picketing in Manchester at this time, but the town was
reported to be "in a state of perfect tranquility, altho' there are still many
factories out of work": Prentice to Melbourne, Jan. 10, 1831. Bouverie
to Phillipps, Jan. 20, 1831: H.O. 40/29.
3. "Truth" to Melbourne, Nov. 3, 1831: H.O. 40/29. There were
many reports of arming and military drilling: William Clark to Melbourne,
Nov. 27, 1831, H.O. 40/29, reporting that at Bath people were fortifying
their houses and laying in arms; Melbourne to Newcastle, Oct. 31, Nov. 6,
16, 30, Dec. 2, 1831, all in H.O. 41/40, ff. 303, 344, 407, 443-44, 455-56.
Also Phillipps to Bouverie, Nov. 12, 1831, Phillipps to Rolleston, Dec. 8,
1831, and Phillipps to T. H. Barber, Dec. 12, 1831: all in H.O. 41/10,
ff. 383, 473, 485. These were not always unconfirmed rumors. There was
a confirmed report that about 60 persons were drilling at night near Manchester: Col. Shaw to Bouverie, Feb. 5, 1832 (copy), H.O. 40/30. A
dagger was found on a man arrested at Manchester: Phillipps to Foster,
Feb. 1, 1832, H.O. 41/11, f. 63.
4. Colonel Macerone, *Defensive Instructions for the People: Containing the New and Improved Combination of Arms, called Foot Lancers:*

In contrast to some local civil officials, Lord Melbourne and his assistants at the Home Office did not react with panic, for they remained skeptical about much that was reported to them. After the Duke of Newcastle reported rumors about military training and arming by a union at Nottingham, Melbourne expressed the hope that in future he would "carefully examine and investigate, whether the representations which are made to you may not be coloured and inflamed by the prevalence of some of the various motives which induce exaggeration upon such subjects." In support of this suggestion he enclosed an extract from a letter received from "A Gentleman of credit residing in Nottingham," who reported that "the arming Branch" of the Union had been disbanded in response to the Proclamation of November 22nd; and that, in response to rumor that there was military drilling in the forest, he had "ascertained that they consisted of Five Men and a Driller." This informant added that, "If all the alarming tales were traced to their sources they would be found as important as the above"; but, he added, "The People are ill off." From Belper near Derby came another and probably related report. A man carrying a gun concealed in a walking stick was arrested, and the Home Secretary was told that there were more than two hundred persons with such weapons, which were procured from Birmingham and completed at Belper. The magis-

---

with miscellaneous instructions on the subject of Arms and Ammunition, Street and House Fighting, etc. (London, Richard Carlile, June, 1834). Macerone's proposals were known late in 1831, for Rotunda speakers refer to them and to a penny pamphlet in which they appear, and they were described in the Morn. Chr., Nov. 12, 1831, p. 3, which printed some of Macerone's letters; and these also were included in an 8-page pamphlet, Project for Armed Unions, n.d., but included in a H.O. bundle for 1830–31: H.O. 64/17; Poor Man's Guardian, Nov. 26, 1831, p. 181. Extracts and illustrations from Macerone's pamphlet were published in a special supplementary number of the Rotunda journal: ibid., April 11, 1832, pp. 345–52. Macerone said that talk of use of arms in the Times, Examiner, and Morning Chronicle at that time inspired him to write it. He also claimed that it sold 200,000 copies, though he does not say over what period of time: Memoirs, 2, 458–59, 468. Somerville's Warning to the People on Street Warfare was directed against Macerone's views.

trates thought their informant reliable beyond doubt. But on inquiry it was discovered that the two gunmakers concerned had abandoned the manufacture of such weapons. The town clerk, reporting this, would not yield his alarmist views, however, for he added that manufacture had ceased because of diminished demand which was due to Nottingham unions having established the practice of giving a musket and bayonet to each new member. Melbourne's endorsement is revealing: "Mr. B. writes, as he talks, very much at random. The Inform. is not worth attending to."[5]

To take another example, in November 1831 various rumors concerning the supply of arms to the Birmingham Political Union were reported to Wellington, who reported them to the King. They involved a London gunmaker, Riviere, and seem to have originated with employees of a Russian merchant engaged in supplying Riviere's guns to the Russian government, and from someone who saw Riviere alighting from the Birmingham coach and who claimed that Riviere himself was the source of the report. Grey's correspondence with Wellington shows skepticism but an open-mindedness to facts. First, he asked for additional information; then he sent a police inspector's report of an interview with Riviere; and finally, acknowledging that some gunmakers might be supplying arms, he expressed great doubt that it could be Riviere. Wellington, even though his informants (Holmes and Rothesay) on further inquiry only confirmed their original reports, admitted privately, but not to Grey, that he had been misinformed.[6] To take still another example, in Manchester, in January 1832, there were reports that the Union had arms and planned to attack the troops while they attended church. But General Bouverie wrote, "I do not believe the Reports, which are all got up by the [one word illegible] employed by the Police to get intelligence." Most of such reports, he said, were "too absurd to be believed." However, he also noted, "that there is a

5. Melbourne to Newcastle, Nov. 30, 1831; Phillipps to Clerk of Magistrates at Derby, Dec. 3, 1831; Town Clerk at Derby to Melbourne, Dec. 2, 23, 1831; all in H.O. 41/10, ff. 443–45 and H.O. 52/12.

6. Wellington, *Despatches, 8,* 30, 57, 60–62, 64–65, 70–71, 73, 78, 86, 111, 113.

great deal of bad feeling . . . but there is no disposition to have their heads broken."[7]

With this kind of sober evaluation to balance the alarmist reports, the Home Secretary did not find it necessary to assume that all reports and rumors were true, nor does he seem to have felt the kind of anxiety that might dipose him to believe them to be true.[8] In the face of a preponderance of alarmist reports, depending upon their credibility Melbourne's reactions varied, but

7. Bouverie to Somerset, Jan. 25, 1832, and Bouverie to Phillipps, Jan. 25, 1832: H.O. 40/30. The illegible word in Bouverie's letter probably refers to spies of some sort. Melbourne found it distasteful to use spies and dangerous as well: Sanders, *Melbourne,* p. 128. But they were employed, almost certainly with his knowledge. On the same day that Bouverie wrote about the use of spies in Manchester, Phillipps, the Under-secretary, wrote to the chief magistrate at Manchester that Melbourne wanted "the best information" regarding the nightly meetings and military exercises reported from Manchester and that "Lord Melbourne will be most ready to supply you with all necessary pecuniary means of obtaining information, which you may think it right to employ." A similar instruction was sent to Bouverie: Phillipps to Foster, Jan. 25, 1832, and Phillipps to Bouverie, Jan. 26, 1832, in H.O. 79/4, ff. 213, 213b. Spies were also employed within the National Union of Working Classes in London. There were at least three, and a person claiming to be a class leader offered his services as well. Although testimony before the Popay inquiry left it uncertain who within the Home Office and Police had authorized spying, it is clear from Melbourne's occasional endorsement that he read the reports and requested particular information from the agent. On at least one occasion his private secretary, T. Young, served as intermediary with the police officer (Stafford) who received the reports and occasionally met the agent who boasted that he was considered by the Rotundaites "to be as good a Revolutionist both in Church and State as they are." *PP,* 1833 (627), XIII, "Report of the Select Committee on the Petition of Frederick Young and Others (Police.)," ques. 4046–48, 4050–51, 4053, 4056, 4063, 4071–74. Secret Service Report of May 30, Dec. 2, 1831: H.O. 64/11; Secret Service Report of Feb. 10, 1832: H.O. 64/12; Anonymous letter of April 21, 1832: H.O. 64/16; Stafford's memo., n.d. [Nov. 3, 1831]: H.O. 52/14.

8. Melbourne has been described as approaching the conflicts of his age with "gravity which bordered on fear": Mather, *Public Order,* p. 35. And as having "shuddered daily" for the security of the metropolis: Torrens, *Melbourne, 1,* 388. But the vigor and decisiveness with which he acted can also be seen as signs of confidence and strength. Cf. Butler, *Reform Bill,* p. 315.

he never experienced panic. While often dubious of alarmist reports, he still recognized that a "mischievous spirit" was abroad. Although he was disposed to rely on the sober evaluations of military officers, he recognized the measure of uncertainty that attended any assessment of the situation, and thus did not discount the possibility of organized rebellion. On the whole he saw the disturbances as scattered outbreaks that could be controlled despite the shortage of troops and the inadequacy of the civil machinery for preserving the peace.

The government's confidence that it could control the disorder and its calm evaluation of its significance contrasts sharply with the frightened and alarmist statements made by some Tory politicians, such as Croker, Winchelsea, Perceval, and even Peel. Not that the government was never apprehensive. But unlike the alarmists, for whom every sign of unrest was a symptom of revolution, the Ministers did not immediately infer revolutionary consequences from every case of agitation. There was one situation, however, in which the government displayed serious concern. This was in November 1831, after the Bristol riots, when some rioting was accompanied by a flood of panic-stricken demands for troops in the mining and industrial areas of Lancashire and Staffordshire. However, it was not the riots or the letters from magistrates that was the immediate cause of apprehension in London. Concern with immediate danger was directed to reports of an organization linking the leaders of the National Union of Working Classes in several towns. The government was confident of its ability to suppress scattered riots that occurred spontaneously, but in view of the shortage of troops knew that it would be difficult to deal with rioting that broke out simultaneously in several places. This meant that organization of dissident groups in several places or any other development that created the possibility of serious riots at the same time in widely separated places would pose a serious threat.

Already in June the Home Secretary had received reports from Foster, the reliable chief magistrate at Manchester, telling of plans for an organization connecting the political unions in several towns around Manchester with those in London and other places. The proposal was to invite deputies from all these towns to assemble in London where they were to call upon Parliament to establish universal suffrage; furthermore, according to the informant's report, the Manchester deputy said, "If he Refusses I shall tell him that he may take the Consequences as the Pipall are dettermined to have there Rights." In addition to the several industrial towns around Manchester, deputies were invited from places in Yorkshire, Cheshire, and Scotland. Acceptances were said to have come from Stockport, Blackburn, Macclesfield, Oldham, Chorley, Huddersfield, and Leeds; and forty deputies were expected in London. This was not only an ambitious fantasy. This information was based on the deliberations of a Manchester meeting of May 27th at which nineteen such deputies attended; a connection with London was already established, as the delegates going to London were directed to Hetherington; and the plans were discussed in an atmosphere of conspiracy, with arrangements "never to meet above twice in one place nor more than twelve in one place at a time for fear of being discovered." Of course, this aspect made it appear ominous, and a sinister touch was given by the free use of abusive and violent language that expressed hostility to King and Church and invited the use of arms. At the time the government did no more than ask for continued surveillance, which it arranged to undertake in London as well, for it asked for the names of the deputies and their London correspondents.[9]

There was additional evidence some months later, after the rejection of the Reform Bill in October. From Manchester came word that Curran and Brooks, the deputies elected by the Working Class Union in June, were sending delegates to the surrounding towns to arrange for a large attendance at a general meeting, its date still to be announced. And one of the leaders flatly announced, "There are Delegates out throughout England and the

9. Foster to Melbourne, June 22, 28, 1831, and David Ramsay to Lavender, Head Officer of Police at Manchester, June 21, 1831: H.O. 52/13. Ramsay was the informant; he clearly attended the meeting of May 27, and Foster thought his report probably accurate. The London N.U.W.C. informant who reported very frequently, sometimes as often as twice a week, gave information on the movements of the Manchester delegates: Secret Service Reports of July 5, 15, 26, 1831: H.O. 64/11.

day is not far off when they will have their way"; and he added, "There will be a meeting held of the Town and Country People and they [his audience] will then know more about it."[10] Therefore, when it was learned from spies and police officers, and later from public announcements and letters opened at the post office, that there were to be two meetings for November 7th, one at Lincoln's Inn Fields and the other at the Rotunda, the latter to march in procession to join their colleagues so that altogether they might march to White Conduit House, to hold still another meeting, the Home Secretary decided to frustrate them. When he made this decision he did not yet know that the Manchester union would decline to participate, as it had too short notice of the plan; so the possibility of such meetings in both London and Manchester was a consideration. But the decision to prevent the meeting was primarily shaped by concern that it might get out of control. The example of Bristol (October 29–31) was immediately before him, and the reports from his informant in the confidence of the Rotunda leaders indicated that the working-class spokesmen and their immediate following were in a belligerent and reckless mood. There was much violent talk and many references to weapons that were to be carried on November 7th. They asked, "what can they do at Bristol that we can't do here ten times over?" It was reported that William Benbow, the most fiery and reckless of the London working-class leaders, was "a leading member of all there [sic] Scheems [sic] and projects." There also were vague but dark allusions to organized combat. At a meeting of the Eastern (Bethnal Green) branch of the union a speaker urged the audience to bring staves, and if they had none, then

> pokers or—(here some of the Committee said Noquett don't go too far)—well he would not say what, but he hoped they would all bring something to defend themselves with. . . . [He also urged them] to repel force by force for indeed there was something else determined on and he could tell them something if he dare. No—no from the Committee. Well he dare not, however he would say they were going to buy firelocks to *Shoot Game*.

10. Foster to Melbourne, Oct. 10, 15, 19, 1831: H.O. 52/13.

These allusions were contradicted by other informants who thought the union did not intend mischief. But all agreed that if the meeting took place the unrestrained belligerency exemplified by Noquett would lead to violence. A police superintendent said, "They would be no paltry window breakers, but *head breakers.*" And another police official thought the danger arose from allowing perhaps 20,000, some of them anxious for mischief, to be brought together to hear long speeches that might encourage rioting. The decision to prevent the meeting was made against the background of reports of unrest elsewhere and the knowledge that the working-class unions in London and Manchester (and perhaps elsewhere) hoped to act together. But what mainly moved the Home Secretary to act was the possibility that the meeting might get out of control. He decided on November 4th to declare the meeting illegal, but hearing that Wakley was alarmed and would attempt to dissuade the Rotundaites from holding the meeting, he postponed action. When on the fifth the Rotunda leaders voluntarily appeared at the Home Office they were informed that they would be prosecuted for treason if the meeting took place. Intimidated, they issued a placard announcing postponement of the meeting. Melbourne's reference to treason indicates how seriously he took this affair.[11]

This did not put an end to the precautions, however. Elaborate preparations were made for November 7th. They were begun be-

11. Home Office to Law Officers, Nov. 2, 1831: H.O. 79/4, f. 208. Somerset to Wellington, Nov. 2, 4, 1831, in Wellington, *Despatches, 8,* 22, 29; Melbourne to Grey, Oct. 30, Nov. 4, 1831, in Grey Collection, Durham. Benbow's proposal for the meeting of Nov. 7 was announced at a meeting of Oct. 31, 1831, and advertised in the *Poor Man's Guardian,* Nov. 5, 1831, pp. 149, 152. Ashmore and Curran to Secy. of London political union, Nov. 5, 1831 (copy), H.O. 44/25. Secret Service Report, Oct. 26, 1831, H.O. 64/11. Reports of Supt. J. Smith, Oct. 31, Nov. 1, 1831; Reports of Supt. T. Hunter, Nov. 2, 1831; Reports of Smith and Hunter, Nov. 3, 5, 1831; Report of Supt. J. Johnston, n.d.; unsigned reports, Nov. 1, 4, 1831; memo. by J. Stafford, Nov. 3, 1831; Law Officers to Melbourne, Nov. 3, 1831; all in H.O. 52/14. *Morn. Chr.,* Oct. 26, 1831, in PCN, Set 17, f. 398. Wilfrid Harris Crook, *The General Strike* (Chapel Hill, Univ. of North Carolina Press, 1931), p. 5 and n. 10. "General Meeting of the Working Classes Postponed" (Nov. 7, 1831); *Poor Man's Guardian,* Nov. 12, 1831, pp. 153–57.

fore Melbourne interviewed the Rotunda leaders; but even after the interview they were not relaxed. With the riots at Bristol fresh in mind, the government was determined to avoid disturbances in London. Military preparations were made. This was the occasion on which the government "scraped together every *disposable Sword and Bayonet* within 50 miles of London," and moved 629 Marines from more distant quarters. In the Court of Aldermen a resolution was passed on November 4th calling upon every member to "immediately enroll and swear in a number of special constables to assist the magistracy upon any tumult, riot, outrage or breach of the peace occurring within the city"; in 70 London parishes and hamlets 7,490 special constables were sworn. Communications were established between police offices and a military command in Regents Park barracks, and arms were sent to the Bank. Arrangements were also made for the arming of 400 Greenwich Pensioners.[12] Gunsmiths' shops were inspected. The police issued placards cautioning people from appearing on the seventh. Also, on November 5th the Home Secretary filed warrants with the Post Master authorizing him to stop letters addressed to the chief members of the National Union of Working Classes, both at London and at Manchester (Cleave, Benbow, and Osborne in London and Ashmore and Curran at Manchester).[13] It seems clear that the events at Bristol as well as intelligence from spies inspired the precautions. "The Bristol affair," Sir James Graham wrote, "would not have been so serious, if it

12. Sir Willoughby Gordon to Sir James Graham, Nov. 9, 1831, and Somerset to Graham, Nov. 5, 1831: Graham Papers, Letters C-H and M-S. Reginald Sharpe, *London and the Kingdom, A History Derived Mainly from the Archives at Guildhall in the Custody of the Corporation of the City of London, 3* (London, 1895), 338. Mepol 1/7, 9,483–9,552. Memo. by Lord Hill, Nov. 7, 1831; Ordnance office to Lamb, Nov. 5, 1831: H.O. 52/14.

13. *Times,* Nov. 8, 1831, p. 2; *Birm. J.,* Nov. 12, 1831, p. 4; Melbourne to Post Master General, Nov. 5, 1831; all in H.O. 79/4, f. 208. Letters directed to the Committee at the Commercial Coffee House, Temple Bar, were also to be stopped. Crook points out that this was at 205 Fleet Street, the same address at which Benbow's pamphlet was printed. He thinks that Benbow may have been the proprietor of the coffee house: Crook, *General Strike,* p. 5.

had been met with more decision and vigor in the first instance: it is an example, which proves what we ought to do on Monday [November 7], if unhappily it be necessary to act."[14]

In the event, next to no disturbance took place. By three o'clock the 2,000 police on duty were relieved. As of six o'clock in the evening on the seventh, the government had "heard of no disposition to riot." "I am happy to say," Graham wrote to the King's secretary, "that the Peace of the Metropolis has not been disturbed: every precaution was taken and an overwhelming force assembled to counteract a seditious movement." He also reported that at no time during the day had more than 500 men (boys and idlers, according to the *Times*) assembled, "and on the occasion of some trifling disturbance taking place, a small body of Police advanced, when the Multitude fled."[15]

The Rotunda leaders ridiculed the government's "extravagant" precautions. "You are aware of the peaceable manner in which the whole of the 'terrible day' passed;—of how the mountain of alarm which the 'wise men' raised, was delivered of a mere mouse."[16] But for the government the precautions were only prudent. And it was such prudence that was responsible for the continuation of their cautious observation of these unions. Already before November seventh the Home Office had information taken from letters opened at the Post Office that seemed to justify its action. From Manchester came a proposal to hold simultaneous meetings of all the unions of the working classes on November 21st and it was hoped that this could be announced at the London meeting on the seventh. The Manchester men also seem to have persuaded Home Office officials that all the Lancashire towns were in cooperation and that "their hearts are nearly screwed up to the striking point." Meanwhile, from Oldham came another report confirming that there were plans "for a grand meeting all over Britain and Ireland at the same day and

14. Graham to Somerset, Nov. 4, 1831: Graham Papers, Letters M-S.
15. *Times*, Nov. 8, 1831, p. 2. Graham to Sir Herbert Taylor, Nov. 7, 1831 (copy): Graham Papers, the King and Sir H. Taylor. Magistrates at White Conduit Tavern to Lamb, Nov. 7, 1831, H.O. 52/14.
16. "National Union. General Meeting of the Working Classes Postponed" (Nov. 7, 1831); *Poor Man's Guardian,* Nov. 12, 1831, p. 156.

hour"; and from Foster came an admission that he would find it difficult to prevent a forcible turnout of the factories, a device the union favored in order to increase attendance at their meetings. A preliminary meeting of delegates from various towns was to be held on the 16th but Foster doubted that he could get accurate information about it, as arrangements for it were conducted with great secrecy. When finally he sent his report, including a copy of the resolutions passed, he was able to tell Lord Melbourne that eighteen or nineteen delegates attended and decided to postpone until November 28th the meetings that were to be held in separate towns. It also passed that those meetings were to choose delegates for a national convention at which a genuine Reform Bill was to be drawn up.[17]

Meanwhile there were developments in London that seemed ominous, if for no other reason than that there was insufficient information about them. A report on a private meeting of the London branch on November 21st suggests that the group was going underground, for it was arranged that they meet in classes of twenty-five with class leaders and that each group meet at the class leader's house "in place of any public establishment." There evidently was something afoot. One of the committee had to deal with a member curious about "something deep and secret going on" in the Committee of the Union; and it was reported that the London group looked forward to "reports from the North with great anxiety."[18] Quite apart from the scraps of evidence that

17. Lamb to Foster, Nov. 7, 1831: H.O. 79/4, ff. 208b–209. Enclosure to J. Holme to Melbourne, Nov. 5, 1831, and Foster to Melbourne, Nov. 12, 19, 1831: H.O. 52/13. Ashmore and Curran to Secy. of London political union, Nov. 5, 1831 (copy made at Post Office): H.O. 44/25. The Manchester union distributed a printed form, dated Nov. 10, 1831; the copy sent to Berwick-upon-Tweed was forwarded to Melbourne: H.O. 52/14.

18. Report of Nov. 23, 1831, signed by Th. Hunter, Supt. and another Supt. whose name is illegible: H.O. 61/5. There already had been reference to class organization at the beginning of the month: Report of Supt. Smith, Nov. 1, 1831: H.O. 52/14. From a personal reference in the report it is clear that they were present and not reporting what other informants had told them. The report refers to the "Halifax Arms Committee," this being the Halifax Arms Branch of the Union (see *Poor Man's Guardian*, Nov. 5,

clearly pointed to the possibility of organized resistance, these men generally were not loath to endorse the use of force. At another small private meeting in London on November 20th a speaker reported that letters received indicated a willingness to "stand or fall to a man"; there were allusions to military training at the class meetings; and the published rules of the Union, having asserted varied rights, stated that, "when a government violates the right of the people, resistance becomes the most sacred, and the most indispensable of duties."[19] And there were allusions to quasi-military organization. One speaker at the Rotunda even suggested that they identify themselves as "a ONE man—a member who had the command of ten, a TEN man— and he who represented a thousand, a *THOUSAND* man, and so on." Moreover, there was communication, and a semblance of organization, among unions in provincial towns such as Preston, Winchester, Huddersfield, and of course Manchester. And at Benbow's class leaders were urged to organize their classes so that at a signal they could be ready to move at a moment's notice.[20]

The signs of organization were such that the Proclamation of November 22 against hierarchical organization in political associations could have been a response to the exclusively working-class unions as well as to Attwood's union, where there also had been a proposal for hierarchical organization. But, unlike the Birmingham Union, the working-class unions aspired to national

---

1831, p. 152), and probably takes its name from a public house. Cleave was present. This is not the public meeting of Nov. 21 reported in the *Poor Man's Guardian,* Nov. 26, 1831, pp. 181–82, which was at the Rotunda. Evidently the private class meetings and the Rotunda meetings were both to take place. The class organization was formed on the model of Wesleyism: W. J. Linton, *James Watson,* p. 40. R. F. Wearmouth, *Some Working Class Movements of the Nineteenth Century* (London, Epworth, 1948), pp. 31, 77.

19. Report of Nov. 23, 1831, H.O. 61/5; *Poor Man's Guardian,* Nov. 26, 1831, p. 182; *The Objects and Laws of the National Union of the Working Classes and Others* (1831), p. 3.

20. *Poor Man's Guardian,* Nov. 26, 1831, p. 182; Dec. 4, 1831, p. 192; Dec. 10, 1831, p. 197. Report of Supts. H and K Divisions, Nov. 20, 1831.

organization and to a degree they did establish links among branches in different towns, especially around Manchester. Only a few days before the Proclamation was issued Foster wrote, expressing the views of the other magistrates, in which he fully concurred, to warn that the unions could still be checked but that if their increase continued they "might ere very long become so powerful and so organized that to controul them would, if not altogether impossible, be at least a task of the greatest difficulty and danger." In addition, the Lancashire unions spoke freely about arms, whereas the Birmingham Political Union, for all its allusions to force and even to arms, did not often get down to recommendations that its members acquire muskets. However, so far as the Proclamation is concerned, the two types of political unions were closely connected, for the Rotunda leaders were using the allusions to arms by the Birmingham Union as an excuse for their own militancy. "If the middle classes were arming under the auspices of the aristocracy," Watson had said, "the working classes ought also to arm," and Lovett, referring to the rival union, noted that, "with our plan of organization I think we shall be ready as soon as they." The Law Officers recognized working-class hostility to the middle class as a reasonable objection to the Birmingham Political Union's plan of organization. "Other classes," they said, "may foresee danger to themselves from the existence of such an association, and may organize and arm themselves in the same manner, to check its movements."[21]

The authorities prepared for the meeting at Camp Field on November 28th by distributing troops at various places throughout the town so as to prevent any attempt to turn out the work-

21. Lovett to Curran, Nov. 14, 1831 (copy made at Post Office and received at Home Office Nov. 18): H.O. 44/24. Law Officers to Melbourne, Nov. 19, 1831: H.O. 48/28, no. 34. Watson in *Poor Man's Guardian,* Nov. 26, 1831, pp. 181–82; Oct. 8, 1831, p. 111, enclosed with J. B. Clark to Melbourne, Oct. 10, 1831: H.O. 52/13. Foster to Melbourne, Nov. 19, 1831: H.O. 52/13. Melbourne did not believe that the Birmingham Union actually had arms (though he recognized the proposed reorganization could facilitate their adoption): Melbourne to Law Officers, Nov. 16, 1831, H.O. 49/7, ff. 433–34. During the week prior to the issuance of the Proclamation Melbourne made inquiries about reports that arms had been shipped

men. But the meetings did not appear formidable to the senior military officer in Manchester, nor to Foster who reported "that nothing has occurred to disturb the public peace." There were one or perhaps two thousand persons present during the period when the factories released men for dinner; after that there were no more than five hundred. The speakers called for abolition of hereditary aristocracy and spoke of the national convention. They also warned they would resist if the meeting was interfered with. But, addressing so small a crowd they also "abused the masters very much for having kept their men at work, attributing to that cause the smallness of the meeting."[22]

If it is judged by the meeting of November 28th, it seems clear that the immediate threat posed by the National Union of Working Classes was not formidable. But what about the government's response to it? Was it an extravagant reaction to an unreal danger? Or was it a precaution that reasonable men ought to have taken?

Although the working-class union did not pose an immediate threat, it did present a few ominous symptoms that were made to appear more serious by the lack of full information. The government's concern had its source in its prudent recognition of the possibility of danger. Here was a small group of Radical politicians who claimed to speak on behalf of the working classes and who were not reluctant to use language suggesting that violence was legitimate. Apart from their talk of arms, it was believed that some of them did in fact possess firearms. In contrast to most other radicals, they also were exponents of a doctrine that

---

to Manchester on Paddington canal barges: W. Adamson to Supt. May, Nov. 19, 1831; Supt. Cardey to H.O., Nov. 19, 1831: H.O. 64/16. An early draft of the Proclamation, apparently in Melbourne's hand, is filed with correspondence dealing with Manchester in 1831: H.O. 52/13; and a 3-column galley from the *Birm. J.* describing the Birmingham plan is in a file of intercepted copies of correspondence between the Manchester and other working-class unions dealing with the attempt to assemble delegates on Nov. 16: H.O. 44/25.

22. Col. Shaw to Bouverie, Nov. 28, 1831: H.O. 40/29. Foster to Melbourne, Nov. 28, 1831: H.O. 52/13. *Manch. Guard.,* Dec. 3, 1831, p. 3.

completely discredited most of the established institutional frame-work—monarchy, hereditary aristocracy, private property, and the Church. And they were as hostile to the middle classes as they were to the aristocracy. Moreover, they were uniformly de-scribed as being "almost without exception composed of men of the lowest description, and altogether unsupported by any per-sons even of ordinary respectability."[23]

What concerned the government above all else, however, was the aspiration—and, to a degree, its realization—for organiza-tion. There was, first, the organization on a local level that gave the unions a quasi-military appearance. In London it was by classes, with class leaders and hierarchical arrangements. Foster reported twenty-seven branches or lodges in Manchester. But still more important was the possibility that unions in different towns might be connected. There was communication between Man-chester and London. And there was persistent talk about a na-tional convention. A speaker at the November 28th meeting boasted that there were such unions in 104 towns. Although this was unconfirmed, at least in the district around Manchester, there were such unions in many of the principal towns, each with about 1,000 members (in one case, 1,600), and Foster reported that in early November they had been increasing in size.[24]

On the other hand, the government also had evidence of the unpopularity of the cause for which the working-class leaders stood. In October, after the rejection of the Bill, when public feelings were generally heightened, the Working Class Union in Manchester twice gave up a plan to hold a meeting for which it would have been sole sponsor. In November Foster reported that among the leaders "much dissatisfaction was expressed that a

23. Melbourne to Law Officers, Nov. 21, 1831, H.O. 49/7, f. 437; and Foster to Melbourne, Nov. 24, 27, 1831, H.O. 52/13.

24. Foster to Melbourne, Nov. 27, 28, 1831: H.O. 52/13. Foster offered the following tentative estimates: Stockport, 1,600 members; Macclesfield, 1,000; Blackburn, 1,000; Preston, 700 to 800; Bolton, 1,000; Oldham, 1,200; for Bury he had no information, but believed the unions to be numerous. At Rockdale, Burnley, Ashton-under-Tyne, Staleybridge, and Dukinfield there were as yet (Nov. 27) no unions, but attempts were being made to form them.

large meeting could not at present be assembled in this neighborhood," and thus the meeting planned for November 21 was put off until the 28th.[25] This made the turnout of the factories necessary for a truly large meeting. The union leaders claimed that only the authorities prevented the men from leaving work to attend a meeting, but privately they acknowledged that at least on routine occasions the men were reluctant to take part in this way. However, there were effective turnouts, for example, at Preston on November 7th, and despite evidence of difficulty faced by the union leaders, it remained uncertain whether subsequent attempts could be effectively resisted.[26]

In the face of this evidence, Melbourne's concern was nourished by word from Foster, who was equally cautious, that the working-class unions around Manchester had been rapidly increasing, that they were still controllable, but that if they continued to increase and spread they would present great difficulties. This estimate, seen in the context of Bristol and the troop shortage, disposed Melbourne to take prompt action. Despite the growing evidence of the unions' weakness, and his own tendency, which he restrained, to see them as absurd and ridiculous, he dealt with them as "a party of individuals who only want opportunity, and perhaps courage, to proceed to the worst (?) extremities." He therefore made plans to deny them that opportunity.[27]

But as events developed it became clear that these unions did not constitute an immediate threat to the social order. In view of the thin attendance at the November 28th meeting, Foster's estimate that the union had 5,000 to 6,000 members in Manchester, 4,000 of them paying the weekly subscription of one penny, was probably incorrect. Already by late November he thought "they

25. Shaw to Somerset, Oct. 17, 1831, and Foster to Melbourne, Oct. 11, 17, Nov. 19, 1831: H.O. 52/13.

26. Lamb to Foster, Nov. 7, 1831, H.O. 79/4, f. 209, and James Dixon, Mayor of Preston, to Melbourne, Nov. 7, 1831. Foster said that men in several mills volunteered to resist a rumored turnout provided the masters would assist them: Foster to Melbourne, Oct. 17, 1831, H.O. 52/13.

27. Melbourne to Grey, June 18, 1831, Jan. 27, 1832: Grey Collection, Durham.

are not now gaining much ground." He also said at this time that he did not much fear the union, though he warned that unemployment, whether caused by depressed trade, industrial disputes, or especially by the spread of cholera, could greatly enhance the danger. However, subsequent events confirm the picture of weakness. The December 26th meeting was of "the most contemptible description," with at most 400 persons attending; it "excited so little attention that were it not for the placards the town in general would be ignorant of its having taken place." The next meetings were held on Sundays (January 22 and 29) in order to allow factory workers, thought to be locked in, an opportunity to attend; but attendance, while it increased somewhat, remained quite meager.[28] The Manchester men might have tried to imitate the London Working Class Union on March 21, 1832, which tried to make the proclaimed Fast Day an occasion for a political rally. But by this time the leaders were in prison, having been convicted on March 12 in connection with previous meetings.[29] As for the working-class unions elsewhere, had there been 104 branches, as claimed, it might be expected that some of them would have followed the example of the London branch on the Fast Day. But if such attempts were made, they attracted no attention.

28. Foster to Melbourne, Nov. 19, 27, Dec. 26, 1831: H.O. 52/13. He also said, "It is not the present power of the Unions that is formidable, but the possibility that circumstances may render them so." Foster estimated that 1,000 were in the vicinity of the Jan. 22 meeting, including many not interested in the proceedings, but a constable thought 2,000 were present in addition to many more in the surrounding streets. Estimates of the size of the Jan. 29 meeting ranged from 300 to 600. Foster to Melbourne, Jan. 22, 29, 1832; Lavender's deposition, Jan. 29, 1832: H.O. 52/18.

29. Eight of them were prosecuted for conspiracy and for holding a riotous and seditious meeting. Evidence was taken with regard to the meetings of Nov. 28, Dec. 26, 1831, and Jan. 22, 29, 1832. All eight were acquitted on the conspiracy charge. Ashmore, Broadhurst, Curran, and Gilchrist were convicted for unlawful assembly and sentenced to one year in prison: *Annual Register for 1832,* Chr., pp. 38–40; *Manch. Guard.,* Dec. 3, 1831, pp. 2–3, and March 17, 1832, p. 3. Three of the London leaders (Benbow, Lovett, Watson) were prosecuted in connection with the Fast Day proceedings; they were acquitted.

The barely secret organization of these unions did not assume large proportions. Far from the 10,000 and even 12,500 members of which the London union boasted, the police estimated its strength at about 3,000. In contrast to the 500 classes claimed by Benbow, there were about 50. An indication of the union's strength and its hopes is perhaps given by the fact that at the beginning of 1832, when it was due to issue new membership cards to old members, it ordered but 500 of them. Its finances were also depressed. In January 1832 its total receipts since March 1831 had been £24; the claims against it, £39.[30] The Home Office spy reported at this time that they "are decidedly on the decline." There were quarrels among the leaders, desertion from the ranks, and difficulty in getting even the faithful to come to meetings and pay their subscriptions. By May 1832 the deterioration had continued, and although the Ministerial crisis brought greater numbers to meetings, by June Watson's class, with 69 the "largest and most honourable," attracted only eight persons.[31] These men and their ideas of course were important in the trade union movement a few years later and among the physical-force Chartists but, apart from the Fast Day meeting in London, they played a small part in the agitation of 1831–32. Their proceedings are significant here for the way they reveal the government's capacity to respond to a potential threat of uncertain magnitude with decision and vigor, yet without panic.

In contrast to its grave concern with this tiny revolutionary minority, the government did not think a serious threat from any other source was very likely. This was evident in the rationale

30. *Poor Man's Guardian,* Dec. 10, 1831, p. 196. Reports of Supt. Smith, Nov. 1 and n.d. [but Nov.] 1831; Report of Supts. Smith and Hunter, Nov. 5, 1831; Memo. of J. Stafford, Nov. 3, 1831; all in H.O. 52/14. Secret Service Report, Jan. 12, 1832: H.O. 64/12. In Nov. Smith estimated 3,270 members, Stafford 2,700. Wearmouth, *Some Working Class Movements,* pp. 68–73, rarely mentions a class numbered above 100; and even assuming that there were 25 to a class, as claimed, and that the classes were numbered consecutively, this would give the union about 2,500 persons.

31. Secret Service Reports, Jan. 3, 12, May 1, 3, 8, 11, 17, 18, June 8, 1832: H.O. 64/12. One of the resolutions drawn up for a January meeting called for complaint against "the apathy of the people."

offered for the Reform Bill, in which it explicitly held that present discontents were only potentially revolutionary. It is also evident in the moderation of government's response to disorder. While it was willing to suppress political meetings of the union suspected of revolutionary intent, the government resisted demands made by some Tories that all political unions be suppressed. The government also attempted to suppress the publications of the National Union of Working Classes, having arrested 500 newsvendors who distributed the unstamped papers presenting its views.[32] In contrast, they resisted frequent Opposition demands that various newspapers be prosecuted for seditious libel. A panic-stricken government would not have had the self-confidence necessary to prosecute the rioters arrested at Bristol and Nottingham and then quickly to carry out some of the sentences and, without fear of appearing weak, reduce the severity of others.[33] The picture of the Home Secretary as "his ordinary smiling self" who struck others by his "coolness" can hardly be reconciled with an image of a government feeling itself on the precipice of revolution.[34]

32. W. J. Linton, *James Watson*, p. 33. Hetherington printed and posted a placard: "Wanted—some hundreds of Poor Men—Out of Employ, who have nothing to risk—some of those persons to whom distress, occasioned by tyrannical government, has made a prison a desirable home. An honest, patriotic, and moral way of procuring bread and shelter. . . . now presents itself to such patriotic Englishmen as will, in defiance of the most odious 'laws' . . . sell to the poor and the ignorant the 'Poor Man's Guardian' and 'Republican,' Weekly 'Papers' for the People": H.O. 64/18. Heywood, a Manchester bookseller, estimated the number to be 750: Thomas Frost, *Forty Years' Recollection* (London, 1880), p. 8, n.

33. Special precautions were taken while the Special Commissions tried those arrested during the riots: Eagles, *Bristol Riots*, p. 57, n; Phillipps to Major General Sir Richard Jackson, Dec. 26, 1831 and Phillipps to Mayor of Bristol, Jan. 2, 1832, in H.O. 41/11, ff. 12, 23. *Records of the Borough of Nottingham, 8,* 402–03; Bouverie to Phillipps, Feb. 3, 1832, H.O. 40/30. There were no disturbances.

34. Cecil, *Melbourne*, p. 181. After the collapse of the proposed meeting for Nov. 7, a colleague said, "Melbourne's odd ways seem on this as on most other occasions to have answered admirably—so much better than the pomp or humbug of Pitt's or Addington's school": Holland to Grey, Nov. 8, 1831, Grey Papers.

"But if one understands by a revolution a violent and sudden change, then England does not seem ripe for such an event"
—Tocqueville (1833)

The government's response to the possibility of national organization among the few radical politicians who talked of violence was a sensible precaution. But there is little evidence that any effective organization existed among Radicals. Yet if a revolutionary threat was to take on reality, it was organization and leadership that were needed. But this sort of organization, as so many other conditions that make up a revolutionary situation, was absent. The so-called working-class unions, which were the only ones openly talking of violence, were few in number and weakly supported and, furthermore, they were divided by personal and tactical disagreement (this anticipating the split between moral and physical-force Chartism).[1] The working-class unions were openly hostile to the political unions that supported the Reform Ministry, even though these unions were the only ones that could at least pretend to have mass support. And these unions were at most loosely connected, the connection between Parkes in Birmingham and Place in London providing the most effective and perhaps the only link between any of them.[2]

1. At both the London meetings conducted by associates of Benbow and in Manchester there were expressions of resentment directed at Hetherington and to those who conducted the "cowardly retreat" in the face of Melbourne's threat of prosecution: "Report of Police Superintendents," Nov. 23, 1831, H.O. 61/5; *Manch. Guard.,* Dec. 3, 1831, p. 3. Secret Service Report, Nov. 7, 1831: H.O. 64/11. There was bitter denunciation of Wakley and the "cowardly apostates": Mansell to Curran, Nov. 6, 1831 (copy): H.O. 44/25. There also were quarrels over Carpenter's softness with regard to the Reform Bill. There was a cleavage created by widely different views of Owenite doctrine. And there were alternating quarrels and reconciliations between Hunt and the others. S.S. Reports, July 5, Oct. 19, 1831: H.O. 64/11; S.S. Reports, Jan. 26, April 23, 1832: H.O. 64/12; Foster to Melbourne, Feb. 7, 1832: H.O. 52/18; Place to James Mill, Oct. 26, 1831: Add. MSS 35,149, f. 123.
2. The political unions in the vicinity of Birmingham (for example, at Walsall), while insignificantly small, apparently were connected by personal ties with the Union at Birmingham. Also, there is reference to a

The lack of any effective organization among the various bodies committed to fundamental change reflected the variety of purposes among extra-Parliamentary politicians, and this was an obstacle to the establishment of that ideological unity that can give leadership and militancy to a revolutionary movement. Among the possible leaders of such a movement, some had political purposes and some economic, some particular grievances and some a broad vision of a new society. In order to get a glimpse of the variety one need only think of the former Tory Thomas Attwood with his belief in paper currency as a panacea for the country's ills; the working-class radicals, such as Cleave, with their socialist views inspired by Hodgskin and Owen; Place, who concealed his general political principles by stating particular grievances and by supporting a particular remedy, the Reform Bill, and for whom the economic views of the working-class radicals were wrong and pernicious; and William Cobbett with a romantically conservative belief in the virtues of rural life that nevertheless required that Parliamentary reform restore the ancient constitution. It was not only variety of purpose and disagreement in principle among the radical politicians that hindered the formation of a revolutionary movement. There was also the resistance to ideological commitment among the public as well. Most reformers were moved by particular grievances and agitated on behalf of particular remedies. Thus there were, in the main, separate "movements" in connection with Catholic Emancipation, the Reform Bill, the Poor Law (that is, reaction to it), and the Corn Laws. There is some continuity in principle and in personnel, but not much. Bentham, whose broad and general principles bore on almost all the institutional arrangements of society, was unusual. The Rotunda Radicals, it is true, were ideologically inspired. But they had no hope of establishing ideological hegemony among English radicals. Tocqueville, on his visit in 1833, recog-

---

Northern Political Union headed by Charles Attwood, but its composition and strength are undetermined. Place did not know Herpath, the leader of the Bristol Political Union, and apparently had no dealings with him in 1831–32: Place to Herpath, April 10, 1834, Add. MSS, 27,790, f. 107.

nized this nonideological aspect of Reform politics; he pointed out that particular grievances were taken up, "one small thing after another, and [reformers] have not in any way conceived one of those general principles which announce the approach of total subversion of the existing order."[3]

Still another consideration reduced the likelihood of revolution. The cleavages and hostilities between classes that exist in all societies can have revolutionary implications if political issues are discussed in a way that facilitates the expression of those hostilities generated by the class system. When this happens the political process draws to itself emotions that might otherwise be restrained or at least be sublimated into other spheres. But the Reform Bill struggle had the opposite effect. The Rotunda Radicals, it is true, attempted to make the Bill an occasion for warfare between middle and working classes, but it is their failure and not their effort to do so that is significant.[4] Hostility to the aristocracy was to be found during this period. Tocqueville noted that it was "not rare to hear an Englishman complain of the extension of aristocratic privileges and to speak with bitterness of those who exploit them." This was evident in the criticisms of

3. Tocqueville, "Last Impressions of England," (entry of Sept. 7, 1833), *Journeys to England and Ireland*, p. 69. Hobsbawm says, "As for the revolutionaries, they were throughout the entire period [1790's–1840's] inexperienced, unclear in their minds, badly organized, and divided": *History Today* (Feb., 1957), 116.

4. Had the political dispute been more closely tied to class cleavages, there would have been a greater tendency toward the mobilization of industrial unrest by the political movement, especially in Oct.–Nov. 1831 and May 1832. But this did not take place. See pp. 189–95 above. The Home Office seems to have been sensitive to the possibility that trade unions could be the means of directing economic grievances into (and thus reenforcing) the political movement. However, in response to its inquiries about this possibility in London, it was told that the National Union of Working Classes "have nothing to do with any trade society as a body." Also, "I have made the strictest inquiry . . . and cannot find that any of the numerous trades on the line of the Thames, or, any other intend meeting with the [political] Union at White Conduit House on [Nov. 7] . . . the great body of the weavers are against it." However, there were many weavers in the National Union of Working Classes. S.S. Report, Oct. 20, 1831: H.O. 64/11; Report of Supt. Smith, n.d. [Nov., 1831]: H.O. 52/14.

the sinecures enjoyed by so many aristocrats, such as those listed in the *Extraordinary Black Book,* which was sufficiently popular to reappear frequently in new editions during these years. Yet the Reform Bill agitation did not mobilize antiaristocratic feelings, for the aristocracy was clearly divided by the Bill, and while it was a majority in the Lords that provided a major obstacle to the passing of the Bill, it was visibly a group of aristocrats in the Lords as well as Commons that led its supporters. Thus Tocqueville also remarked that one could easily find someone who "will complain of such-and-such a Lord, or the course which the House of Lords has adopted, but it does not seem to have entered his head that one could do without Lords."[5] It is noteworthy that the Benthamites, who had been among the most doctrinaire critics of aristocratic government during the 1820's, now supported Lord Grey's Ministry.[6] There were very few suggestions of abolition of the House of Lords during the Reform Bill agitation; the remedy for the Lords' opposition to the Bill was the creation not the abolition of peers.[7] It was principally the working-class unions that saw the Reform Bill as a class measure; in their view it was for the exclusive benefit of the middle class, and this is the interpretation that has found greatest appeal among his-

5. *Journeys,* pp. 70–71. "The English aristocracy can . . . never arouse those violent hatreds felt by the middle and lower classes against the nobility in France where the nobility is an exclusive caste, which while monopolising all privileges and hurting everybody's feelings, offers no hope of ever entering into its ranks. The English aristocracy has a hand in everything; it is open to everyone; and anyone who wishes to abolish it or attack it as a body, would have a hard task to define the object of his onslaught." On the other hand, "The English aristocracy will fall more slowly and less violently than the French, but I think that it will fall as inevitably." Also—"if you speak to a member of the middle classes; you will find he hates some aristocrats but not the aristocracy. On the contrary he himself is full of aristocratic prejudices": ibid., pp. 67–70.

6. James Mill, "Edinburgh Review," *Westminster Review, 1* (1824), 211, 213; John Stuart Mill, "Speech on Parliamentary Reform at the Mutual Improvement Society, 1823 or 1824," *Realist, 1* (Sept. 1929), 54–55.

7. Among the notable exceptions were speakers before the National Union of Working Classes who occasionally proposed the abolition of hereditary aristocracy.

torians. But the working-class radicals, even if they were correct, failed to persuade their contemporaries that the Bill ought to have been exclusively discussed in terms of its effects on social and economic classes. Indeed, class labels are not at all prominent in discussions of the Reform Bill, and the agitation for it did not become the occasion for sharpening those class cleavages that of course existed.[8]

There was one area—the Church—which became involved with the political struggle in a way that did add violent passion to the popular cause. Although this was not sufficient to create a revolutionary situation, it does illustrate that political conflict can activate latent hostilities that are independent of the political issue, bringing them to the surface, giving them focus, and giving the persons who possess them an excuse to organize. The result is to make them more destructive, and this can be especially dangerous if these destructive impulses are directed against the institutions closely associated with the ideas and beliefs by which legitimacy of the political system is maintained. The only recurring symptom of such hostility to a national institution in 1831–32 involved the Church, or at least its bishops, twenty-one of whom, of the twenty-three who voted, declared against the Reform Bill in October 1831, providing the margin by which it was defeated (it lost by 41 votes). It was after this that the Bishop's Palace was attacked at Bristol, with Davis, the Bristol rioter, concentrating his violent abuse on the bishops. During October and November there were several occasions on which effigies of bishops were burned; at a Newcastle meeting a banner showed

---

8. Of course Macaulay and Durham occasionally referred to the middle classes in speeches but they never posed as spokesmen for the middle class, and their justification for the Bill had little to do with the interests of the middle class or, for that matter, any class. The prolific literature of the Birmingham Political Union of course insisted that the Bill was in the interest of "the people" and that seeing the society as divided into separate classes was unnatural. It should be added that the articles in the *Westminster Review* in 1832 that do connect the Bill with a separate middle class are not a reflection of Millite views. James Mill and his son and disciples by this time had quarreled with Bowring and had broken their connection with the *Review*.

a figure of death, its foot trampling the mitre.[9] Much of this hostility arose from varied sources not directly related to the Reform Bill, but which existed by virtue of the role of the Church Establishment in the context of social life and even in the economy. This hostility coalesced with political feelings, each reinforcing the other, and the result was the most impassioned expression of hostility during these years. But it was not enough to bring down the political edifice. For one thing, the bishops, though symbolically important, were not the Church; nor was the Established Church the entirety of organized religion. Furthermore, anger was not confined to the populace, as Grey's quarrel with Philpotts made clear; thus the unpopularity of the bishops was not a means of discrediting the entire elite. In addition, the bishops were denied an opportunity to repeat their performance in May 1832. Above all, there were other institutions, especially the crown, that were more important in giving legitimacy to the political system, which escaped the kind of attack to which the bishops were subjected. The King, despite his ambivalence about Reform and his opposition to political unions and the creation of peers, achieved the appearance of being favorable to Reform. One of the favorite slogans of the Bristol rioters was "The King and Reform."[10] Indeed, apart from the bishops, the political conflict, far from encouraging hostility, often gave an opportunity for affirmation of the existing order.

It has been noted that the outbreak of revolution is signaled by an otherwise insignificant event that "precipitates a separation of the repressors . . . from the repressed." The effect of this is to bring people into alignment in accordance with a cleavage in society which previously had not been explicitly acknowledged. The historical importance of these events, such as the storming of the Bastille or the St. Petersburg strike in February 1917, is derived

9. *Newcastle Courant,* Oct. 22, 1831, p. 2.

10. *Trial of Pinney,* pp. 39, 306. When, after passage of the Bill on June 19, 1832, the King was struck by a stone, but not injured, Peel tried to find an explanation in political excitement and loose talk of physical force as a remedy for grievances; but he produced no evidence of such a connection. Althorp insisted that there was universal indignation about it: *Hansard, 13,* 910–13.

"entirely from the social cleavage which they reveal." This phenomenon is also emphasized by another observer who, looking to its psychological dimension, notes that in genuine revolutionary situations, "feeling was so tense that almost any additional exasperation would probably have provoked the outbreak." Thus in Paris in 1848 a political banquet was canceled and "its proscription unloosed all the battered-down discontent of the people." The actual rising began "as the direct and immediate and spontaneous result" of a musket shot coming from one of the angry crowds; the troops, taking this as the beginning of an attack, responded with a volley of fire against the crowd. "That night the barricades were up all over Paris and the spatter of musketry fire announced that the people had passed the Rubicon between demonstration and armed revolt. . . . The tinder was so well dried and laid that the merest friction only was necessary to make a spark and ignite it."[11] If this was to have happened in England in 1831, the outburst at Bristol would have done it. If revolutionary feeling had been sufficiently aroused, the events at Bristol which, at least for a time, revealed the weakness of authority and symbolized hostility to the established order, would have served as a trigger to release strong but previously restrained feelings in other parts of the country. And, indeed, this was the time when dissident elements were encouraged. Guy Fawkes Day, following in the wake of the exaggerated rumors that spread from Bristol, became the occasion for the gathering of crowds, and on November 5th there were several cases of fires, burning of Bishops' effigies, and other disturbances, especially in the Southwest. But the events at Bristol also stimulated the nervousness of local officials and, more important, the rational fears of the Home Secretary. Thus the main impact was not to trigger the release of hostile feelings, nor to lay bare a previously concealed cleavage in society. "The Bristol affair," Edward Ellice wrote to his son, "seems to have produced one good consequence—rallying the supporters of peace and the men of property and industrial pursuits all over the Kingdom, for the maintenance of order and

11. Lyford Edwards, *The Natural History of Revolution* (Univ. of Chicago Press, 1927), p. 98; Chorley, *Armies and the Art of Revolution,* p. 25. The example of Paris in 1871 is also given.

quiet."[12] Hobhouse said the riots "had tended to cool the ardour of most politicians."[13] The author of a plan for a new way of organizing special constables thought "the feelings created by the calamities at Bristol" provided a special opportunity for enlisting volunteers from the populace who under ordinary circumstances would stand aloof.[14]

The reaction to Bristol reflected a general attitude to violence that was an obsacle to the spread of revolutionary organization, and it was not confined to the aristocracy and wealthy middle classes. When the Bristol and Nottingham rioters were tried and some of them convicted, there was no loud outcry against the judgments nor any attempt to interfere with the execution of the sentences (though before the trials some houses had been chalked, "a House for a neck"). When three of the Nottingham rioters were executed in February 1832, troops were available in the event of disturbance, but the "dense crowd" gave no difficulty.[15] At

12. Edward Ellice to Edward Ellice, Jr., Nov. 7, 1831: Ellice MS. E. 61, f. 22.

13. Broughton, *Recollections, 4,* 153. Greville noted that "The Bristol business has done some good, inasmuch as it has opened people's eyes (at least so it is said)" (Nov. 11, 1831): Strachey and Fulford, eds. *Greville Memoirs, 2,* 212. Roebuck said of Bristol, "It concentrated into one incident many of the horrors of revolutionary violence, and seriously alarmed the thinking men of all parties": *History of the Whig Ministry, 2,* 235. Schelling has described how, in the absence of overt leadership, an "incident" can serve as a signal and thus serve to coordinate the actions of many persons who share "converging expectations." But this is just what the Bristol riots did not do: Thomas C. Schelling, *The Strategy of Conflict* (Cambridge, Harvard Univ. Press, 1960), pp. 90–91.

14. Capt. Bowles, "Suggestions for the organization of Special Constables," Nov. 9, 1831: H.O. 61/5.

15. A. Bagnell to Melbourne, Dec. 27, 1831, H.O. 40/28, f. 308; *Annual Register for 1832,* Chr., pp. 9–13, 17. Bouverie reported that at Nottingham "the execution of the three unfortunate men . . . took place without the slightest appearance of any (thing?) likely to create tumult, and the concourse of people which is stated by Lt. Col. Thackwell to have been very large, dispersed immediately." Military preparations had been made but concealed, and special constables had been sworn. These together "would in all probability have been sufficient to have deterred the Populace from making any attempt at Rescue or disturbance, had they been so inclined, but for some time past no apprehension of such attempts has been felt, by those who have had the best means of judging": Bouverie to Phillipps, Feb. 3, 1832, H.O. 40/30.

Bristol, where four convicted rioters were executed on January 27, 1832, military aid was also provided, but "no disposition to outrage was manifested in any quarter."[16] The absence of identification even by the politically aroused public with the convicted men, who in other circumstances might have achieved the status of martyrs, can be inferred from the editorial protests that came from various Radical sources. Cobbett in his *Register* expressed the hope that the punishments would not be more severe than necessary to deter others from such crimes, and he suggested that neither capital punishment nor transportation was required. An organ of the National Political Union only protested against the application of capital punishment. "The sacrifice of life . . . will be the greatest blot in the whole affair. Enough is done, in shipping off a hundred to the other side of the earth [i.e. by transportation], to make the impression necessary on the multitude, that such scenes cannot be safely embarked on." It was only the severity of the punishment that was criticized; but the propriety of some severe punishment short of execution was accepted by all but the minuscule working-class unions which called the sentences "legal murder."[17] This reaction was in keeping with the abhorrence of violence that was to be found among large sections of the populace. This reflected the spread of "bourgeois" values that was already reaching the artisan and other working-class groups during this period. As for the middle classes, Tocqueville noticed their "horror" of riotous proceedings at an election, and this attitude would certainly have carried over to disturbances of any sort.[18]

16. Eagles, *Bristol Riots,* p. 275.

17. *Cobbett's Weekly Political Register, 75* (Jan. 28, 1832), 304–05; *Union,* No. 10 (Jan. 28, 1832), 145; *Poor Man's Guardian,* Feb. 4, 1832, pp. 265, 271.

18. Tocqueville, *Journeys to England and Ireland,* p. 45 (entry of Aug. 15, 1833). Place was greatly interested in the gradual bourgeoisification of the working classes. "Fifty years ago all got drunk. . . . None then excepting literary men read much. . . . Few saved money, certainly not one then for fifty now, all were improvident, gross, dirty, slovenly, negligent to a great extent": Place to Wade, July 9, 1833, Add. MSS 35,149, f. 214. General historical and sociological works mention other conditions of revolution than those introduced in the foregoing discussion. But

Despite all the talk of revolution in 1831–32, there does not appear to have been much reality behind the alleged threat. Adopting this view, however, does not mean that the social structure was perfectly harmonious, or that the country was without problems and its people without discontent. There was economic distress in 1831 arising from unemployment and increased food prices.[19] There were discontents that were made abundantly evident in the strikes in the mining areas, in the disturbances among the technologically unemployed handloom weavers, and among the farm laborers who felt threatened by the introduction of threshing machines. The disturbances attending these and other dislocations in the economy were part of the broad changes attending industrialization, and in the short run they could only reduce the stability of society. But to acknowledge this does not require that the society at any moment be viewed as resting on crumbling foundations.[20] Yet there has been a tendency to make just this assumption. This is exemplified in an extreme way by the Hammonds, whose judgment of the instability of the social

---

in most cases they were clearly absent in 1831–32; for example, it is difficult to find much evidence of desertion by the intellectuals, or self-distrust among the ruling class, or of ineptitude in the government's use of force. See Crane Brinton, *The Anatomy of Revolution* (New York, Vintage, 1957), pp. 28–52, 263–66. On economic conditions see n. 19 below.

19. W. W. Rostow, *British Economy of the Nineteenth Century* (Oxford, Clarendon, 1949), pp. 118, 121, 124–25. Davies has suggested that one condition of revolution is a prolonged period of objective economic development followed by a short period during which there is a sharp reversal. This might have been the circumstance in 1831–32, at least for certain segments of the populace. However, this is not a sufficient condition for, as Davies indicates, there are cases in which it is met without revolutionary consequences. The critical variable is the psychological effect of such changes: James C. Davies, "Toward a Theory of Revolution," *American Sociological Review, 27* (1962), 6, 17–19.

20. On extraeconomic sources of disturbance see Smelser, *Social Change in the Industrial Revolution*, pp. 226–32, 245–50, 322–31, and especially chap. 14: "The Question of Explanation in Working-class History." Smelser observes (p. 248) that "business conditions determined the *Timing*, structural pressures the *Content* of the violence." Smelser also shows that there were various nonviolent responses to the structural pressures. Hobsbawm

order was strongly influenced by the emphasis they gave to the economic deprivation and social disorganization that were among the consequences of industrialization. They visualized the working class as having been "naturally contented" in an earlier age, and as "naturally discontented" in the nineteenth century. Now politicians had to practice the "art of preserving discipline among a vast population destitute of the traditions and restraints of a settled and conservative society, dissatisfied with its inevitable lot and ready for disorder and blind violence."[21] This view of a society which in its nature made men "ready" for disorder gives an exaggerated significance to whatever symptoms of disorder are found. Various circumstances gave credence to such a view. For example, there was the rioting. There were many expressions of genuine fear of revolution. And there was the prominent use of a rhetoric that held out threats of violent revolution. But the rioting, which is usually mentioned to show the presence of a revolutionary situation, may have indicated nothing more than an inadequate police force. Had professional police forces existed throughout the country it is unlikely that the evidence of revolution provided by a riotous populace would have been available. It is worth noting that London, which had such a police force, had the reputation for being apathetic at the very time that other

---

has shown how a variety of impulses and social circumstances can lead to mob activities: *Primitive Rebels,* pp. 2, 5, 7, 110–11, 118–20. Also see Rudé, *The Crowd in the French Revolution,* pp. 235–38; Smelser, *Theory of Collective Behavior* (New York, Free Press, 1963), Chap. 8, "The Hostile Outburst."

21. J. L. Hammond and B. Hammond, *The Town Labourer 1760–1832 —The New Civilization, 1* (London, Guild Books, 1949), 101. Another example of this theoretically derived predisposition to believe that the social structure was particularly fragile can be found in Polanyi's study of the rise of the market economy. "The old social tissue was destroyed," the "fabric of society was being disrupted," the "Industrial Revolution was merely the beginning of a revolution as extreme and radical as ever inflamed the minds of sectarians, but the new [market economy] creed was utterly materialistic," and the "market system was more allergic to rioting than any other economic system we know": Karl Polanyi, *Origins of Our Time; the Great Transformation* (London, Gollancz, 1945), pp. 41, 43, 48, 187.

towns, without police, gave the appearance of being insurrectionary. With regard to the fears of revolution felt by many persons
at the time, it should be said that such fears were a permanent
part of the early Victorian mentality, especially among upper-
middle class, intellectually oriented persons whose impressions
were likely to be recorded; in themselves they do not verify a
hypothesis concerning the existence of a revolutionary situation
in 1831–32.[22] As for those who talked much about the imminence of revolution, at least in some cases "much was said that
no one really believed," and such rhetoric was not confined to
occasional speeches at public meetings, for it made its way to the
government and it appeared in some of the most influential newspapers as well.[23] Yet, given theoretical views that assume the
likelihood of revolution, such rhetoric (like the expressions of
fear or the petty rioting), becomes evidence of the existence of a
revolutionary situation. Once such theoretical dispositions are
given up, the evidence is seen in a different light. Thus Clapham,
having done just this, said that he has "never been able to find
any moment in the nineteenth century at which, so far as I could
judge, the risks of violent revolution, or of anything like it, were
so great as to make it necessary for historians to explain why no
violent revolution took place. . . . the risk was never high."[24]
In keeping with this view, Tocqueville, who was anything but
insensitive to symptoms of revolution, altered his judgment after

22. For example, Kingsley writing in 1862 and Mark Rutherford in
the 1880's provide some of the most striking evidence presented by
Houghton to show that such fears were endemic: *Victorian Frame of
Mind,* pp. 57–58.

23. The implications of this for the use of evidence from the Place
manuscripts as well as from newspapers are clear. Yet Place's manuscript
accounts, some of which were written after the event, have been much
used to interpret the enactment of the Reform Bill as a consequence of
a revolutionary situation.

24. J. H. Clapham, "Conservative Factors in Recent British History,"
Authority and the Individual, Harvard Tercentenary Publications (Cambridge, Harvard Univ. Press, 1936), p. 117. This is somewhat different
from Halevy's interpretation. He saw a potential for revolution that was
paralyzed by Nonconformity which, as the religion of the middle class,
deprived the working class of leadership. Hobsbawm disputes Halevy's

visiting England in 1833. He arrived "under the impression that the country was on the point of being thrown into the troubles of a great revolution." And he recognized that a broad "social transformation" of revolutionary proportions was taking place. "But," he added, "if one understands by a revolution a violent and sudden change, then England does not seem ripe for such an event, and I see many reasons for thinking that it will never be so."[25]

---

analysis but not his final conclusion, for he acknowledges the absence of certain necessary conditions for revolution. But he insists that there was "a good deal of revolutionary feeling in large parts of the Country": "Methodism and the Threat of Revolution in Britain," *History Today* (Feb. 1957), p. 116; Halevy, *Victorian Years 1841–1895,* with a supplementary section by R. B. McCallum, Eng. tr. E. I. Watkin (London, Benn, 1951), pp. 394–96.

25. Tocqueville (entry of Sept. 7, 1833), *Journeys to England and Ireland,* p. 66. Tocqueville (p. 68) noted that it was "generally believed in France" that England was threatened with revolution, and evidently this had shaped the expectation with which he arrived in England.

CHAPTER 6

The Millite Radicals, Public Opinion, and the Passing of the Reform Bill

The Millite Radicals and such radically inclined Whigs as Ellice and Durham, with whom they cooperated, thought of themselves as having had a large and perhaps decisive influence on the passing of the Reform Bill, and they thought it had been achieved through the use of intimidation tactics. Roebuck boasted about the "wholesome terror" that had been fabricated; and Fonblanque seems to have been alluding to this when he wrote that victory had been achieved "by the mere Whiff and wind of the country."[1] This must also have been in Place's mind when, later during the 1830's, while alluding to the Reform Bill, he reminded Fonblanque that "without . . . 'crooked and disingenuous means' " the working people "might have talked and petitioned for an age to come."[2] A similar view of their role was held by Edward Ellice, who in later years wrote to Parkes: "How little any of the Cabinet of 1832 understood the means by which the Reform was carried! You saw, and were party to the making of the Comee. [committee] of public safety in Richmond Terrace [Ellice's London address] in those days, which shaped, and regulated, and often controlled

1. *Exam.,* May 20, 1832, p. 321.
2. *The Examiner and the Tax on Newspapers* (London, 1836), p. 8. Place is quoting Fonblanque, who had fallen into disagreement with the Benthamite Radicals during the mid-thirties, accusing them of advocating "crooked and disingenuous means." Place's use of this phrase perhaps explains why he destroyed his correspondence in May 1832.

the opinion out of doors, so as [to] obtain all the advantages of its support, and prevent the dangers of its excesses."[3]

It has sometimes been suggested that the relationship between the Radicals and the Whig government was not so much one of influence as of collusion, where the leaders of the Whig government were willing and cooperative allies. If this had been the case, claims to decisive influence would immediately be invalidated. The possibility of collusion is suggested by several considerations. Both Whigs and Millite Radicals sought peaceful change. In 1831-32 (though at no other time) they were roughly agreed as to the magnitude and kind of change to be sought. Furthermore, the government stood to gain by the machinations of those using Millite tactics. Even at the time the charge of collusion was made, Tory politicians and journalists claimed that there was "connivance" between the government and the forces of popular radicalism (with which, in Tory eyes, the Millite Radicals were identified). Wetherell said the "Government have connived at the acts of violence encouraged by their own organ, the leading journal *The Times,* which has been daily exciting and irritating the people"; it was said "that Ministers will use the disturbances, as the vehicle and means of carrying their Reform Bill."[4] Ministers were also accused of conniving with the Birmingham Political Union, as when Russell and Althorp responded

3. Ellice to Parkes, July 31, 1852 (copy): Ellice MS. E. 43, f. 64. Ellice in 1835 said that "Lord Grey is . . . vowing that he will have nothing to do with any person *in communication* with the Radicals: Who carried his Bills, and who established his fame?": Ellice to Durham, March 19, 1835, in A. Aspinall, *Lord Brougham and the Whig Party* (Manchester Univ. Press, 1927), p. 294. Ellice lived at No. 3 Richmond Terrace: Montagu H. Cox and P. Norman, eds., *Survey of London, 13, The Parish of St. Margarets, Westminster—Part 2* (London, Batsfords, 1930), pp. 251-52; Parkes included the following statement in Ellice's obituary: "No man knew better by experience the difficulty and danger of a Government in proposing organic reforms not supported by the feeling of a nation." *Times,* Sept. 21, 1863, p. 7.

4. *Hansard, 8* (Oct. 12, 1831), 618, 620. Harrowby referred to the Whigs' "skilful party manoeuvre". Wharncliffe said the government party "made a stalking-horse of Reform for their own purposes": ibid., *13* (June 4, 1832), 356, 369.

gratefully to the expressions of support that had come from the Union.[5]

If collusion is understood to mean that the Ministers deliberately conspired with agitators in order to create situations that would provide evidence either of riotous conduct or pro-Reform sentiments, it is difficult to substantiate such charges. The Whigs' genuine fear of revolution prevented them from encouraging discontent and actual revolutionary developments. They were also too concerned about the political unions to conspire in their organization or to encourage their agitation beyond the conventional techniques of extra-Parliamentary politics. The unions were feared because they claimed to represent the people, and they thus challenged the authority of Parliament. They also were seen as symptoms of extreme discontent and as the means of mobilizing such discontents. It seems unlikely, therefore, that the Ministers would encourage the growth of unions or any organization that facilitated the expression of the very discontents they were seeking to appease.[6]

At the same time, the Ministers welcomed evidence of widespread popular support as a means of influencing the King and the Opposition majority in the House of Lords, to say nothing of their marginal supporters in the House of Commons and the almost reluctant supporters of the "whole Bill" in their own ministerial ranks. In seeking such support the Ministers engaged in negotiations that did involve something akin to collusion. Althorp, with the Prime Minister's permission, secretly communicated with Parkes in an effort to arrange that the Council of the Birmingham Political Union give up the plan to adopt a military

5. Russell, *Early Correspondence, 2,* 25.

6. Sanders, *Melbourne,* pp. 133, 137; Lord Cockburn, *Life of Lord Jeffrey, 1* (Edinburgh, 1852), 330–32, and *2,* 239–40; Melbourne to Brougham, Oct. 31, 1831, Brougham Papers, 20,386. Cf. Moore, "Other Face of Reform," *Victorian Studies, 5* (1961), 29–30, where it is suggested that possibly there was complicity of certain Ministers in the riots that occurred in the autumn of 1831; and where it is said that Ministers played on fears of others, implying that they had none of their own. Cf. Graham's memorandum, Nov. 25, 1831, in Parker, *Graham, 1,* 130–33 and n. 28 below.

posture, for this would have required prosecution. Several considerations probably moved Althorp to take this step. He may have thought that prosecution would increase the risk of disturbances; also, the evidence of popular support provided by the Union helped maintain his uncertain majority in the House of Commons; and in wanting to maintain it he could not have been indifferent to the prospects for his party as well as the fate of his country. Once the government came into conflict with the unions, he explained to Parkes, "the Reform Bill will be lost, and as a necessary consequence we go out too." Althorp tried to conceal his dealings with the Union. To Parkes, who was not formally a member of the Union at this time, he wrote, "not from me but from yourself try to influence Mr. Attwood not to proceed."[7] There is no evidence that Parkes shared the confidence with Attwood or the Council of the Union. But this arrangement does not show that there was collusion in other matters, for in attempting to alter the Union's plans, Althorp was trying to control a force that appeared threatening but that also just possibly could be useful. On Parkes' side this was hardly collusion for, with his manipulative approach to the situation, he used the opportunity to shape a particular image of public feeling in Althorp's mind, while Althorp, trusting him, saw him in an altogether different role. Therefore, while the Ministers did not conspire to encourage agitation, they were willing to use any evidence of pro-Reform sentiment that happened to be available, and they were even willing quietly to intervene in the affairs of the Union in order to achieve this end.[8]

The nearest evidence of collusion that can be found involves three radically inclined Whigs—Hobhouse, Ellice, and Durham— who appear to have been acting on their own initiative rather than on instruction from the government. Ellice, in a passage already quoted, identified himself with a committee that "shaped,

---

7. Althorp to Parkes, Nov. 21, 1831: Parkes Papers.

8. On Althorp's judgment that Parkes was trustworthy, see Buckley, *Parkes,* p. 85. However, Melbourne did not share Althorp's judgment; see p. 270 below. Scholefield was privy to Althorp's role in the proceedings: Parkes to Grote, Nov. 28, 1831 (copy), Add. MSS 35,149, ff. 128.

and regulated, and often controlled" public opinion, and in later years he also addressed Parkes as an "ancient Colabarateur [sic]" whom he had employed as an "intermediary . . . with the Political Unions."[9] That Hobhouse was aware that the "language of menace" was being used—and misused—is indicated by his request, made after he took office in February 1832 as Secretary for War, that Place give him testimony of public feeling that could be used to bolster confidence among his ministerial associates. (Describing his reply, Place said he "put the following menaces on paper.")[10] Since this occurred after Place had confessed that both the London and Birmingham Unions were "mere moonshine," Hobhouse presumably knew how accurate Place's testimony in this situation would be. Yet these are isolated cases, and Ellice, Durham, and Hobhouse appear to have been acting on their own, not as agents of the Cabinet. Like Parkes and Place, they were attempting to manipulate the situation, including the Cabinet. Their cooperation with Parkes and Place, therefore, does not implicate the Cabinet in collusion with the Millite Radicals.[11]

9. Ellice to Parkes, Oct. 26, 1831 (copy), and Nov. 24, 1851 (copy): Ellice MS. E. 43, ff. 1, 47–50. See Disraeli's open letter to Ellice in which he ironically speaks of "your contempt for all intrigue and subterranean practices": "The Letters of Runnymede" (1836), in *Whigs and Whiggism, Political Writings,* ed. William Hutcheon (London, 1913), p. 303.

10. Butler, *Reform Bill,* p. 411; Wallas, *Place,* pp. 277, 314–17. Such transactions may have been in Place's mind when he wrote in a public letter to Hobhouse, with whom he was quarreling, "I know not why I should have any secrets on political matters, and I have none, at least none of my own": Place to Hobhouse, Nov. 19, 1832, in *A Letter to the Electors of Westminster from Francis Place* (London, 1832), p. 8. However, Hobhouse had been the object of Place's attempts to intimidate as late as Oct. 1831, as their letters of Oct. 11 and 14 indicate: Add. MSS 35,149, ff. 83b–87.

11. For indications of Durham's cooperation with Parkes and Place, see Wallas, *Place,* p. 292; Butler, *Reform Bill,* pp. 265–66. Parkes organized election campaigns for many Whig candidates during the thirties and as a solicitor served many of them professionally. Thus occasionally he has been labeled a Whig. However, he certainly did not think of himself in this way. He said that "Bowring's introduction of me to Bentham, and Gregory's to George Grote and Mill, created all the power and moral

Most of the Ministers, uncertain of the consequences and thus of the wisdom of the Bill, were even more uncertain about public order; had they been convinced that reports of popular unrest were exaggerated, they would have been less insistent in December and the following May about carrying a Bill as extensive as the one first introduced in March 1831. Grey's willingness to negotiate with Lord Wharncliffe indicates that he would consider compromise, provided public feeling permitted. It thus seems unlikely that there was collusion to fabricate evidence of strong public feeling, since a not wholly palatable measure was reluctantly supported in deference to public feeling. Indeed, with regard to Parkes and Place, far from there being collusion, Melbourne thought it possible that they were secretly connected with the working-class unions and directed inquiries about them to Home Office spies operating within the Rotunda groups. This was hardly a condition that would have allowed for collusion.[12] On the other side, the Millite Radicals looked upon most of the Ministers, not as men with whom they were in collusion but as the objects of their manipulations. It was a situation in which each group thought it was using the other for its own purposes; this did not even involve a tacit agreement, for each felt that the other was at

---

courage I have brought to bear in favour of the people": H. Grote, *Life of George Grote,* p. 80. However, as a nondoctrinaire Radical, he promoted cooperation between Radicals and liberal Whigs, for which, he complained, he was "much blagguarded and nicknamed 'Whig' for doing so among my Movement [i.e., radical] bretheren": Parkes to E. J. Stanley, April 8, 1839 (copy), Parkes Papers.

12. Secret Service Report, Nov. 29, 1831, H.O. 64/11 (reporting on the groups connected with the Rotunda, particularly Carlile's circle, Benbow's, and Watson's); Report of Supt. J. Smith, Oct. 31, 1831, H.O. 52/14 (reporting on a group that met at the Philadelphia Chapel). It is clear from occasional endorsements on these reports and from T. Young's role as intermediary that Melbourne originated the inquiries to which the agents replied. Melbourne suspected that Parkes and Place had been secretly supplying funds to the Rotunda Radicals. The agent explained that there were private individuals, unknown to him, who sent money; apart from this possibility, Parkes' name was unknown and Place, while known to his associates, was unconnected with the Rotunda union.

best difficult to control, and that it was a continuous and uncertain struggle to do so.[13]

If the Millite Radicals were not in outright collusion with the Whig government, what was their relationship to it? What of their claim that they had a decisive influence in passing the Reform Bill? That they played an important part is generally acknowledged, although the exact boundaries of their influence cannot be mapped. It is, however, possible to specify the ways in which they exercised their influence.

Their influence was exercised through their participation in extra-Parliamentary politics. This meant that it was concerned with "public opinion." But "public opinion" remains amorphous, with no fixed relationship to the political process until it is articulated so as to give it shape and substance. Until this happens it remains a varied aggregation of sentiments, aspirations, and dissatisfactions which, with regard to any general topic, are held with differing degrees of salience, varying degrees of intensity, and are justified with varying amounts and kinds of information. These "opinions" are given shape by self-appointed spokesmen who formulate the grievances and the demands of the people on behalf of whom they speak. And the plausibility of the claims made by these spokesmen is roughly established by their organizing large numbers of followers in public meetings and associations who apparently endorse and clearly do not challenge the formulation of grievances and demands uttered on behalf of their chosen "constituents." Since there is no one formulation that is peculiarly appropriate, the leadership has some discretion, and this is enlarged to the extent that the constituents are permissive; that is, without preconceived ideas and beliefs. Of course, to the extent that there are rival leaders, this discretion is re-

13. Roebuck acknowledged that it was well known, "or at least surmised," that the Ministers welcomed the use of "violent language" when the Bill was in danger. But he did not credit the belief that there was collusion, for he saw the Whigs as men who "found the people excited," and who, for party purposes, "kept that excitement alive" and even increased it; but then they were "in an agony of terror at the result." In contrast, the Radicals were democrats who used the Reform Bill as a stepping-stone to their ultimate goals: Roebuck, *History of the Whig Ministry*, 2, 238, 290–91; *Hansard, 36,* 30.

duced. Since leadership gives a uniformity of demand and attributes a unanimity of interest and concern to the constituency where previously "opinion" varied among individuals and was collectively amorphous, this kind of leadership has a creative role in the process of making public opinion relevant to the institutions of government.

Parkes and Place to a degree played this role, although the men who contributed most by these means were Attwood, as the leading figure in the Birmingham Political Union, and those journalists, such as Cobbett and Thomas Barnes of the *Times,* who pressed for Reform in widely circulated papers. Mill and Place, like Bentham before them, as publicists of long standing, did have an indirect influence on the rhetoric of Radicalism as it was used by popular journalists and politicians.[14] But active leadership in the mobilization of opinion was not their main contribution, although in this sphere it is necessary to recognize that Place was the leading organizer of the National Political Union which, though insignificant by comparison with Attwood's Union, was important for having been the means by which Place successfully carried on his struggle against the Working Class Union and thereby denied the opposition to the Bill an opportunity of easily contradicting the government's contention that support for the Bill was practically unanimous. It was also Place's associates in the Union who organized and addressed meetings in the metropolitan area in order to provide some evidence of popular support for the Bill. Place was well qualified to engage in these activities, which Parkes described as "the dragooning and assailing system out of doors" about which gentlemen feel "natural disgust."[15]

The Millite Radicals had an impact that reached beyond this. Unlike many other Radicals, such as Attwood, Cobbett, Burdett, and Hunt, who mainly aspired to shape the opinions and intensify

14. Of course this should not be exaggerated, but one thinks of Wooler, Black, Fonblanque, Burdett, Hume, Hobhouse, O'Connell, and Hodgskin, who all were closely associated with Bentham, Mill, or Place at one time or another. There is evidence of this kind of influence in Carpenter's *Political Catechism* and Dolby's *Cyclopaedia.*

15. Parkes to Ellice, Jan. 8, 1837: Lambton Papers.

the feelings of the populace, Parkes, Place, and their associates were also concerned to shape the beliefs of the governing classes as to what the opinions and feelings of the populace were, and in this role they made their distinctive contribution to the passing of the Reform Bill. Their purpose, of course, was to create a convincing image of the populace as being unanimous in its demands and threatening in its attitude toward the government that might dare to disappoint it. They (in Edward Gibbon Wakefield's words) "put forward images of revolution." This, they calculated, would give public opinion genuine impact. They pursued this goal in two ways. First, by personally conveying information to Ministers, either by correspondence, such as Parkes had with Althorp or Place with Melbourne (or his aides); or by leading deputations, such as Mill to Brougham or Parkes to Althorp or Place to Grey. Place's deputation, for example, may have helped to persuade the Cabinet into recalling Parliament without too great a delay after the Lords' rejection so as to have it publicly commit itself to an equally extensive Reform Bill.[16]

But the second method—that of using the press—was probably more important. By this means they published characterizations of public opinion which emphasized the barely restrained violent disposition of the populace. Parkes, and in some cases Mill and Place as well, had access to the editorial columns of the *Morning Chronicle,* the *Examiner* (and to a lesser degree to the *Spectator* and the *Times*) where events were interpreted in order to substantiate this image.[17] But their reporting of "news" was even more useful to them. Its importance for Parkes is indicated by recalling that, so far as Birmingham was concerned, he had a near-monopoly of news such as a single wire service might have today. Ellice was appreciative of it. Referring to a Birmingham meeting, he told Parkes it "will do great good—one might have preferred it on the Saturday than on the Monday, as the House meets early on the Monday—but the apprehension of the coming thunder, is often greater than the fear of the actual storm, and I suppose you will take all reasonable means to announce it."

16. Halevy, *Triumph of Reform,* p. 41. E. G. Wakefield, *England and America, 1* (London, 1833), 178.

17. *History of the Times 1785–1841,* pp. 275–76, 457–63.

The situation allowed him to boast that there was "perhaps no one having so wide and quiet a relation to that *Power* [of the press], and few more (from all the passages in my past life) knowing more of the Provincial Press."[18] This power he used to shape the image of public opinion held by the governing classes. Parkes saw the press, like the other methods used, as being analogous to the action of a steam engine. "What James Watt was in science in the application of the power of steam, we now want in the political science." The purpose was to channelize the steam of public opinion in order to maximize its thrust as it affected the political process.[19]

Of course, the few Millite Radicals were not solely responsible for the use of menacing language. Predictions of the dire consequences that would follow rejection of the Reform Bill were made quite often. Evidence of their handiwork can be found in certain key newspapers; but Barnes' adoption of the language of menace was not based only on Parkes' reports. Attwood also used such language, but the extent of Parkes' influence on him and others in Birmingham remains undetermined.[20] The intimidating language, which the Millite Radicals used so systematically

18. Parkes to Durham, July 21, 1835: Lambton Papers. Ellice to Parkes, April 28, 1832: Ellice MS. E. 43, f. 4.

19. Parkes to Grote, Oct. 26, 1831: Add. MSS 35,149, f. 118. G. C. Lewis distinguishes among three ways by which the press exercises influence: from authority, from argument on behalf of particular opinions, and from publication of statements of fact that substantiate particular opinions. Mill advocated and Parkes practiced journalism that exemplified the latter method: G. C. Lewis, *An Essay on the Influence of Authority in Matters of Opinion* (London, 1849), p. 343.

20. Parkes looked on Attwood and the Birmingham Political Union as instruments for the promotion of his views. He was not a member. His manipulative approach to the Council is evident in his letter thanking Place for sending letters, including one that was "anonymous." "I made good use of all. They were so many trains of your powder. The Union soaked them in": Parkes to Place, Oct. 15, 1831, Add. MSS 35,149, f. 96. Parkes thought he had used Attwood: "Some of us, without his discovery, used him between 1830 and 1832 to graft on his humbug object [currency scheme] the democratic movement." "Some of us tacked [the Reform Bills] upon his 'Political Union,' using 'Tom Attwood' as a steam tug": Parkes to Cobden, Dec. 30, 1839, Cobden Papers.

and self-consciously, also appeared in many provincial papers where their influence was not direct. Indeed, certain stereotyped interpretations of situations, and sometimes uniform phraseology, seem to have spread from central sources. In part this can be accounted for by their methods of distributing news. The national distribution of London papers (which happened to include publications with which they were connected) and the widespread practice of reprinting news items that originally appeared in them, greatly facilitated their infiltration of the press. Thus, for example, the *Scotsman* frequently quoted the *Morning Chronicle's* statements on reform politics. Charles Buller noted that "news contained in such papers as *The Times* and *Morning Chronicle*" was "being transferred, in a few hours after the publication of these papers, to other prints." In addition, Parkes made a practice of distributing the pamphlet-size reports of Union meetings to various newspapers over the country. Thus the editor of the *Weekly Dispatch* admitted receiving early reports of the proceedings of the Birmingham Political Union from the editor of the *Birmingham Journal*.[21] But still more important was the disposition to take the cues and print the accounts such as Parkes and Place distributed. They offered an interpretation that implicitly acknowledged the existence of anxieties about violence and anarchy, and it also reassuringly outlined the political remedy that would remove the danger. Journalists and other public figures, often isolated and uncertain and thus hungry for news, were disposed to accept and repeat such an interpretation. Given prevailing anxieties and aspirations, it appeared plausible in addition to being, in many cases, in accord with their political preferences. Thus when Bowyer was seeking publicity for the London reform

21. *Scotsman,* May 12, 1832, p. 2; *Weekly Dispatch,* June 24, 1832, p. 204. Buller, *Hansard, 35* (July 18, 1836), 274. Some of the "language of menace" probably reflected the "romantic approach" that Prof. Kitson-Clark has described; it produced a "romantic oratory" with wild talk of revolution, but did not encourage a "very clear appreciation of what words about force really implied." But this markedly contrasts with the calculated and sophisticated use of words about violence by such men as Parkes and Place. G. A. R. Kitson-Clark, "The Romantic Element, 1830 to 1850," in *Studies in Social History: A Tribute to G. M. Trevelyan,* ed. J. H. Plumb (London, Longmans, 1955), pp. 234–36.

procession of October 12, paragraphs "of a sufficiently sounding and exciting nature were written and immediately conveyed to the Editors of the Daily Journals as articles of News," and he was agreeably surprised when he found that they were "greedily received and published." To take another example, Perry, at a time when by his own account the union was experiencing difficulties, sent a letter to the *Times* "describing our success, [and] they incorporated a good part of the letter in a leader." The disposition of the editors was as essential as the initiative taken by Bowyer and Perry. It had similar effects on other occasions when it was Parkes and Place who were the initiators, allowing Parkes to observe that "the Press in these times makes a loud echo."[22]

The claim that the Millite Radicals influenced the passing of the Reform Bill in this way rests on the assumption that concern about the possible revolutionary consequences of not passing it was an important consideration affecting the many actors on the Parliamentary stage. While it is not easy to identify the motives and assumptions for the backbench support led by Lord Ebrington, it would be difficult to assume that the alleged threat of revolution had no role in shaping the determination of at least marginal supporters who had no strong convictions prompting them to support the Bill. In May, as during the previous October, excited talk of civil war and anxious allusions to the insurrectionary mood of the people were to be heard at Westminster, and it is impossible to believe that the lobbies were immune from it.[23] One member took note of the accounts from different parts of the country that told of "the desire of the lower orders to come to blows"; he also thought (on May 18) that "if the government had after all gone out nothing could have prevented an immediate explosion in the country."[24]

22. Bowyer's Narrative, Add. MSS 35,149, f. 344b; Parkes to J. Abercrombie, Jan. 12, 1834, Grey Papers. Perry, Add. MSS 27,822, f. 32b.

23. Aspinall, ed., *Three Diaries,* pp. 246, 251, 255, 258, 263, from the diary of Le Marchant who, as Brougham's secretary, spent much time in the House of Commons, in order to make a précis of its debates for the Chancellor.

24. Sir Thomas Byam Martin's diary (M.P. for Plymouth), Martin Papers: Add. MSS 41,369, ff. 8, 9b (entries of May 18 and 19, 1832). Mrs. Arbuthnot, referring to "the most furious articles in the radical

Neither were the Tories uninfluenced by the fear of revolutionary consequences. Had they formed a government they would have been committed to a reform bill of their own and, while the King's demand was in part responsible for this, the belief that "it would neither be safe nor consistent with the peace and tranquility of the country" to ignore popular demand also played a part.[25] But this outlook also influenced their inability to form a government, which paved the way for Grey's return. For it is by no means clear that the Tory members who withheld their support from Wellington were moved only by the wish to evade the charge of inconsistency and mere office seeking.[26] There was also the King, on whom any Parliamentary solution depended, who was also subject to fears of revolution.

Most important was the Whig government, which was anything but immune to fears of violent revolution. Its most persistent concern, it is true, was directed to the possibility of revolution in the foreseeable but distant future, and its rationale for the Bill rested mainly on the need to create a capacity to resist

---

papers" and their threats of "rows and insurrections," said "none of [these things] will happen but the fear of [them] will, I dare say, influence many votes in Parliament": *Journal of Mrs. Arbuthnot*, eds., Bamford and Wellington, *2*, 414.

25. Baring, *Hansard, 12* (May 10, 1832), 799. Arbuthnot writing (May 11) to his son, who was an army officer serving with troops used to help maintain public order, thought it worth repeating Wellington's belief that "Paris was lost [in July 1830] by frittering away the troops in isolated small bodies," and suggested, in case of risings, that this mistake be avoided: *The Correspondence of Charles Arbuthnot*, ed. A. Aspinall (London, Royal Historical Society, 1941), p. 159 (Camden, 3d ser., *65*).

26. Le Marchant believed that "Peel dreaded Civil War." At least in late 1831 Peel said that "dissolution would mean revolution." Peel, having armed his servants at Tamworth, indicates that at least he could not have been indifferent to the possibility of violence: Aspinall, ed., *Three Diaries*, p. 255; K. Feiling, *The Second Tory Party 1714–1832* (London, Macmillan, 1938), pp. 391, 394–96; C. S. Parker, ed., *Sir Robert Peel, 2* (London, 1899), 191. Brock states that when Wellington "stopped a civil war in 1829 his majority saw him through: when he looked like starting one in November, 1830 and May, 1832, they left him": M. G. Brock, "Wellington: The Statesman," in *Wellingtonian Studies*, ed. Michael Howard (London [?] 1959), p. 76.

long before the expected attack. This means that the Ministers mainly saw unrest as a symptom of vulnerability to future but not imminent revolution. But at the same time, as responsible politicians, they could not ignore the possibility that the threat might be real. Without showing intense fright, neither were they indifferent to the turbulence of their times. Melbourne, for example, wrote to the Prime Minister after the riots at Nottingham and Derby, "Such violence and outrage are I believe quite new and unprecedented in this Country; at least I never remember to have heard of Country homes being attacked, plundered, and set on fire in any former times of political ferment." He did not sense disaster; but neither was this normalcy, and therefore he was uneasy.

This added to his difficulty in evaluating both the symptoms and the diagnosis offered by the Millite Radicals, and even though he was in the best position to form a judgment about the threat, yet even he felt genuine uncertainty. As has been noted, he was able calmly to discount alarmist reports; and when someone like Place was identified as the source of "the most serious fears" he observed that "eager advocates" of the Bill might "be biassed by their wishes and inclinations," and he skeptically commented that such evidence "must be received with some allowance." On the other hand, he also said that it was "by no means to be rejected," and he confessed to feeling "solicitude and uneasiness." Indeed, suspecting as he did that Place might be connected with the working-class radicals and thus capable of being involved in a seditious and perhaps treasonable conspiracy, he could not easily assume that Place's talk of revolution merely consisted of exaggerated, empty threats. Therefore, even when he recognized that bias or strategy might lead to exaggeration, he remained uncertain. His uncertainty also stemmed from the belief that it was "impossible beforehand to estimate or conjecture" about the depth of public feeling and its implications for popular action.[27] His cautious attitude was evident in the preparations made in

27. Melbourne to Grey, Oct. 29, 1831, Grey Papers; Melbourne to Sir Herbert Taylor, Sept. 24, 1831, in Sanders, *Melbourne*, pp. 129–30; see p. 270, n. 12.

anticipation of the possibility of difficulties from the working-class union in November 1831. It is not surprising that others, less calm and less well-informed, might also experience uncertainty and serious concern. Indeed, where Melbourne was uncertain many of his colleagues were plainly apprehensive and therefore more explicit in identifying their fears. Thus Graham thought the resignation of the Ministry in October 1831 would have been "the signal for anarchy," and that another rejection of the Bill by the Lords "would be followed by the most fatal consequences."[28] Without being panic stricken, to responsible politicians the possibility of revolution, even if it did not appear to be very great, could reasonably have been a consideration affecting their decision.

Of course, there were other considerations as well—calculations of party advantage, backbench pressure, the wish to exploit the opportunity provided by disagreements within the Tory party. But if there had not been serious concern about the consequences of not passing the Bill, why would they have persisted in seeking passage of a measure not really palatable to many in the Cabinet? And why would they have persisted in seeking passage by means (creating peers) that were not acceptable to many who otherwise approved of the Bill? There was a possibility of compromise in November 1831 when Wharncliffe was negotiating with Grey. Yet the Cabinet overcame its reluctance and distaste and remained determined to have a bill no less efficient than the one rejected in the Lords. They did this because they thought it either desirable or necessary; or, desirable because necessary. And here the threat of revolution played a part. It

28. See pp. 238–47 above; memorandum by Sir James Graham (to Grey and Althorp), Nov. 25, 1831, in Parker, *Graham, 1,* 130–31. The draft on which the memo was based spelled out the fatal consequences. A second rejection, he wrote, would be "followed by the immediate destruction of our present Form of Government; that life and Property would be insecure, and that Society itself would be reduced into its first Elements": Graham Papers, Letters, 1810–31. Also see Durham to Grey, March 22, 1831; Jeffrey to Grey, Oct. 10, 1831, Jan. 14, 1832; Grey to Jeffrey, Jan. 17, 1832; all in Grey Papers. *Correspondence of Grey and William IV, 1,* 376, 378, 425; *2,* 69, 197.

was conveyed in many ways, in surly looks as well as in serious riots; it was made explicit by nervous magistrates and spokesmen of the "language of menace"; and it was made plausible by obvious reasons for discontent as well as by the fear that it inspired. After sober evaluation these symptoms usually were discounted (and rightly so). But a residue of uncertainty, sometimes a considerable residue, remained to give the possibility of revolution, no matter how small the risk or remote the possibility, an influence on the ultimate decision.[29]

There were several circumstances that contributed to the kind of influence exercised by Parkes and Place and their associates. For one thing, the approval of reform that prevailed among the public greatly facilitated their influence. If reform had been any less salient it would have been difficult to give credence to their descriptions of the popular demand for it. Had it been more salient and opinions more intense, their descriptions of it as unanimous as well as intense might well have been challenged. Equally important was the Whigs' traditional concern about revolution and their sensitivity to its symptoms. To this must be added the "terrible apprehensions" of revolution that were quite common throughout this period.[30] This feeling that society rested on crumbling foundations made men ready to believe rumors and to exaggerate symptoms that pointed to the possibility of revolution. This atmosphere was not congenial to the hard-headed detached attitude that would have directed considerable skepticism at the claims and machinations for which the Millite Radicals were responsible. Finally, the circumstances surrounding Catholic

29. Cf. Ferguson, *Victorian Studies, 3* (1960), 273, where the threat of insurrection of May in which Place was involved is artificially isolated from the whole atmosphere of danger and the vague expectation of violence that was evident in much political discussion of the time and which is the context in which specific threats should be seen. Ferguson holds that it was "immaterial because the whole tone of the threat was transparent." While some of the threats were not intended to be carried out, it does not follow that they did not influence even perceptive politicians who were vulnerable to them because of their insecurity about the stability of the social order.

30. Houghton, *Victorian Frame of Mind,* pp. 55–57; Christie, *Transition from Aristocracy,* pp. 48, 51.

Emancipation also helped create an environment favorable to the practice of Millite tactics. For the events of 1829 are said to have helped "establish the tradition that that which can no longer be defended except at the cost of civil strife, must be surrendered."[31] To the extent that this was an operative principle, it put a premium on the threat of civil strife, whether real or rhetorical, and it could hardly be expected that shrewd politicians would not recognize this.

Against this background the Millite Radicals should be seen as men who attempted to play upon the uncertainties and anxieties of Parliamentary politicians. In this way they exercised an influence that was much more specific and of a different character than the influence usually ascribed to them. But while it is possible to specify the kind of influence they had and the way they achieved it, it is not possible to establish its exact magnitude. Various conditions enhanced their effectiveness; but at the same time, there were limits to what could have been achieved. Thus the more extravagant boasts about having created "wholesome terror" (Roebuck) and having "shaped, and regulated, and often controlled opinion out of doors" (Ellice) claim too much. However, on the whole they saw themselves in a large perspective. Even Roebuck, who went farthest in suggesting that what appeared to be public opinion was a mere fabrication, also acknowledged the existence of genuine concern for the Bill as well as occasional popular outbursts of real excitement and even furious anger.[32] Parkes frequently commented on the relationship of public opinion to Parliamentary politics in a way that makes it clear he saw it as something to be shaped and directed but not altered in its fundamental character.[33] The Millite Radi-

31. Aspinall and Smith, *English Historical Documents 1783–1832*, p. 55. The Conservative Party was learning that "the way to avert revolution was to abandon opposition to inevitable change": ibid.

32. Roebuck, *History of the Whig Ministry*, 2, 208–09, 216–17.

33. In 1841 he said, "when the law of Public Opinion bursts out it finds a channel, tho' one can't foresee the course": Parkes to Stanley, Dec. 16, 1841, Parkes Papers. To Ellice he wrote that "the Anti Corn Law Question is the fanaticism of the day. If Peel staves off the Question . . . he will be agitated to death, . . . I see the storm brewing in the

cals achieved this effect by conducting themselves with energy and skill and above all by using that knowledge of what Parkes called "the ins and outs of Parties, Press, and Public meetings" which made the British Constitution appear "as elastic as a ball of India rubber."[34]

---

talk of Cobden and Co.—Cobden and Co. are the Tom Attwoods of 1831–2. The out-door men have always scattered the Tories, and always will. Fanaticism is as essential in Politics as in Religion": Parkes to Ellice, Sept. 16, 1841, Ellice MS. E. 38, ff. 30–39.

34. Parkes to Durham and Ellice, Sept. 6, 1835: Lambton Papers.

Index

Yale Studies in Political Science